lonely planet

COSTA RICA

TOP SIGHTS, AUTHENTIC EXPERIENCES

Ashley Harrell,
Jade Bremner, Brian Kluepfel

Contents

Plan Your Trip

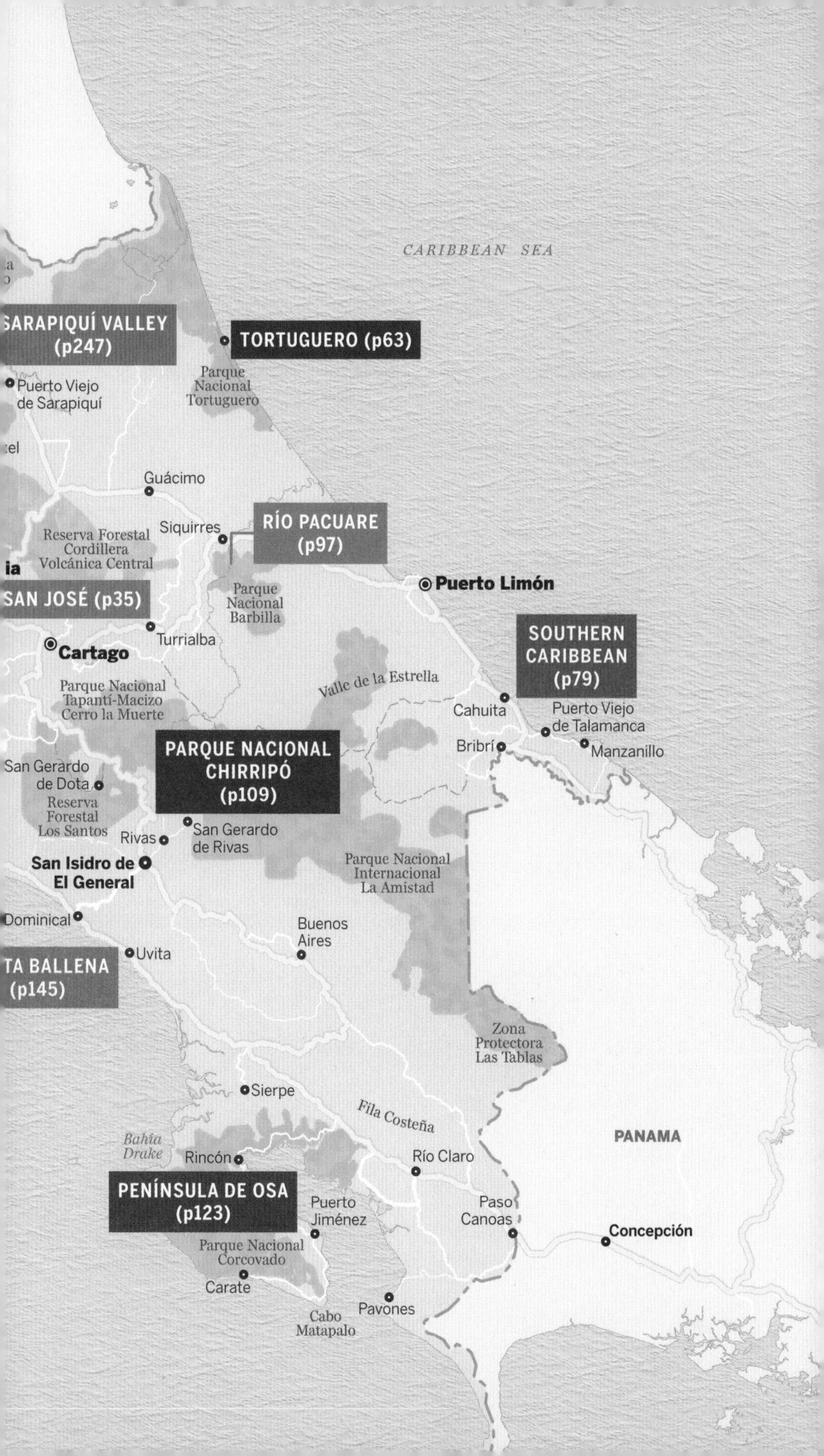

CARIBBEAN SEA
SARAPIQUÍ VALLEY (p247)
TORTUGUERO (p63)
Parque Nacional Tortuguero
Puerto Viejo de Sarapiquí
Guácimo
Siquirres
RÍO PACUARE (p97)
Reserva Forestal Cordillera Volcánica Central
Puerto Limón
SAN JOSÉ (p35)
Parque Nacional Barbilla
Turrialba
Cartago
SOUTHERN CARIBBEAN (p79)
Valle de la Estrella
Parque Nacional Tapantí-Macizo Cerro la Muerte
Cahuita
Puerto Viejo de Talamanca
Bribrí
Manzanillo
PARQUE NACIONAL CHIRRIPÓ (p109)
San Gerardo de Dota
Reserva Forestal Los Santos
Rivas
San Gerardo de Rivas
San Isidro de El General
Parque Nacional Internacional La Amistad
Dominical
Buenos Aires
Uvita
TA BALLENA (p145)
Zona Protectora Las Tablas
Sierpe
Fila Costeña
PANAMA
Bahía Drake
Rincón
Río Claro
PENÍNSULA DE OSA (p123)
Puerto Jiménez
Paso Canoas
Concepción
Parque Nacional Corcovado
Carate
Pavones
Cabo Matapalo

Welcome to Costa Rica

Discovering a sleepy sloth in the rainforest or scaling a misty mountain peak, braving a rushing white-water rapid or riding a world-class surf break, in Costa Rica the heart is set a-flutter. The only limit is your return date.

If marketing experts could draw up an ideal destination, Costa Rica might be it. The 'rich coast' has earned its name and stands apart from its Central American neighbors on the cutting edge of peace-keeping policy, farm-to-table restaurants and sustainable tourism. The dizzying suite of out-door adventures offers thrills of every shape and size – from the squeal-inducing rush of a canopy zipline to a sun-kissed afternoon at the beach. National parks offer glimpses into rainforest and cloud forest life, volcanoes simmer amid other-worldly vistas, and reliable surf breaks are suited to beginners and experts alike.

Meanwhile, wildlife that seems almost cartoonish abounds: keel-billed toucans ogle you from treetops and scarlet macaws raucously announce their flight plans. Blue morpho butterflies flit amid orchid-festooned trees, while colorful tropical fish, sharks, rays, dolphins and whales thrive offshore – all as if in a conservationist's dream. One-quarter of the country's wild lands are pro-tected by law, while developing infrastructure is balanced by green energy such as wind and hydro. And with no standing army, Costa Rica allows visitors to relax into the pure life, or as the locals say at every opportunity, *pura vida, mai.*

> *relax into the pure life...*
> *pura vida*

Cloudbridge Nature Reserve (p116)
CHRISONTOUR84/SHUTTERSTOCK ©

Peñas Blancas

Lago de
Nicaragua

San
Carlos

NICARA

La Cruz

Islas
Solentiname

Santa
Cecilia

Los Chiles

Upala

Refugio de
Vida Silvestre
Caño Negro

Area de
Conservación
Guanacaste

Parque Nacional
Volcán Tenorio

VOLCÁN ARENAL
(p225)

Refugio
Silvestr
Maqu

◉ Liberia

Bagaces

Laguna
de Arenal

La Fortuna

La Virgen

El Castillo

Potrero

Cañas

Santa Elena

MONTEVERDE
(p199)

Sa

Puerto Humo

Tamarindo

Zarcero

San Antonio

Manzanillo

San Ramón

Paraíso

Alajuela ◉   H

Puntarenas ◉

Sámara

Paquera

Santiago
de Puriscal

Ciudad
Colón

SOUTHERN NICOYA
(p181)

Tárcoles

**COSTA
RICA**

Santa Teresa

Montezuma

Mal País

Jacó

Parrita

Quepos

Manuel
Antonio

MANUEL ANTONIO
(p161)

PACIFIC   OCEAN

N   0
     0

100 km

50 miles

Costa Rica's Top 12

N K/SHUTTERSTOCK ©

Southern Nicoya

Wild ocean meets lush jungle

If you dig laid-back beach culture and lounging on sugar-white coves, head for Southern Nicoya. In the little surf towns of Mal País and Santa Teresa, the sea is full of wildlife and the waves are near-ideal in shape. There's easy access to Cabo Blanco reserve or Montezuma's triple-tiered waterfall, and some of the country's best restaurants await. Left: Montezuma (p192); Right: Capuchin monkeys

1

Baby three-toed sloth
MARK KOSTICH/GETTY IMAGES ©

Tortuguero
Sea-turtle spotting and canal tours

Canoeing the canals of Parque Nacional Tortuguero is a boat-borne safari. Get up close to caimans, river turtles, crowned night herons, monkeys and sloths. Under the cover of darkness, watch the ritual of turtles building nests and laying eggs. Between wetlands and the wild Caribbean Sea, this is among the country's premier places for wildlife. Top: Basilisk lizard; Bottom: Baby green turtle

SIMON DANNHAUER/GETTY IMAGES ©

Costa Ballena

Whale-watching, wave riding and pure deliciousness

South of Quepos, the well-trodden central Pacific trail tapers off, evoking the Costa Rica of yesteryear – surf shacks and empty beaches, roadside ceviche vendors and a little more space. Intrepid travelers stumble on deserted beaches and great surf spots, and the long, coconut-strewn Costa Ballena beaches feel like an isolated desert island (great for whale-watching). Parque Nacional Marino Ballena (p148)

3

4

Península de Osa
Secluded wilderness and wildlife for days

Muddy and intense, the vast, largely untouched rainforest of Parque Nacional Corcovado is no walk in the park. Here travelers with a sturdy pair of rubber boots thrust themselves into the unknown and emerge with stories of a lifetime. The further into the jungle you go, the better it gets: the best wildlife-watching, most desolate beaches and vivid adventures lie down these seldom-trodden trails.
Parque Nacional Corcovado (p126)

5

Manuel Antonio
Alive with the call of birds and monkeys

Although droves of visitors pack Parque Nacional Manuel Antonio, the country's most popular (and smallest) national park remains an absolute gem. Capuchin monkeys scurry across its idyllic beaches, brown pelicans dive-bomb its clear waters and sloths watch over its trails. It's a perfect place to introduce youngsters to the wonders of the rainforest; indeed, you're likely to feel like a kid yourself. Brown pelican, Parque Nacional Manuel Antonio (p164)

SIMON DANNHAUER/SHUTTERSTOCK ©

Southern Caribbean

Laid-back charm and surf scene

By day, lounge in a hammock, cycle to uncrowded beaches, hike
to waterfall-fed pools and visit remote indigenous territories. By
night, dip into zesty Caribbean cooking and sway to reggaetón at
open-air bars cooled by ocean breezes. An outpost of this unique
mix of Afro-Caribbean, Tico and indigenous culture, this area is also
a perfect base for jungle and ocean adventures. Playa Cocles (p82)

6

MACDUFF EVERTON/GETTY IMAGES ©

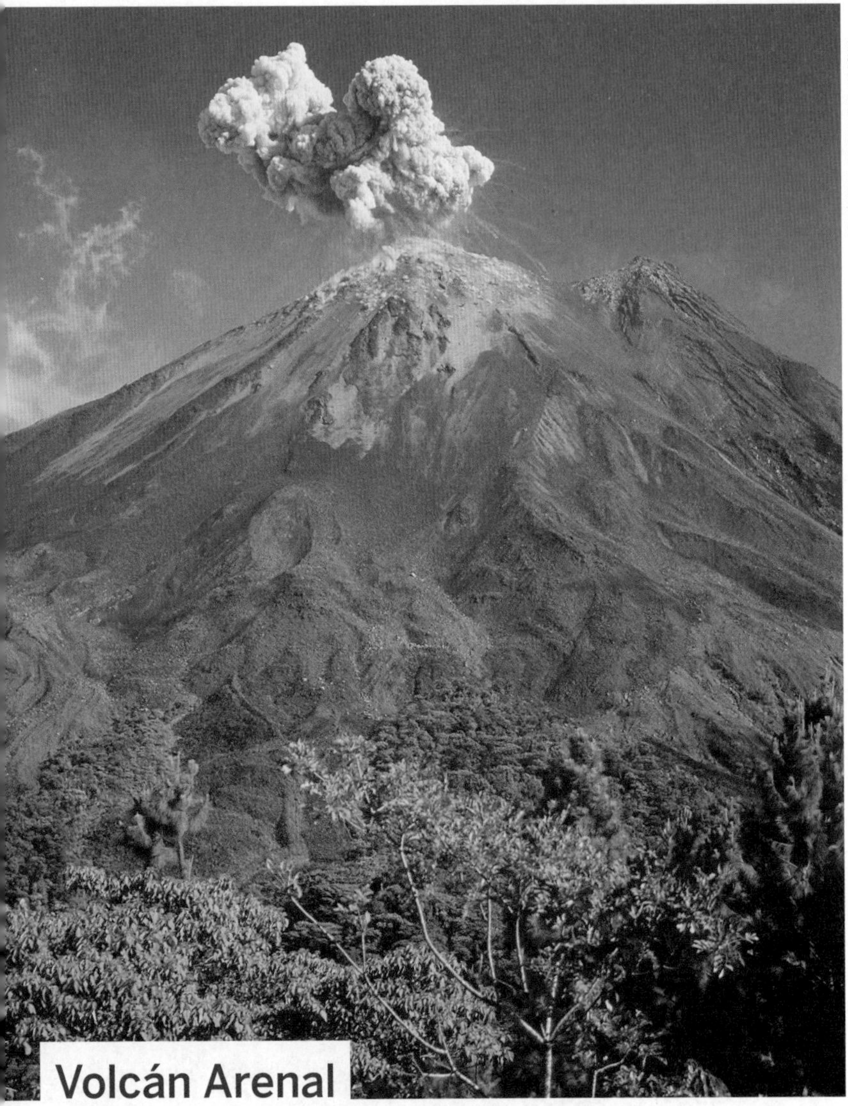

Volcán Arenal

Iconic volcano, bubbling springs, a stunning lake

While the molten night views are gone, this mighty, perfectly conical giant is still considered active and worthy of a pilgrimage. Shrouded in mist or bathed in sunshine, Arenal has several beautiful trails to explore, and at its base you're just a short drive away from its many hot springs, in which sore muscles are destined to be soothed.

7

Río Pacuare

Costa Rica's wildest white-water ride

Dedicated adrenaline junkies and white-water novices alike will appreciate heart-pounding Río Pacuare. Rapids range from Class I to Class V, with fun runs, fast rapids and smooth stretches allowing rafters to take in the luscious jungle scenery and animal life amid the glorious gorges. All you need is a life jacket, a helmet and some chutzpah.

9

Monteverde
A pristine expanse of virgin forest

Monteverde Cloud Forest owes much of its impressive natural beauty to Quaker settlers, who helped foster conservationist principles with Ticos of the region. But fascinating as the history is, the real romance is in nature: a mysterious Neverland shrouded in mist, draped with mossy vines, sprouting ferns and bromeliads, gushing creeks, blooming with life and nurturing rivulets of evolution. Far left: Monteverde Cloud Forest (p202); Left: Red-eyed tree frog

Parque Nacional Chirripó

Spectacular views above the clouds

The view from Costa Rica's highest peak – of wind-swept rocks and icy lakes – may not resemble the postcards, but the two-day hike above the clouds is one of the country's most satisfying excursions. A pre-dawn expedition rewards hardy hikers with a chance to catch the fiery sun rise and see both the Caribbean Sea and Pacific Ocean from 3820m. Top: Cerro Chirripó (p112); Above left: Parque Nacional Chirripó (p109); Above right: Yellow mushrooms

Sarapiquí Valley
Kayaking and rafting white-water adventures

Sarapiquí Valley rose to fame as a principal port in the nefarious old days of United Fruit dominance, only to be reborn as a paddler's paradise, thanks to the frothing serpentine magic of its namesake river. These days it's still a mecca for adventure-seekers; it's also dotted with fantastic ecolodges and private forest preserves in that steaming, looming, muddy jungle.

San José
Historic neighborhoods, vibrant culture, local cuisine

The heart of Tico culture lives in San José, as do university students, intellectuals, artists and politicians. While not the most attractive capital in Central America, it does have graceful neo-classical and Spanish-colonial architecture, leafy neighborhoods, museums housing pre-Columbian jade and gold, and sophisticated restaurants. Street art adds unexpected pops of color and public discourse to the cityscape. Ceramics, Museo Nacional de Costa Rica (p41)

Plan Your Trip
Need to Know

When to Go

Tamarindo
GO Nov–Apr

Puerto Limón
GO Jan–Apr

San José
GO Dec–Apr

Parque Nacional Manuel Antonio
GO Dec–Feb

Puerto Jiménez
GO Feb, Mar, Sep & Oct

■ Tropical climate, rain year-round
■ Tropical climate, wet and dry seasons

High Season (Dec–Apr)

○ 'Dry' season still sees some rain; beach towns fill with domestic tourists.

○ Accommodations should be booked well ahead; some places enforce minimum stays.

Shoulder (May–Jul & Nov)

○ Rain picks up and the stream of tourists starts to thin.

○ Roads are muddy and rivers begin to rise, making off-the-beaten-track travel more challenging.

Low Season (Aug–Oct)

○ Rainfall is highest, but storms bring swells to the Pacific and the best surfing conditions.

○ Rural roads can be impassable due to river crossings.

○ Accommodations prices lower significantly.

○ Some places close entirely; check before booking!

Currency

Costa Rican colón (₡)
US dollar ($)

Language

Spanish, English

Visas

Most nationalities do not need a visa for stays of up to 90 days. Check the visa requirements for your country at www.costarica-embassy.org.

Money

US dollars accepted almost everywhere and dispensed from most ATMs; carry colones for small towns, bus fares and rural shops. Credit cards generally accepted.

Cell Phones

Both 3G and 4G systems are available, but those compatible with US plans require expensive international roaming; prepaid SIM cards are cheap and widely available. See https://opensignal.com/networks for coverage details for each of the four cellular providers (Claro, Kolbi, Movistar, TuYo).

Time

Central Standard Time (GMT/UTC minus six hours)

Daily Costs

Budget: Less than US$40

- Dorm bed: US$8–15
- Meal at a *soda* (inexpensive lunch counter): US$3–7
- DIY hikes without a guide: free
- Travel via local bus: US$2 or less

Midrange: US$40–100

- Basic room with private bathroom: US$20–50 per day
- Meal at a restaurant geared toward travelers: US$5–12
- Travel on an efficient 1st-class shuttle van like Interbus: US$50–60

Top End: More than US$100

- Luxurious beachside lodges and boutique hotels: from US$80
- Meal at an international fusion restaurant: from US$20
- Guided wildlife-watching excursion: from US$40
- Short domestic flight: US$50–100
- 4WD rental for local travel: from US$60 per day

Useful Websites

Anywhere Costa Rica (www.anywhere.com/costa-rica) Excellent overviews of local destinations.

Essential Costa Rica (www.visitcostarica.com) The Costa Rica Tourism Board website has planning tips and destination details.

The Tico Times (www.ticotimes.net) Costa Rica's English-language newspaper's website; its searchable archives can be helpful for trip planning.

Lonely Planet (www.lonelyplanet.com/costa-rica) Destination information, hotel bookings, traveler forum and more.

Opening Hours

The following are high-season opening hours; hours will usually shorten in the shoulder and low seasons. Generally, sights, activities and restaurants are open daily.

Banks 9am to 4pm Monday to Friday, sometimes 9am to noon Saturday.

Bars and clubs 8pm to 2am.

Government offices 8am to 5pm Monday to Friday. Often closed between 11:30am and 1:30pm.

Restaurants 7am to 9pm. Upscale places may open only for dinner. In remote areas, even the small *sodas* might open only at specific meal times.

Shops 8am to 6pm Monday to Saturday.

Arriving in Costa Rica

Aeropuerto Internacional Juan Santamaría (San José) Buses from the airport to central San José (about US$1.50) run hourly all day. Taxis charge from US$30 and depart from the official stand; the trip takes from 20 minutes to an hour. Interbus runs between the airport and San José accommodations (US$17 per adult). Book ahead.

Getting Around

Air Inexpensive domestic flights between San José and popular destinations such as Puerto Jiménez, Quepos and Tortuguero will save you the driving time.

Bus Very reasonably priced, with extensive coverage of the country, though travel can be slow and some destinations have infrequent service.

Shuttle Private and shared shuttles such as Interbus and Gray Line provide door-to-door service between popular destinations and scheduling to your needs.

Car Renting a car allows you to access more remote destinations that are not served by buses, and frees you to cover as much ground as you like. Cars can be rented in most towns. Renting a 4WD vehicle is advantageous (and essential in some parts of the country); avoid driving at night.

For more on **getting around**, see p306

Plan Your Trip
Hot Spots for...

SEKAR BALASUBRAMANIAN/GETTY IMAGES ©

Wildlife-Watching

World-class parks, dedication to environmental protection, and mind-boggling biodiversity enable Costa Rica to harbor scores of rare and endangered species.

Península de Osa (p123)
Parque Nacional Corcovado teems with wildlife, including scarlet macaws, tapirs and four species of monkey.

What to Spot
Macaws along the Agujitas–Corcovado trail.

Tortuguero (p63)
The list of birds and amphibians is a mile long at this wildlife-rich park.

What to Spot
Turtles, herons, kites, kingfishers and macaws.

Parque Nacional Manuel Antonio (p164)
This park may be tiny, but it's full of wild creatures that are easily encountered.

What to Spot
Sloths, anteaters, four species of monkey.

GROGL/SHUTTERSTOCK ©

Surfing

Point and beach breaks, lefts and rights, reefs and river mouths, warm water and year-round waves make Costa Rica a favorite surfing destination.

Dominical (p154)
Countless foreigners show up here to surf – and can't bring themselves to leave.

Surf Lessons
Costa Rica Surf Camp (p157) can help you learn.

Southern Caribbean (p79)
Salsa Brava is the country's biggest break – in December waves get up to 7m.

Surf Lessons
Caribbean Surf School (p83) has top instructors.

Santa Teresa (p188)
The best beach break in Southern Nicoya, especially when there's an offshore wind.

Surf Lessons
Learn to ride waves with Nalu Surf School (p191).

Yoga

Something about yoga and Costa Rica go together, and beachfront studios are catering to this niche (fantastic views included).

SHELLYGRAPHY/SHUTTERSTOCK ©

Dominical (p154)
With big festivals and plenty of counter-culture, Dominical is a hotspot for spiritual stretching.

Where to Practice
Danyasa (p155) is the area's top yoga studio/stay.

Southern Nicoya (p181)
Away from it all, Southern Nicoya is an ideal place to relax, breathe and hold uncomfortable positions.

Where to Practice
Casa Zen (p194) is Santa Teresa's loveliest studio.

Montezuma (p192)
This laid-back beach town attracts a wellness-seeking set, with plenty of yoga studios and resorts.

Where to Practice
Montezuma Yoga (p194) is a top studio.

White-water Rafting

With Costa Rica's waterways and excellent operators, the opportunities for rushing down frothing white-water rapids will satisfy even the greatest thirst for adventure.

MARK NEWMAN/GETTY IMAGES ©

Río Pacuare (p97)
Take on runs of Class II to IV rapids on the country's best white water.

Tour Operator Exploradores Outdoors (p77) or Rios Tropicales (p101).

Río Sarapiquí (p250)
Less populated by people but crowded with wildlife, this is a great place to raft or kayak.

Tour Operator
Sarapiquí Outdoor Center (p251) is based in La Virgen.

Río Savegre (p170)
Gentle rapids that intensify in the rainy season are a great intro to rafting; trips depart from Quepos.

Tour Operator
For kayaking or tubing, try H2O Adventures (p170).

Plan Your Trip
Local Life

©JONATHAN GREGSON/LONELY PLANET ©

Activities

Miles of shoreline, endless warm water and a multitude of national parks and reserves provide an inviting playground for active travelers. Whether it's the solitude of absolute wilderness, family-oriented hiking and rafting adventures, or surfing and jungle trekking you seek, Costa Rica offers fun to suit everyone.

Be sure to pack for your adventure. Although the coastal areas are sunny, hot and humid, calling for a hat, shorts and short sleeves, you'll want to bring a sweater and lightweight jacket for popular high-elevation destinations such as Monteverde. If you plan to hike up Chirripó, bring lots of layers and a hat and gloves. Additionally, while hiking through the rainforest is often a hot and sweaty exercise, long sleeves and lightweight, quick-drying pants help keep the bugs away. A lightweight rain poncho comes in handy in quite a few places.

Shopping

Costa Rica has everything from full-on urban mall experiences to cute craft stores and stands in tourist towns, featuring well-made artisanal wares.

Avoid purchasing animal products, including turtle shells, animal skulls and anything made with feathers, coral or shells (it's illegal to export them).

Wood products can also be highly suspicious: make sure you know where the wood came from. Tropical-hardwood items include salad bowls, plates, carving boards, jewelry boxes, carvings and ornaments.

Coffee is a prevailing souvenir, available pretty much everywhere, even at the local grocery store. The most popular alcohol purchases are Ron Centenario, Café Rica (a coffee liqueur) and *guaro* (the local firewater).

Eating

A typical eating establishment is the *soda*. These are small, informal lunch counters dishing up a few daily *casados*

GUSTAVO MIRANDA HOLLEY/GETTY IMAGES ©

(set meals). Other cheapies include the omnipresent fried- and rotisserie-chicken stands.

A regular *restaurante* is usually higher on the price scale and has slightly more atmosphere. Many serve *casados,* while the fancier places refer to the set lunch as the *almuerzo ejecutivo* ('executive lunch').

For something smaller, *pastelerías* and *panaderías* are shops that sell pastries and bread, while many bars serve *bocas* ('mouthfuls'; snack-sized portions of main meals).

Drinking & Nightlife

In the more touristy areas of Costa Rica, there's no shortage of bars and night-clubs. San José has the most going on, with all the dive bars, lounges and dance clubs you could ask for. Most spots open at around 10pm, and don't truly get going until after midnight. When leaving a bar late at night, keep your wits about you and take a taxi.

★ Best for Nightlife

Club Vertigo (p57)

Costa Rica Craft Brewing (p56)

Lazy Mon (p92)

Roca Mar (p192)

Fuego Brew Co (p158)

At the beach, Santa Teresa and Puerto Viejo are top spots to tie one on, but almost every beach town in the country has at least one lively local night spot.

Entertainment

Live music, dance performances, parades, soccer matches and bullfights are the primary forms of entertainment. All can be found in San José on a regular basis. Nearly every town has its own festival, with carnival games, rides and rodeos.

From left: Surfing, Guanacaste province; *Casado* (set meal)

Plan Your Trip
Month by Month

January

Every year opens with a rush, as North American and domestic tourists flood beach towns to celebrate. January sees dry days and occasional afternoon showers.

🍷 Las Fiestas de Palmares

Ten days of boozing, horse shows and other carnival events take over the tiny town of Palmares in the second half of the month. There's also a running of the bulls – um, opt out.

February

February is the perfect month, with ideal weather and no holiday surcharges. The skies above Nicoya are particularly clear, and it's peak season for some species of nesting turtle to do their thing.

🎭 Envision Festival

Held in Uvita in late February, this is a festival with a consciousness-raising, transformational bent. It brings together fire dancers and performance artists of all stripes, yoga, music and spiritual workshops. Also takes place during the first week of March, in Dominical.

March

Excellent weather continues through the early part of March, though prices shoot up during Semana Santa, the week leading up to Easter and North American spring break (aka Holy Week and Unholy Week).

🎭 Día del Boyero

A colorful parade, held in Escazú on the second Sunday in March, features colorfully painted *carretas* (oxcarts, the national symbol) and includes a blessing of the animals. Plaid shirt and cowboy hat optional.

🎭 Feria de la Mascarada

During the Feria de la Mascarada, begun in 2002, people don massive colorful masks

Above: Dancers, Costa Rican Independence Day (p24)

(weighing up to 20kg) to dance and parade around the town square of Barva. Usually held during the last week of March.

April

Easter and Semana Santa can fall early in April, which means beaches fill and prices spike. Nicoya and Guanacaste are dry and hot, with little rain.

✤ Día de Juan Santamaría

Commemorating Costa Rica's national hero (the main airport is named for him), who died in battle against American colonist William Walker's troops in 1856, this day of celebration on April 11 includes parades, concerts and dances.

May

Attention, budget travelers: wetter weather begins to sweep across the country in May, heralding the country's low season. So, although conditions are pleasant, prices drop.

★ **Best Festivals**
Las Fiestas de Palmares, January
Envision, February
Día de Juan Santamaría, April
Independence Day, September
Día de los Muertos, November

✗ Día de San Isidro Labrador

Visitors can taste the bounty of San Isidro and neighboring villages during the nation's largest agricultural fairs, in honor of the growers' patron saint, on May 15. A chance to see soccer-playing priests? Don't miss it.

June

The Pacific Coast gets fairly wet during June, though this makes for good surfing. The beginning of the 'green season,' this time of year has lots of discounted rates.

Above: Envision Festival

LINDSAY FENDT/ALAMY STOCK PHOTO ©

✣ Festival de las Artes (FIA)

This multidisciplinary, multiday festival featuring international artists takes flight all across San José and has recently been moved to June or July.

July

July is mostly wet, particularly on the Caribbean coast, but the month also occasionally enjoys a brief dry period that Ticos call *veranillo* (summer). Expect rain, particularly late in the day.

✣ Día de Guanacaste

The 1824 annexation of Guanacaste from Nicaragua is celebrated with rodeos, bullfights, cattle shows and general bovine madness. It takes place on July 25.

August

The middle of the rainy season doesn't mean that mornings aren't bright and sunny. Travelers who don't mind some rain will find great hotel and tour deals.

✣ La Virgen de los Ángeles

The patron saint of Costa Rica, the Black Virgin or Black Madonna, is celebrated with an important religious procession from San José to Cartago on August 2.

September

The Península de Osa gets utterly soaked during September, which is the heart of the rainy season and what Ticos refer to as the *temporales del Pacífico*. It's the cheapest time to visit the Pacific.

✣ Costa Rican Independence Day

The center of the Independence Day action is the relay race that passes a 'Freedom Torch' from Guatemala to Costa Rica. The torch arrives at Cartago on the evening of the 14th, when the nation breaks into the national anthem.

October

Many roads become impassable as rivers swell and rain continues to fall in one of the wettest months in Costa Rica. Lodges and tour operators are sometimes closed until November.

✣ Día de la Raza

Columbus' historic landing on Isla Uvita has traditionally inspired a small carnival in Puerto Limón on October 12, with street parades, live music and dancing.

November

The weather can go either way in November. Access to Parque Nacional Corcovado is difficult after several months of rain, though the skies clear by month's end.

✣ Día de los Muertos

Families visit graveyards and hold religious parades in honor of the dead in this lovely and picturesque festival on November 2.

December

Although the beginning of the month is a great time to visit – with clearer skies and relatively uncrowded attractions – things ramp up toward Christmas and reservations become crucial.

✣ Festival de la Luz (Festival of Light)

San José comes to life as it marks the beginning of the Christmas season on the second Saturday of the month, with marching bands, spectacular floats, and various colorful light displays and artworks throughout downtown (www.festivaldelaluz.cr).

✣ Las Fiestas de Zapote

In San José between Christmas and New Year's Eve, this weeklong celebration of all things Costa Rican (rodeos, cowboys, carnival rides, fried food and booze) draws tens of thousands of Ticos to the bullring in the suburb of Zapote every day.

Plan Your Trip
Get Inspired

Read

Tropical Nature: Life and Death in the Rain Forests of Central and South America (Adrian Forsyth and Ken Miyata; 1987) Easy-to-digest natural-history essays on rainforest phenomena, written by two biologists.

There Never Was a Once Upon a Time (Carmen Naranjo; 1989) Ten stories, narrated by children and adolescents, by Costa Rica's most widely translated novelist.

Costa Rica: A Traveler's Literary Companion (Barbara Ras, foreword by Óscar Arias; 1994) A collection of stories reflecting distinct regions of Costa Rica.

Watch

El Regreso (The Return; 2011) Featuring a realistic, contemporary plot, this is the first Tico film to earn international acclaim. Hernán Jiménez wrote, directed, starred in and crowdfunded it.

Agua Fría de Mar (Cold Ocean Water; 2010) Directed by Paz Fábrega, this social commentary unfolds at a paradisiacal Pacific beach; the film won several international awards.

Caribe (Caribbean; 2004) The first Costa Rican film ever to be submitted for Oscar consideration; it's a drama set in Limón.

Listen

Various Artists, SíSan José (2011) A collaboration between a WFMU engineer and nine of Costa Rica's best indie rock acts.

Chavela Vargas, Coleccion Original RCA (1946) With the original long out of print, this 2011 re-issue from Costa Rican–born singer Vargas features hauntingly beautiful folk ballads.

Malpaís, Un Día Lejano (2009) Costa Rica's innovative and now defunct rock band mixes calypso, jazz and Latin American balladry.

Various Artists, Calypsos: Afro-Limonese Music From Costa Rica (1991) A raucous collection that captured the heart of Costa Rico's Afro-Caribbean folk scene.

Above: Scarlet macaw

Plan Your Trip
Five-Day Itineraries

Pacific Dreams

Spend your days exploring dreamy beaches, swimming in turquoise waters and spying on playful monkeys. Spend your nights indulging in amazing seafood, sunset views and rollicking nightlife.

San José (p35) Devote a day to exploring the neighborhoods, perusing the museums and sampling the dining and drinking scene.
✈ 1 hr to Quepos

Montezuma (p192) Hike to waterfalls, ride the surf and do sun salutations in open-air studios. This is the good life.

Manuel Antonio (p161) The national park is prime for hiking, wildlife-watching, swimming and kayaking, followed by sundowners at nearby bars. 🚌 to Jacó, then ⛴ 1 hr to Montezuma

Eastern Escapade

Raging rivers, jungle-clad canals, and post-card perfect beaches... Take a jaunt into the east and enter another world, where the power of the earth is palpable.

Tortuguero (p63) Paddle through luscious, greenery-draped canals, where birds and animals hide around every corner. ⚓ 3½ hrs to Moín, then 🚗 1 hr to Puerto Viejo

Sarapiquí Valley (p247) Prime territory for riding rapids, sampling local specialties and wildlife-watching.
🚗 2 hrs to La Pavona, then
⚓ 1 hr to Tortuguero

Puerto Viejo de Talamanca (p86) Relax into a hammock on the beach, feast on delicious Caribbean fare, and hike through steaming jungles.

10-Day Itinerary

Essential Costa Rica

This is the trip you've been dreaming about: a romp through paradise with seething volcanoes, tropical parks, ghostly cloud forests and sun-kissed beaches.

Playa Santa Teresa (p188) Next up: beach time. In this charming coastal enclave, surfing, snorkeling and swimming are at your doorstep. **3**

MATYAS REHAK/SHUTTERSTOCK ©

2

Volcán Arenal (p225) Head for La
Fortuna, where adventure awaits. Hike
to crater lakes, swim beneath
waterfalls and spot a sloth.
🚗 4 hrs to Monteverde

Monteverde (p199) Zip through the
treetops on a canopy tour or learn
about your favorite morning drink on a
coffee tour. 🚗 5 hrs to Santa Teresa

Plan Your Trip
Two-Week Itinerary

Southern Adventure

Satisfy your adventurous spirit with a journey to the lesser traveled southern sector. Climb the country's highest peak, then recover on its glorious beaches.

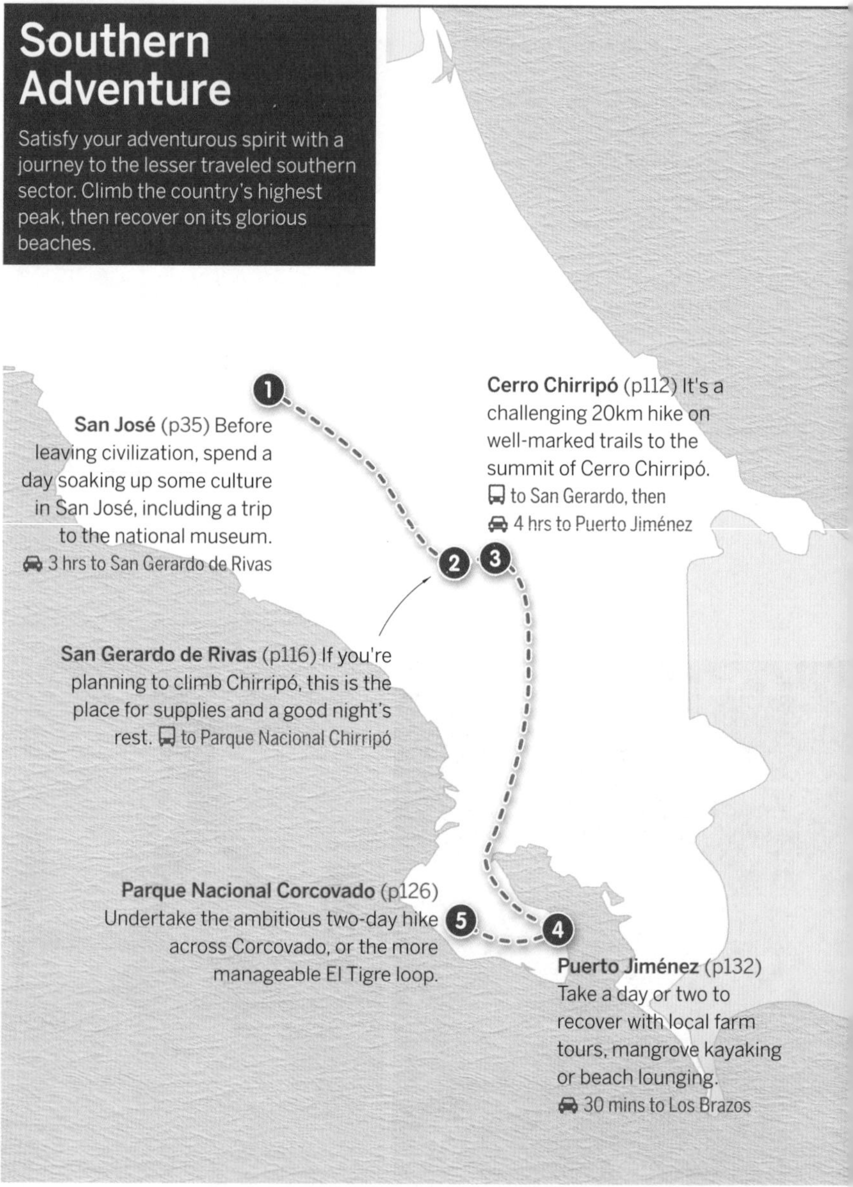

1

San José (p35) Before leaving civilization, spend a day soaking up some culture in San José, including a trip to the national museum.
🚙 3 hrs to San Gerardo de Rivas

Cerro Chirripó (p112) It's a challenging 20km hike on well-marked trails to the summit of Cerro Chirripó.
🚌 to San Gerardo, then
🚙 4 hrs to Puerto Jiménez

2 3

San Gerardo de Rivas (p116) If you're planning to climb Chirripó, this is the place for supplies and a good night's rest. 🚌 to Parque Nacional Chirripó

Parque Nacional Corcovado (p126) Undertake the ambitious two-day hike across Corcovado, or the more manageable El Tigre loop.

5 **4**

Puerto Jiménez (p132) Take a day or two to recover with local farm tours, mangrove kayaking or beach lounging.
🚙 30 mins to Los Brazos

Plan Your Trip
Family Travel

Mischievous monkeys and steaming volcanoes, mysterious rainforests and palm-lined beaches – Costa Rica sometimes seems like a comic book made real. The perfect place for family travel, it's a safe, exhilarating tropical playground that will make a huge impression on younger travelers. The country's myriad possibilities for adventure cover the spectrum of age-appropriate intensity levels – and for no intensity at all, some kids might like the idea of getting their hair braided and beaded by a beachside stylist in Puerto Viejo de Talamanca. Whatever you do, the warm culture is extremely welcoming of little ones.

In addition to amazing the kids, this small, peaceful country has all the practicalities that rank highly with parents, such as great country-wide transportation infrastructure, a low crime rate and an excellent health-care system. But the reason to bring the whole family is the opportunity to share unforgettable experiences such as spotting a dolphin or a sloth, slowly paddling a kayak through mangrove channels, or taking a night hike in search of tropical frogs.

Eating

o Hydration is particularly crucial in this tropical climate, especially for children who aren't used to the heat and humidity. Fortunately, Costa Rica's tap water is safe everywhere (except for the rare exception, usually in remote areas).

o If you're traveling with an infant or small child, stock up on formula, baby food and snacks before heading to remote areas, where shops are few and far between.

o Kids love refreshing *batidos* (fresh fruit shakes), either *al agua* (made with water) or *con leche* (with milk); the variety of novel tropical fruits may appeal to older kids.

o Coconut water might be old news back home, but watching a smiling Tico hack open a *pipa fría* (cold young coconut) for you with a machete is another thing entirely. It's often cheaper than bottled water.

BRANDON ALMS/SHUTTERSTOCK ©

○ Many restaurants have kids menus, but these tend to offer international rather than Costa Rican food.

Getting Around

○ Children under the age of 12 receive a discount of up to 25% on domestic flights, while on some carriers children under two fly free (provided they sit on a parent's lap).

○ Children aged three and up pay full fare with most bus companies.

○ Car seats for infants are not always available at car-rental agencies, so bring your own or make sure you double- (or triple-) check with the agency in advance.

Family Activities

Jaguar Centro de Rescate (p86) No jaguars were here at the time of research, but you may get to hold a howler monkey or a baby sloth. You'll also see colorful snakes, raptors and frogs.

★ Best Wildlife-Watching

Parque Nacional
Manuel Antonio (p164)
Parque Nacional Tortuguero (p72)
Parque Nacional
Marino Ballena (p148)
Monteverde (p199)

Frog's Heaven (p252) A frog-lover's heaven, this tropical garden is filled with all sorts of brightly colored (and transparent!) amphibians, including the iconic red-eyed tree frog.

Ecocentro Danaus (p234) Walk the trails to look for monkeys and sloths, visit a pond with caimans and turtles, delight in the butterfly garden and ogle frogs in the ranarium (frog pond).

Alturas Wildlife Sanctuary (p154) Meet various rescued critters here, from macaws and monkeys to Bubba the famous coatimundi.

From left: Monteverde (p199); Red-eyed tree frog

SAN JOSÉ

Central San José

The city's congested center is where you'll find its cultural and commercial hubs. (p44)

Barrio Escalante

Home to some of San José's trendiest bars and restaurants. (p52)

Río Virilla

Río Torres

Estación del Atlántico

PLAZA DE LA CULTURA

PLAZA DE LA DEMOCRACIA

Cementerio General

Estación del Pacífico

Río María Aguilar

Parque Recreativo La Paz

Los Yoses & San Pedro

These contiguous neighborhoods are home to a rollicking nightlife scene. (p52)

Central San José Map (p46)
La Sabana Map (p51)

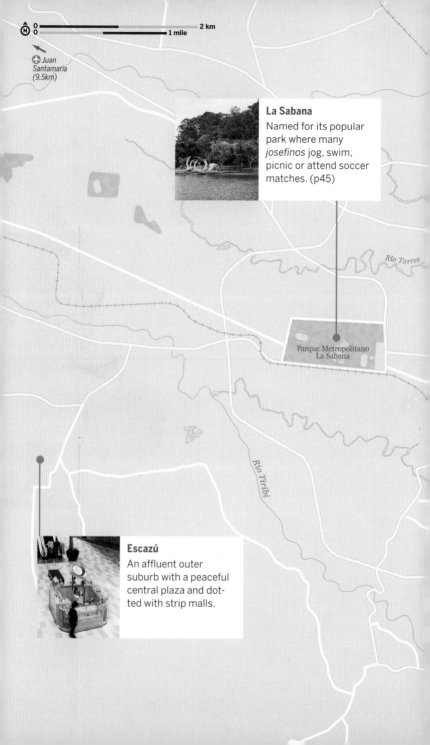

La Sabana
Named for its popular park where many *josefinos* jog, swim, picnic or attend soccer matches. (p45)

Río Torres

Parque Metropolitano
La Sabana

Río Tiribí

Escazú
An affluent outer suburb with a peaceful central plaza and dotted with strip malls.

Juan
Santamaría
(9.5km)

2 km
1 mile

San José at a Glance...

It's no secret that Chepe, as San José is affectionately known, doesn't make a great first impression, with its unremarkable concrete structures and honking traffic. Dig deeper, though, and you'll discover countless, untold charms. Poke around historic neighborhoods, where colonial mansions have been converted into contemporary art galleries, restaurants and boutique hotels. Stroll the bountiful farmers market, join the Sunday crowds in Parque La Sabana, dance the night away, or visit the museums of gold, jade, art and natural history. Only then will you begin to recognize the multidimensional appeal of Costa Rica's largest city and cultural capital.

One Day in San José

Begin with a peek inside the 19th-century **Teatro Nacional** (p38) and an espresso at its atmospheric **cafe** (p39). Then peruse pre-Columbian treasures at the **Museo de Oro Precolombino y Numismática** (p39). Take lunch at **Rávi Gastropub** (p53) in the city's culinary hub Barrio Escalante, then wander historic Barrio Amón and sample local microbrews at **Stiefel** (p56). Do dinner and cocktails at the fabulous **Café de los Deseos** (p50).

Two Days in San José

Start day two with a primer on Costa Rican history at the **Museo Nacional de Costa Rica** (p41), then visit the newly expanded **Museo de Jade** (p40). Head up to the **Mercado Central** (p44) for cigars and local snacks.

Grab dinner at the city's top restaurant, **Park Café** (p51), then venture east for a rooftop drink at **Azotea Calle 7** (p56), then catch a local band at **Mundoloco El Chante** (p58).

Music Temple, Parque Morazán (p42)

Arriving in San José

International flights arrive at Aeropuerto Internacional Juan Santamaría in nearby Alajuela. An official, metered taxi from the airport to downtown San José costs around US$30. There are also Interbus shuttles and public buses operated by Tuasa and Station Wagon that run between downtown and the airport. The drive takes 20 minutes to an hour, sometimes longer on the bus.

Sleeping

Accommodations in San José run the gamut from simple but homey hostels to luxurious boutique retreats. If you're flying into or out of Costa Rica from here, it may be more convenient to stay in Alajuela, as the town is minutes from the international airport.

For information on what each neighborhood has to offer, see p61.

Teatro Nacional

MIHAI-BOGDAN LAZAR/SHUTTERSTOCK ©

Plaza de la Cultura

This architecturally unremarkable concrete plaza in the heart of downtown is usually packed with locals slurping ice-cream cones and observing street life: juggling clowns, itinerant vendors and cruising teenagers.

Great For...

☑ Don't Miss

The Teatro Nacional's most famous painting, *Alegoría al café y el banano*.

Teatro Nacional

On the southern side of the Plaza de la Cultura resides the **Teatro Nacional** (Map p46; ☑2010-1110; www.teatronacional.go.cr; US$10; ☺9am-7pm), San José's most revered building. Constructed in 1897, it features a columned neoclassical facade that is flanked by statues of Beethoven and famous 17th-century Spanish dramatist Calderón de la Barca. The lavish marble lobby and auditorium are lined with paintings depicting various facets of 19th-century life. The hourly tours here are fantastic, and if you're looking to rest your feet, there's also an excellent on-site cafe.

The theater's most famous painting is *Alegoría al café y el banano*, an idyllic canvas showing coffee and banana harvests. The painting was produced in Italy and shipped to Costa Rica for installation in

Sculpture at Teatro Nacional

❶ Need to Know

Map p46; Avs Central & 2 btwn Calles 3 & 5

✕ Take a Break

Enjoy an espresso at the Teatro Nacional's atmospheric **Alma de Café** (Map p46; ☏2010-1119; www.teatronacional.go.cr/ Cafeteria; mains US$6-11; ⊙9am-7pm Mon-Sat, to 6pm Sun).

★ Top Tip

Tours are offered every hour on the hour in Spanish and English.

Performances

Costa Rica's most important theater stages plays, dance, opera, symphony, Latin American music and other major events. The main season runs from March to November, but there are performances throughout the year.

Museo de Oro Precolombino y Numismática

This three-in-one **museum** (Map p46; ☏2243-4202; www.museosdelbancocentral.org; adult/student/child US$11/8/free; ⊙9:15am-5pm) houses an extensive collection of Costa Rica's most priceless pieces of pre-Columbian gold and other artifacts, including historical currency and some contemporary regional art. The museum, located underneath the Plaza de la Cultura, is owned by the Banco Central and its architecture brings to mind all the warmth and comfort of a bank vault. Security is tight; visitors must leave bags at the door.

the theater, and the image was reproduced on the old ₡5 note (now out of circulation). It seems clear that the painter never witnessed a banana harvest because of the way the man in the center is awkwardly grasping a bunch (actual banana workers hoist the stems onto their shoulders).

Tours

On this fascinating **tour** (☏ext 1114 2010-1100; www.teatronacional.go.cr/Visitenos/ turismo; Av 2 btwn Calles 3 & 5; tours US$10; ⊙9am-5pm), guests are regaled with stories of the art, architecture and people behind Costa Rica's crown jewel, the national theater. The best part is a peek into otherwise off-limits areas, such as the Smoking Room, which feature famous paintings, lavish antique furnishings and ornate gold trim.

Sphere, Museo Nacional de Costa Rica

Plaza de la Democracia

Between the national museum and the Museo de Jade is the stark Plaza de la Democracia, which was constructed by President Óscar Arias in 1989 to commemorate 100 years of Costa Rican democracy.

Great For...

☑ **Don't Miss**

Mural by César Valverde Vega in the Museo de Jade.

Museo de Jade

Reopened in its brand-new home in mid-2014, this **museum** (Map p46; ☎2521-6610; www.museodeljadeins.com; US$15; ☺10am-5pm) houses the world's largest collection of American jade (pronounced 'ha-day' in Spanish). The ample exhibition space (five floors offer six exhibits) allows the public extensive access to the museum's varied collection. There are nearly 7000 finely crafted, well-conserved pieces, from translucent jade carvings depicting fertility goddesses, shamans, frogs and snakes to incredible ceramics (some reflecting Maya influences), including a highly unusual ceramic head displaying a row of serrated teeth.

Pre-Columbian jade jewelry, Museo Nacional de Costa Rica

WOLFGANG KAEHLER/GETTY IMAGES ©

❶ Need to Know

Map p46; Avs Central & 2 btwn Calles 13 & 15

✕ Take a Break

Touristy **Nuestra Tierra** (Map p46; ☏2258-6500; cnr Av 2 & Calle 15, Escazú; mains US$6-22; ☺6am-midnight; ♟) is a fine spot for lunch and sangria after a visit to the nearby museums.

★ Top Tip

The elevated terraces provide lovely views of the mountains surrounding San José (especially at sunset).

Museo Nacional de Costa Rica

Entered via a beautiful glassed-in atrium housing an exotic butterfly garden, this **museum** (Map p46; ☏2257-1433; www.museocostarica.go.cr; Calle 17 btwn Avs Central & 2; adult/child US$9/4; ☺8:30am-4:30pm Tue-Sat, 9am-4:30pm Sun) provides a quick survey of Costa Rican history. Exhibits of pre-Columbian pieces from ongoing digs, as well as artifacts from the colony and the early republic, are all housed inside the old Bellavista Fortress, which historically served as the army headquarters and saw fierce fighting (hence the pockmarks) in the 1948 civil war.

It was here that President José Figueres Ferrer announced, in 1949, that he was abolishing the country's military. Among the museum's many notable pieces is the fountain pen that Figueres used to sign the 1949 constitution.

Don't miss the period galleries in the northeast corner, which feature turn-of-the-20th-century furnishings and decor from when these rooms served as the private residences of the fort's various commanders.

Mercado Artesanal

The **Mercado Artesanal** (Crafts Market; Map p46; ☺9am-5pm) is a touristy open-air market that sells everything from handcrafted jewelry and Bob Marley T-shirts to elaborate woodwork and Guatemalan sarongs.

Asamblea Legislativa

Costa Rica's congress meets in the grand **Asamblea Legislativa** (Legislative Assembly; Map p46; cnr Av 8 & Calle 33) in the center of San José.

San José Walking Tour

Historic Barrio Amón abounds with 19th-century *cafetalero* (coffee grower) mansions and brightly painted tropical Victorians, many of which house hotels, cafes and boutiques.

Start Parque España
Distance 1.4km
Duration 2 hours

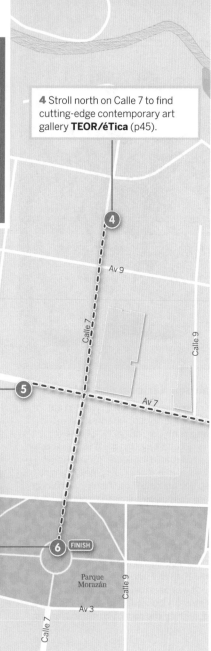

4 Stroll north on Calle 7 to find cutting-edge contemporary art gallery **TEOR/éTica** (p45).

Av 9

Calle 7

Calle 9

Av 7

5 Back on Av 7, **Galería Namu** (p49) has the country's best selection of indigenous handicrafts.

6 End your tour at **Parque Morazán**, which is particularly lovely in the evenings.

6 FINISH

Parque Morazán

Calle 9

Av 3

Calle 7

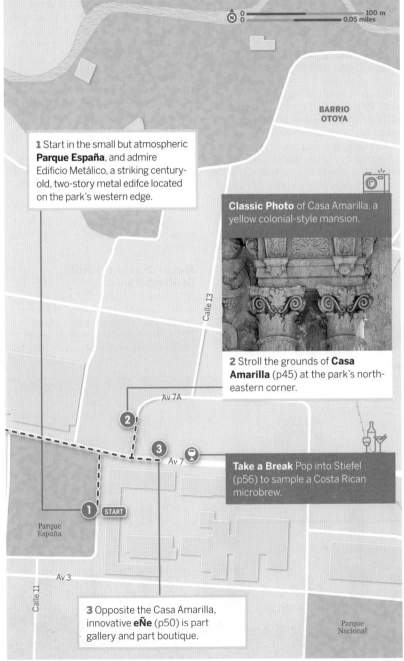

1 Start in the small but atmospheric **Parque España**, and admire Edificio Metálico, a striking century-old, two-story metal edifce located on the park's western edge.

Classic Photo of Casa Amarilla, a yellow colonial-style mansion.

2 Stroll the grounds of **Casa Amarilla** (p45) at the park's north-eastern corner.

Take a Break Pop into Stiefel (p56) to sample a Costa Rican microbrew.

3 Opposite the Casa Amarilla, innovative **eÑe** (p50) is part gallery and part boutique.

BARRIO OTOYA

Calle 13

Av 7A

Av 7

Av 3

Calle 11

Parque España

Parque Nacional

START

100 m
0.05 miles

2. LINDA WHITWAM/GETTY IMAGES © 5. HUMBERTO OLARTE CUPAS/ALAMY STOCK PHOTO © 6 E. ROJAS/GETTY IMAGES ©

⊙ SIGHTS

◎ Central San José

Barrio Amón   Area

North and west of Plaza España lies this pleasant, historic neighborhood, home to a cluster of *cafetalero* (coffee grower) mansions constructed during the late 19th and early 20th centuries. In recent years, many of the area's historic buildings have been converted into hotels, restaurants and offices, making this a popular district for an architectural stroll. You'll find everything from art-deco concrete manses to brightly painted tropical Victorian structures in various states of upkeep. It is a key arts center.

Barrio Escalante   Area

Formerly a residential enclave, the streets of this increasingly hip neighborhood are now lined with dozens of restaurants, cafes, bakeries and bars. The largest concentration of eateries stretches along Calle 33 and has been dubbed Paseo Gastronómico La Luz (La Luz Restaurant Promenade) in honor of a small grocery store that used to stand on the street's corner facing Avenida Central. Crowds of foodies descend on Barrio Escalante on weekend evenings, when finding parking becomes a very tall order.

Mercado Central   Market

(Map p46; Avs Central & 1 btwn Calles 6 & 8; ◷6:30am-6pm Mon-Sat) Though *josefinos* mainly do their shopping at chain supermarkets, San José's crowded indoor markets retain an old-world feel. This is the main market, lined with vendors hawking everything from spices and coffee beans to *pura vida* souvenir T-shirts made in China. It's all super cheap, and likely made in China or Nicaragua.

In December Mercado Central sometimes has extended hours and is open on Sundays.

Museo de Arte y Diseño Contemporáneo   Museum

(MADC; Map p46; ☏2257-7202; www.madc.cr; cnr Av 3 & Calle 15; US$3, Tue free; ◷9:30am-5pm Tue-Sat) Commonly referred to as MADC, the Contemporary Art & Design Museum is housed in the historic National

Museo de los Niños

Liquor Factory building, which dates from 1856. The largest and most important contemporary-art museum in the region, MADC is focused on the works of contemporary Costa Rican, Central American and South American artists, and occasionally features temporary exhibits devoted to interior design, fashion and graphic art.

TEOR/éTica
Gallery

(Map p46; ✆2233-4881; www.teoretica.org; cnr Calle 7 & Av 11; ⏱9am-5pm Mon, Tue & Thu, to 6pm Wed, to noon Fri, 10am-4pm Sat) **FREE** This contemporary-art museum is the bricks-and-mortar gathering space for the TEOR/éTica Foundation, a nonprofit organization that supports Central American art and culture. Housed in a pair of vintage mansions across the street from one another, each of its elegant rooms exhibits cutting-edge works by established and emerging figures from Latin America and the rest of the world.

Casa Amarilla
Historic Building

(Map p46; Av 7 btwn Calles 11 & 13) On Parque España's northeast corner, this elegant colonial-style yellow mansion (closed to the public) houses the Foreign Affairs Ministry. The ceiba tree in front was planted by John F. Kennedy during his 1963 visit to Costa Rica. If you walk around to the property's northeast corner, you can see a graffiti-covered slab of the Berlin Wall standing in the rear garden.

◎ La Sabana & Around

Parque Metropolitano La Sabana
Park

Once the site of San José's main airport, this 72-hectare green space at the west end of Paseo Colón is home to a museum, **Museo de Arte Costarricense** (Map p51; ✆2256-1281; www.musarco.go.cr; east entrance of Parque La Sabana; ⏱9am-4pm Tue-Sun; 👶) **FREE**, a lagoon and various sporting facilities – most notably Costa Rica's National Stadium (p58). During the day, the park's paths make a relaxing place for a stroll, a jog or a picnic.

 San José for Children

If you're hanging out in San José for a day – or two or three – with your kids, here are some activities they will enjoy.
Museo de Ciencias Naturales La Salle (Map p51; ✆2232-1306; www.museolasalle. ed.cr; Sabana Sur; adult/child US$2/1.60; ⏱8am-4pm Mon-Sat, 9am-5pm Sun; 👶) Ever wanted to see a spider-monkey skeleton? This natural-history museum near Parque La Sabana's southwest corner has an extensive collection of taxidermic animals and birds from Costa Rica and far beyond, alongside animal skeletons, minerals, preserved specimens and a vast new collection of butterflies.
Museo de los Niños & Galería Nacional (Map p46; ✆2258-4929; www. museocr.org; Calle 4, north of Av 9; adult/child US$3.80/3.50; ⏱8am-4:30pm Tue-Fri, 9:30am-5pm Sat & Sun; 👶) If you were wondering how to get your young kids interested in art and science, this unusual museum is an excellent place to start. Housed in an old penitentiary built in 1909, it is part children's museum and part art gallery. Small children will love the hands-on exhibits related to science, geography and natural history, while grown-ups will enjoy the unusual juxtaposition of contemporary art in abandoned prison cells.
Spirogyra Jardín de Mariposas (Map p46; ✆2222-2937; www.butterflygardencr. com; Barrio Amón; adult/child US$7/4; ⏱9am-2pm Mon-Fri, to 3pm Sat & Sun; 👶; 🚌to El Pueblo) Housing more than 30 species of butterflies in plant-filled enclosures, this small butterfly garden is a great spot for kids. Visit in the morning to see plenty of fluttering. The garden is 150m east and 150m south of Centro Comercial El Pueblo, which can be reached on foot (about a 20- to 30-minute walk from downtown), by taxi or by bus.

Central San José

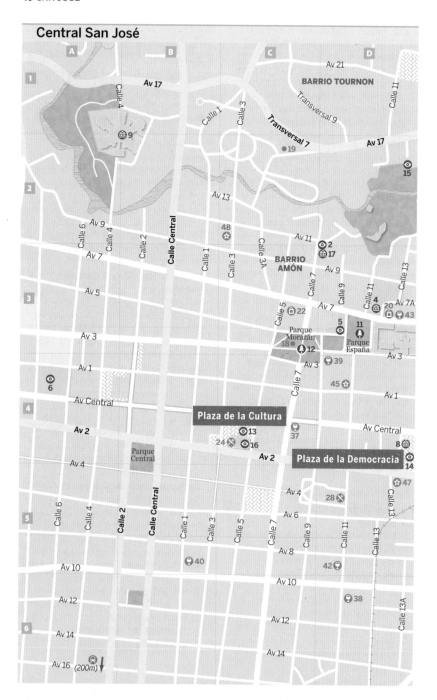

BARRIO TOURNON

Av 21

Av 17

Transversal 9

Transversal 7

Av 17

BARRIO AMÓN

Parque Morazán

Parque España

Plaza de la Cultura

Plaza de la Democracia

Parque Central

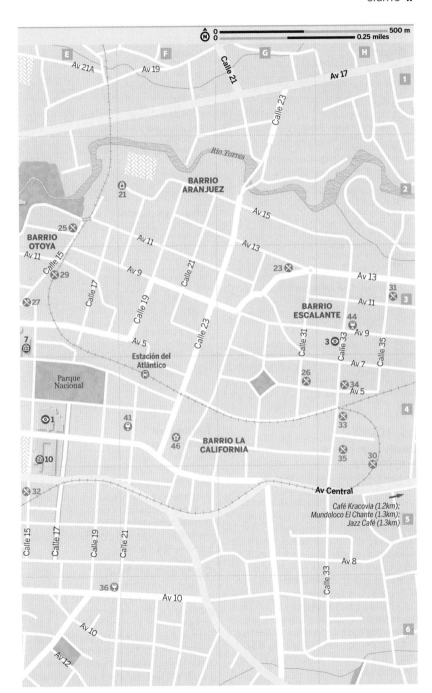

0   500 m
0   0.25 miles

Av 21A

Av 19

Calle 21

Av 17

Río Torres

BARRIO ARANJUEZ

21

Av 15

25

BARRIO OTOYA

Av 11

Av 11

Av 13

Calle 15

Av 9

Calle 21

23

Av 13

29

Calle 23

Av 11

31

27

Calle 17

Calle 19

BARRIO ESCALANTE

44

Av 9

7

Av 5

3

Calle 33

Calle 35

Estación del Atlántico

Calle 31

Av 7

26

Av 5

34

Parque Nacional

1

41

33

46

BARRIO LA CALIFORNIA

35

30

10

32

Av Central

Café Kracovia (1.2km);
Mundoloco El Chante (1.3km);
Jazz Café (1.3km)

Calle 15

Calle 17

Calle 19

Calle 21

Av 8

Calle 33

36

Av 10

Av 10

Av 12

Central San José

⊙ TOURS

Really Experience Community
Tours

(Triángulo de la Solidaridad Slum Tour; ☑2297-7058; www.boywithaball.com; US$12-25 per person, $100 minimum group rate) Nonprofit Boy with a Ball wants to be clear: Really Experience Community is not your average slum tour. It may seem exploitative, but visiting El Triángulo, a squatter development of 2000 people north of San José, is anything but. Promising young residents lead tours, introducing guests to neighbors and community entrepreneurs. No cameras are allowed, but the conversations make a lasting impression.

Note that this tour has a minimum cost of $100, making it ideal for groups. Boy With a Ball requires that you book at least three days in advance.

Barrio Bird Walking Tours
Walking

(Map p46; ☑6280-6169; www.toursanjosecostarica.com; tours from US$29) Knowledgeable and engaging guides show visitors San José's famous and not-so-famous sights, providing history and insight on the city's architecture, markets and urban art. Specialized tours also cater to foodies and culture enthusiasts.

Costa Rica Art Tour
Tours

(☑8359-5571, in USA 877-394-6113; www.costaricaarttours.com; per person US$150) This small outfit run by Molly Keeler conducts private tours that offer an intimate look at artists in their studios, where you can view (and buy) the work of local painters, sculptors, printmakers, ceramicists and jewelers. Lunch and San José city hotel pickup is included in the price. Reserve at least a week in advance. Discounts are available for groups.

Swiss Travel Service Walking
(Map p46; ☑2282-4898, 8310-7636; www.swisstravelcr.com; price dependent on group size) This long-standing agency offers a four-hour afternoon city tour of San José that hits all the key sites. Not offered on Mondays.

Carpe Chepe Tours
(☑8347-6198; www.carpechepe.com; guided pub crawls US$20; ◷8pm Fri & Sat) For an insider's look at Chepe's nightlife, join one of these Friday- and Saturday-evening guided pub crawls, led by an enthusiastic group of young locals. A shot is included at each of the four bars visited. There are other offerings as well, including a hop-on-hop-off nightlife bus, food tours, a craft-beer tour and free walking tours of San José. Note that the tours may not run on time and can feel a bit disorganized.

🔒 SHOPPING

Whether you're looking for indigenous carvings, high-end furnishings or a stuffed sloth, San José has no shortage of shops, running the gamut from artsy boutiques to tourist traps stocked full of tropical everything. Haggling is not tolerated in stores (markets are the exception).

**Feria Verde
de Aranjuez** Market
(Map p46; www.feriaverde.org; Barrio Aranjuez; ◷7am-12:30am Sat) For a foodie-friendly cultural experience, don't miss this fabulous Saturday farmers market, a weekly meeting place for San José's artists and organic growers since 2010. You'll find organic coffee, artisanal chocolate, tropical-fruit ice blocks, fresh produce, leather, jewelry and more at the long rows of booths set up in the park at the north end of Barrio Aranjuez.

Don't miss the mouthwatering samples of cured trout and fish dip, which an enthusiastic German expat loves feeding to passersby.

🔖 **Biesanz Woodworks**

Located in the hills of Bello Horizonte in Escazú, the workshop of **Biesanz Woodworks** (☑2289-4337; www.biesanz.com; 33 Calle Pedrero; ◷8am-5pm Mon-Fri, 9am-2pm Sat) can be difficult to find, but the effort will be well worth it. This shop is one of the finest woodcrafting studios in the nation, run by celebrated artisan Barry Biesanz.

His bowls and other decorative containers are exquisite and take their inspiration from pre-Columbian techniques, in which the natural lines and forms of the wood determine the shape and size of the bowl. The pieces are expensive (from US$45 for a palm-size bowl), but they are unique – and so delicately crafted that they wouldn't be out of place in a museum.

IMAGE SUPPLIED BY BIESANZ WOODWORKS ©

Galería Namu Arts & Crafts
(Map p46; ☑2256-3412, in USA 800-616-4322; www.galerianamu.com; Av 7 btwn Calles 5 & 7; ◷9am-6:30pm Mon-Sat year-round, plus 1-5pm Sun Dec-Apr) This fair-trade gallery brings together artwork and cultural objects from a diverse population of regional ethnicities, including Boruca masks, finely woven Wounaan baskets, Guaymí dolls, Bribrí canoes, Chorotega ceramics, traditional Huetar reed mats, and contemporary urban and Afro-Caribbean crafts. It can also help arrange visits to remote indigenous territories in different parts of Costa Rica.

eÑe
Arts & Crafts

(Map p46; ☏2222-7681; laesquina13y7@gmail.com; cnr Av 7 & Calle 11A; ☺10am-6:30pm Mon-Sat) This hip little design shop across from Casa Amarilla sells all manner of pieces crafted by Costa Rican designers and artists, including clothing, jewelry, handbags, picture frames, zines and works of graphic art.

 EATING

From humble corner stands dishing out gut-filling *casados* (set meals) to contemporary bistros serving fusion everything, in cosmopolitan San José you'll find the country's best restaurant scene. Dedicated foodies should also check out the dining options in Los Yoses and San Pedro, as well as Escazú and Santa Ana.

Top-end restaurants are often busy on weekend evenings; make a reservation.

 Central San José

Café de los Deseos
Cafe $

(Map p46; ☏2222-0496; www.facebook.com/Cafedelosdeseos; Calle 15 btwn Avs 9 & 11; mains US$5-12; ☺11:30am-10pm Tue-Thu, to 11pm Fri & Sat; ☎) Abuzz with artsy young bohemians, this colorful Barrio Otoya cafe makes a romantic spot for drinks (from wine to cocktails to smoothies), *bocas* (handmade tortillas with Turrialba cheese, salads, teriyaki chicken, individual pizzas), and tempting desserts. Walls are hung with the work of local artists and rooms are adorned with hand-painted tables, beaded curtains and branches entwined with fairy lights.

Kula
Cafe $$

(Map p46; ☏8583-0786; cnr Calle 15 & Av 7; mains $7-12; ☺10:45am-5:45pm) This sunny yellow cafe is newly perched in a second-story space, its plant-draped windows framing a particularly scenic corner of Barrio Amón. The food is fresh and inventive, with highlights including a *pejibaye* (peach palm fruit) and heart of palm salad, and mouthwatering *arepas*

filled with mushrooms and cheese. Don't miss the *churro* truffles for dessert.

La Esquina de Buenos Aires
Argentine $$$

(Map p46; ☏2223-1909; www.laesquinadebuenosaires.com; cnr Calle 11 & Av 4; mains US$15-29; ☺11:30am-3pm & 6-10:30pm Mon-Thu, 11:30am-11pm Fri, 12:30pm-11pm Sat, noon-10pm Sun; ☎) White linens and the sound of old tango evoke the atmospheric bistros of San Telmo, as does the menu, featuring grilled Argentine cuts of steak, house-made *empanadas* and an extensive selection of fresh pastas in exquisite sauces. The excellent South American–centric wine list and attentive service make this an ideal place for a date. Reservations recommended.

La Terrasse
French $$$

(Map p46; ☏8939-8470; chef.patricia.frenchcuisine@gmail.com; Calle 15 btwn Avs 9 & 11; mains US$17-32) Hidden away in the living room of a 1925 Barrio Otoya home, this intimate French restaurant regularly welcomes well-heeled locals with something to celebrate. Gracious Gerald plays host while his wife, the talented chef Patricia, reveals her fine sensibilities in thick, creamy soups and cheeses, hearty meat dishes and imaginative presentation. Order French wine and a few dishes to share.

 La Sabana & Around

Lubnan
Lebanese $$

(Map p51; ☏2257-6071; www.facebook.com/lubnancr; Paseo Colón btwn Calles 22 & 24; mains US$8-25; ☺11am-3pm & 6pm-midnight Tue-Fri, noon-4pm & 6pm-midnight Sat, 11am-5pm Sun; ℗) This atmospheric Lebanese place is a great date spot, with creamy hummus, flavorful tabbouleh and an array of succulent meats – some cooked, some deliciously raw. Waiters wear fezzes and a live belly-dancing performance goes down every Thursday at 8:30pm. DJs perform on Saturday night.

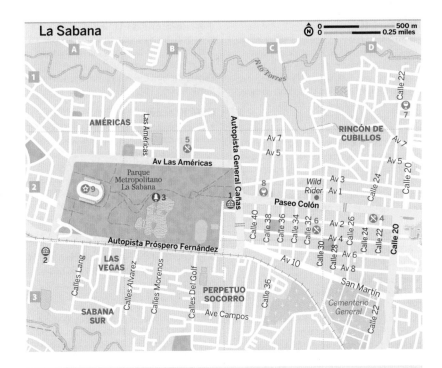

La Sabana

◎ Sights

Park Café European $$$

(Map p51; ☏ 2290-6324; www.parkcafecosta
rica.blogspot.com; Calle 48; tapas US$6-12,
mains US$17-35; ⊙5-9:15pm Tue-Sat) At this
felicitous fusion of antique shop and French
restaurant, Michelin-starred chef Richard
Neat offers an exquisite menu of smaller
sampling plates (Spanish tapas–style),
normal-sized mains, and a thoughtful wine
list. The romantic candlelit courtyard is
eclectically decorated with Asian antiques
imported by Neat's partner, Louise France.

It's near Parque La Sabana's northeast cor-
ner (100m north of Rostipollos restaurant).

The tantalizing menu includes classic fla-
vor combinations – carpaccio of beef with
mustard dressing – alongside innovative of-
ferings such as crab ravioli with asparagus
and ginger cappuccino, crispy leg of duck
with cucumber-mint salad or Gorgonzola
gnocchi with prune-stuffed pork fillet, all
prepared with passion and flair by Neat
himself. An eight-table limit magnifies the
intimate atmosphere.

**Restaurante
Grano de Oro**   Fusion $$$

(Map p51; ☎2255-3322; www.hotelgranodeoro.com; Calle 30 btwn Avs 2 & 4; lunch mains US$15-29, dinner mains US$19-42; ⏱7am-10pm)
Known for its Costa Rican–fusion cuisine, this stately, flower-filled restaurant is one of San José's top dining destinations. The menu features unique specialties such as sea bass breaded with toasted macadamia nuts or seared duck crowned with caramelized figs, and there's an encyclopedic international wine list. For dessert, don't miss the coffee cream mousse. Dinner reservations recommended.

✪ Los Yoses, Barrio Escalante & San Pedro

**Mantras Veggie
Cafe and Tea House**   Vegetarian $

(Map p46; ☎2253-6715; www.facebook.com/mantrasveggiecafe; Calle 35 btwn Avs 11 & 13; mains US$8-10; ⏱8:30am-5pm; 🌱) Widely recognized as the best vegetarian restaurant in San José (if not all of Costa Rica), Mantras draws rave reviews from across the foodie spectrum for meatless main dishes, salads and desserts so delicious that it's easy to forget you're eating healthily. It's in Barrio Escalante, and there's a great brunch on Saturdays and Sundays.

Café Kracovia   Cafe $

(☎2253-9093; www.cafekracovia.com; Paseo del la Segunda Republica; snacks US$4-10, mains US$8-14; ⏱10:30am-9pm Mon, to 11pm Tue-Sat; 🛜) With several distinct spaces, from the low-lit, intimate downstairs to the outdoor garden courtyard, this hip cafe has something for everyone. Contemporary artwork and a university vibe create an appealing ambience for lunching on crepes, wraps, salads, Polish food and craft beer. It's 500m north of the Fuente de la Hispanidad traffic circle, where San Pedro and Los Yoses converge.

**Sofia
Mediterráneo**   Mediterranean $$

(Map p46; ☎2224-5050; www.facebook.com/SofiaMediterraneo; cnr Calle 33 & Av 1; mains US$8-22; ⏱6-11pm Tue-Fri, noon-11pm Sat, noon-5pm & 6:30-9pm Sun; 🌱) This Barrio

Escalante gem serves a superb mix of authentic Mediterranean specialties, including house-made hummus, tortellini, grilled lamb and a rotating selection of daily specials, accompanied by sweet, delicate baklava for dessert. The restaurant doubles as a community cultural center where owner Mehmet Onuralp hosts occasional themed dinners featuring musicians, chefs and speakers from around the world.

Rávi Gastropub
Gastropub $$

(Map p46; ☑2253-3771; www.facebook.com/ravicostarica; cnr Calle 33 & Av 5; mains US$9-18; �spnoon-11pm Tue-Thu, to midnight Fri & Sat) This cool corner pub in Barrio Escalante is awash in bright murals, with seating in cushy blue booths, intimate back rooms or on the convivial bar stools up front. A menu of *bocas*, sandwiches, pizzas and more is served with craft brew on tap and homemade tropical-fruit sodas served in cute little bell jars.

At lunchtime, pick from the rotating menu of appetizers and main dishes and throw in a homemade soda, all for US$10.

Olio
Mediterranean $$

(Map p46; ☑2281-0541; www.facebook.com/Restaurante.olio; cnr Calle 33 & Av 3; tapas from US$7, dishes US$12-22; �11:30am-11pm Mon-Wed, to midnight Thu & Fri, 6pm-midnight Sat; ☑) This cozy, Mediterranean-flavored gastropub in a century-old brick building in Barrio Escalante serves a long list of tempting tapas, including divine stuffed mushrooms, goat-cheese croquettes, and pastas. The enticing drinks list includes homemade sangria and a decent selection of beers and wine. It's a romantic spot for a date, with imaginative, conversation-worthy quirks of decor and beautiful patrons.

Al Mercat
Gastronomy $$

(Map p46; ☑2221-0783; http://almercat.com; Av 13, Barrio Escalante; US$8-25; �spnoon-5pm Tue & Wed, noon-5pm & 6:30-10pm Thu-Sat, noon-3pm Sun; ☑) This exquisite Barrio Escalante restaurant serves whatever is fresh from the market. Family-style dishes of corn and sweet potato *chalupas* or grilled vegetables with smoked cheese are fresh and flavorful. Although vegetarians are well served, meat eaters will appreciate the fine cuts of meat. The service

★ **Top Five for Foodies**

Park Café (p51)

La Esquina de Buenos Aires (p50)

Cocina Eclectica (p54)

Maxi's By Ricky (p55)

Café de Los Deseos (p50)

From left: Empanadas; Market eatery; Tile painting outside the Don Carlos Hotel

Parque Nacional Volcán Poás

Just 37km north of Alajuela, by a winding and scenic road, is Parque Nacional Volcán Poás, the home of a 2704m active volcano. Violent eruptions hadn't taken place for more than 60 years when rumblings began in 2014; there were further significant eruptions in April and June 2017, and at the time of research the park was closed due to these events.

In previous years it was possible to peer into the crater, measuring 1.3km across and 300m deep, and watch the steaming, bubbling cauldron belch sulfurous mud and water hundreds of meters into the air. This may be possible again in future, but for now the best place to view Poás is from afar, in the scenic, uncluttered countryside.

La Paz Waterfall Gardens (☑2482-2720, reservations 2482-2100; www.waterfallgardens.com; adult/under 13yr US$42/26, package tours from San José US$88/78; ☉8am-5pm; P✦) ✦, a storybook garden complex just east of Volcán Poás, offers the most easily digestible cultural experience in the Central Valley. Guests walk 3.5km of well-maintained trails to five scenic waterfalls, and can also wander around zoo-like displays including a butterfly conservatory, get up close to hummingbirds and hand-feed toucans. It's ideal for families; stay on-site at the **Peace Lodge** (☑2482-2720; www.waterfallgardens.com; d standard/deluxe/villa/deluxe villa US$430/510/710/940, additional adult/child US$40/20; P✦✦).

Hummingbird, La Paz Waterfall Gardens
JAKUB KYNCL/SHUTTERSTOCK ©

here is impeccable and the atmosphere is enlivened by vertical gardens.

More recently, the chef has added smaller and less expensive plates to the menu, such as tacos and *ceviche*.

Kalú Café & Food Shop
International $$$

(Map p46; ☑2253-8426, 2253-8367; www.kalu.co.cr; cnr Calle 31 & Av 5; mains US$15-21; ☉noon-10pm Tue-Fri, 9am-10pm Sat, 9am-4pm Sun; ✦) Sharing a sleek space with **Kiosco SJO** (Map p46; ☉noon-8pm Tue-Fri, from 10am Sat, 10am-4pm Sun) ✦ in Barrio Escalante, chef Camille Ratton's exceptional cafe serves a global fusion menu of soups, salads, sandwiches, pastas and unconventional delights. These include the fish taco trio filled with mango-glazed salmon, red-curry prawns and macadamia-crusted tuna. Don't miss the mind-meltingly delicious passion-fruit pie.

Lolo's
Pizza $$$

(Map p46; ☑2283-9627; pizzas US$14-24; ☉6pm-midnight Mon-Sat) Fans of bohemian chic will appreciate this quirky pizzeria, hidden in a mustard-yellow house (No 3396) along the railroad tracks north of Av Central in Barrio Escalante. The vibrantly colorful, low-lit interior, hung with an eclectic collection of plates and other knickknacks, creates an artsy, romantic setting for sangria and pizzas fired up in the bright-red oven out back.

Escazú & Santa Ana

Cocina Eclectica
International $$

(☑8529-2509; www.facebook.com/CocinaEclecTicaEscazu/; Trejos Montealegre, Escazú; meals/mains US$12-20; ☉noon-8pm) The Escazú residence of Joanna Stein, identifiable only by a small 'J' on the door, might not seem like a restaurant. In fact it's much more. All day long, dressed in an apron and inked with dozens of tattoos, the self-taught cook pirouettes around her well-stocked kitchen preparing her personal vision of haute cuisine with local produce and exotic ingredients.

When guests arrive, she works out their dietary needs and desires, considers what's available and inspiring, and commences her labor of love. Our visit involved a soul-warming soup of cardamom, carrot and quinoa, delicious home-cured trout *ceviche*, and hearty chicken *chicharrón* with pear butter and fried potatoes. Dessert was homemade passion-fruit ice cream. The experience cost just US$12. Joanna also rents rooms in her lovely abode for US$20 to US$35 a night.

Maxi's By Ricky   Caribbean $$
(📞2282-8619; Calle San Rafael, Santa Ana; appetizers US$1.50-8, mains US$9-30; ⊙noon-midnight) If you can't get to the Caribbean coast, this restaurant is a good substitute. Manzanillo native Ricky transported his lip-smacking restaurant to the Central Valley in 2014 and everybody started showing up to feast on the traditional rice-n-beans, Caribbean chicken and *rondón* soup. The latest addition to the menu: small plates, so everybody can try a little of everything. Delish! It's tricky to find: ask locally for directions.

Saúl Bistro   Mediterranean $$
(📞2228-8685; www.facebook.com/SaulBistro CostaRica; Calle Real; appetizers US$10-16, mains US$11-25; ⊙7am-10pm Sun-Thu, to midnight Fri & Sat) There are life-sized plastic zebras in the dining room at this snazzy open-air restaurant that appeared (and became a sensation) in 2015. An extension of Saúl Mendez, the Guatemala-based empire of men's fashion, the restaurant is adorned with curious art, bubbling fountains and vertical gardens, and it serves delicious Mediterranean cuisine, savory crepes, fine wine and exquisite cocktails. It's quite the scene; recently a newer location opened in fabulous Barrio Escalante (p44).

Container Platz   Gastronomy $$
(📞6050-1045; www.facebook.com/Container Platz/; Calle 5, Santa Ana; mains $6-15; ⊙11:30am-10pm Mon-Thu, 11am-midnight Fri & Sat, 11am-8pm Sun) In this recently launched gastronomic experiment, about a dozen mini-businesses have sprung to life in brightly painted shipping containers in Santa Ana. The effort earns high marks for innovation and reasonably priced, artisanal fast-food, with everything from a circus-themed nacho place to a *churros* factory and a *'hummuseria'* that serves delectable pita triangles with its homemade hummus.

Preparing *arepas* (p50)

ACONGAR/SHUTTERSTOCK ©

★ Top Five for Live Music

El Lobo Estepario (p59)

Mundoloco El Chante (p58)

El Sótano (p58)

Club Vertigo (p57)

8ctavo Rooftop (p59)

From left: Barrio Amón (p44); Blackberry smoothie;
Flower stall, Mercado Central (p44)

Communal picnic tables foster a sense of camaraderie, as does the craft-beer container.

🍺 DRINKING & NIGHTLIFE

Whatever your poison, San José has plenty of venues to keep you lubricated.

Stiefel   Pub

(Map p46; ☑8850-2119; www.facebook.com/StiefelPub; Av 5; ⊙6pm-2am Mon-Sat) Two-dozen-plus Costa Rican microbrews on tap and an appealing setting in a historic building create a convivial buzz at this pub half a block from Plaza España. Grab a pint of Pelona or Maldita Vida, Malinche or Chichemel; better yet, order a flight of four miniature sampler glasses and try 'em all!

Costa Rica Craft Brewing   Brewery

(☑2249-4277; www.facebook.com/craftbeer costarica; Calle Cajeta; ⊙10am-10pm Mon-Wed, to midnight Thu-Sat, noon-6pm Sun) Just when everyone thought it would be Imperial versus Pilsen forever, this artisanal brew

pub paved the way for craft beer in Costa Rica. The brewery's newer location in Brasil, a suburb of San José, offers tours and tastings of its fine products, which include staple ales such as Libertas and Segua, along with more experimental barley wines and Russian Imperial stouts. It's out of town; ask locally for directions.

Azotea Calle 7   Cocktail Bar

(Map p46; ☑2010-0000; www.facebook.com/pg/azoteacalle7; Calle 7, Hotel Presidente; ⊙4-10pm Sun-Wed, to midnight Thu-Sat) Featuring stylish indoor and verdant outdoor spaces, along with a sweeping view of the city, this rooftop cocktail bar fills nightly with guests from **Hotel Presidente** (☑2010-0000, in USA 1-877-540-1790; www.hotel-presidente.com; Av Central; r US$100-189; P ❄ 🛜) 🏊 and well-heeled professionals. Great craft cocktails, too.

Castro's   Club

(Map p51; ☑2256-8789; cnr Av 13 & Calle 22; ⊙1pm-4am) Chepe's oldest dance club, this classic Latin American disco in Barrio México draws crowds of locals and tourists to its large dance floor with a dependable mix of salsa, *cumbia* and merengue.

Antik   Club

(Map p46; Av 10; cover US$10; ⏲11:30am-3pm
& 6-11pm Tue-Thu, 11:30am-3pm & 6pm-6am Fri,
6pm-6am Sat) Set in a historic mansion that
once belonged to a Venezuelan general,
Antik offers a tri-level experience, with a
basement catering to the EDM crowd, a
main-level pizza restaurant and an upper
floor featuring Latin dance rhythms and
a sweet balcony with city views. There are
a couple of bars offering craft beer and
excellent, reasonably priced cocktails. The
music often continues until dawn.

Club Vertigo   Club

(Map p51; ☏2257-8424; www.vertigocr.com;
Paseo Colón btwn Calles 38 & 40; cover US$6-
15; ⏲10pm-dawn Fri & Sat) Located on the
ground floor of the nondescript Centro
Colón office tower, the city's premier club
packs in Chepe's beautiful people with
a mix of house, trance and electronica.
Downstairs is an 850-person-capacity
sweatbox of a dance floor; upstairs is a
chill-out lounge lined with red sofas. Dress
to the nines and expect admission charges
to skyrocket on guest-DJ nights.

Chubbs   Sports Bar

(☏2222-4622; 2nd fl, Calle 9 btwn Avs 1 & 3;
⏲11am-2am) In the heart of the San José
tourist belt, this little sports bar has
reasonably priced drinks, tasty burgers
and a stack of TVs displaying the game. It's
popular with expats and has unsurprisingly
opened a second location on the old road
between Santa Ana and Escazú.

Mercado
La California   Beer Garden

(Map p46; www.facebook.com/MercadoLaCali
fornia/; Calle 21; cocktails US$5-15, beer US$3;
⏲6pm-3:30am Thu-Sat, 4pm-1:30am Sun)
Inspired by Madrid's 'Mercado San Miguel,'
El Mercadito (as the locals say) is a recent
addition to the up-and-coming Barrio La
California. The line regularly snakes down
the block from the entrance to this nightlife
plaza's food kiosks, cocktail stands and
craft-beer vendors, and the people in that
line are often stunning to behold.

The plaza is lit up and lively, with
seating areas for hanging out and feasting
on gourmet tacos, pizza and BBQ-pork
sandwiches.

Wilk   Brewery

(Map p46; www.facebook.com/wilkcraftbeer; cnr Calle 33 & Av 9; ⏰4pm-1am Tue-Sat) This Escalante pub attracts a mixed crowd of Ticos and gringos who share an appreciation for craft brews and seriously delicious burgers (veggie included). The wide selection includes 27 craft beers on tap, including inventive concoctions of Costa Rica Craft Brewing (p56) and Treintaycinco. On each month's first Thursday, a crowd gathers to watch a local brewmaster invent a new beer.

⭐ ENTERTAINMENT

Pick up *La Nación* on Thursday for listings (in Spanish) of the coming week's attractions. The free publication GAM Cultural (www. gamcultural.com) and the website San José Volando (www.sanjosevolando.com) are also helpful guides to nightlife and cultural events.

Mundoloco
El Chante   Live Performance

(⏰2253-4125; www.facebook.com/Mundoloco Restaurante/; Av Central, San Pedro; ⏰4pm-2:30am Mon-Thu, from noon Fri & Sat) Grab a

craft beer and some vegetarian grub, such as stuffed mushrooms, at this super-cute San Pedro restaurant and bar. Then head to the spacious and comfortable back room for the entertainment, which rotates from stand-up comedy to dance performances and live music of all kinds. Great acoustics here: it's an ideal place to catch a local band.

Estadio Nacional
de Costa Rica   Stadium

(Map p51; Parque Metropolitano La Sabana) Costa Rica's graceful, modernist 35,000-seat national soccer stadium, constructed with funding from the Chinese government and opened in 2011, is the venue for international and national Division-1 *fútbol* (soccer) games.

Its predecessor, dating back to 1924 and located in the same spot in Parque Metropolitano La Sabana, hosted everyone from Pope John Paul II to soccer legend Pelé and Bruce Springsteen over its 84-year history.

El Sótano   Live Music

(Map p46; ⏰2221-2302; www.facebook.com/ sotanocr; cnr Calle 3 & Av 11; ⏰3pm-2am Mon-Sat)

Costa Rican soccer fans

WENN.COM/AGE FOTOSTOCK ©

One of Chepe's most atmospheric night-spots, Sótano is named for its cellar jazz club, where people crowd in for frequent performances including intimate jam sessions. Upstairs, a cluster of elegant rooms in the same mansion have been converted into a gallery space, a stage, and a dance floor where an eclectic mix of groups plays live gigs.

El Lobo
Estepario   Live Music
(Map p46; 2256-3934; www.facebook.com/loboestepariocr; Av 2; 4pm-12:45am Sun-Thu, to 2am Fri & Sat) This artsy, two-story dive serves up good vegetarian fare and attracts some of the top local talent for live-music gigs. The ceiling is also a blackboard, filled nightly with messages and drawings of the patrons' choosing.

8ctavo Rooftop   Live Music
(4055-0588; www.facebook.com/8voRooftop; Autopista Próspero Fernández, Hotel Sheraton San José) See and be seen at this swanky rooftop lounge, where international DJs regularly perform. If you want to show up early and dine first, this place is also a hit for the city views, the eclectic menu and the spicy cocktails. It's right off Hwy 27 on the west side of Escazú.

Jazz Café   Live Music
(2253-8933; www.jazzcafecostarica.com; Av Central; cover US$6-13; 6pm-2am Mon-Sat) This intimate San Pedro venue presents a different band every night. Countless performers have taken to the stage here, including legendary Cuban bandleader Chucho Valdés and Colombian pop star Juanes. Its sister club in **Escazú** (2288-4740; Autopista Próspero Fernández, north side; cover US$5-10; 6pm-2am) features a similar mix of local and international bands.

Cine Magaly   Cinema
(Map p46; 2222-7116; www.facebook.com/CineMagaly; Calle 23 btwn Avs Central & 1) Screens the latest releases in a large, recently renovated theater, along with independent films in English. The attached Kubrick Gastro Bar (noon to 10pm Monday to Saturday, from 1pm Sunday) serves up delicious

 LGBT San José

The city is home to Central America's most thriving gay and lesbian scene. As with other spots, admission charges vary depending on the night and location (from US$5 to US$10). Some clubs close on various nights of the week (usually Sunday to Tuesday) and others host women- or men-only nights; inquire ahead or check individual club websites for listings. Many clubs are on the south side of town, which can get rough after dark. Take a taxi.

La Avispa (Map p46; 2223-5343; www.laavispa.com; Calle 1 btwn Avs 8 & 10; 8pm-6am Thu-Sat, 5pm-6am Sun) A lesbian disco bar that has been in operation for more than three decades, La Avispa (the Wasp) has a bar, pool tables and a boisterous dance floor that's highly recommended by travelers.

BO Club (Map p46; 2221-0500; cnr Calle 11 & Av 10; 8pm-6am Fri & Sat) A club that features everything from classic disco to electronica, as well as special themed nights. It's on the south side of town.

Pucho's Bar (Map p46; 2256-1147; cnr Calle 11 & Av 8; 8pm-2am Tue-Sat) This gay male outpost is more low-rent (and significantly raunchier) than some; it features scantily clad go-go boys and over-the-top drag shows.

salads, pizza, desserts and an assortment of flavored teas. It's the perfect spot for a sweet treat before or after the movie.

Casino Club Colonial   Casino
(Map p46; ☏2258-2807; www.casinoclubcolonial.
com; Av 1 btwn Calles 9 & 11; ⏰24hr) San José's
most elegant casino.

 INFORMATION

EMERGENCY

Fire	☏118
Red Cross	☏128
Traffic Police	☏2523-3300, 2222-9245, 2222-9330

GAY & LESBIAN TRAVELERS

In recent years attitudes toward LGBT locals and
travelers have shifted towards acceptance. Gay
pride parades take place regularly, and the city's
youth are leading the country's tolerance movement. A good site for all things gay travel is www.
costaricagaymap.com, which offers listings of bars
and hotels that cater to the LGBT community.

 GETTING THERE & AWAY

International flights leave from Juan Santamaría
(SJO) airport outside Alajuela.

Aeropuerto Internacional Juan Santamaría
(p305) Handles international flights and **Nature
Air** (☏2299-6000, in USA 1-800-235-9272;
www.natureair.com) domestic flights in its main
terminal. Domestic flights on **Sansa** (☏2290-
4100; www.flysansa.com) depart from the Sansa
terminal.

Aeropuerto Tobías Bolaños (☏2232-2820;
Pavas) In the San José suburb of Pavas; services
private charter and a few national flights.

 GETTING AROUND

Central San José frequently resembles a parking
lot – narrow streets, heavy traffic and a complicated one-way system mean that it's often quicker
to walk than to take the bus. The same applies to
driving: if you rent a car, try to avoid downtown. If
you're in a real hurry to get somewhere that's more
than 1km away, take an Uber or a taxi.

If traveling by bus, you'll arrive at one of several bus terminals sprinkled around the western
and southern parts of downtown. Some of this
area is walkable provided you aren't hauling a

lot of luggage and are staying nearby. But, if
you're arriving at night, take a taxi, since most
terminals are in dodgy areas.

CAR

It is not advisable to rent a car just to drive around
San José. Traffic is heavy, streets are narrow
and meter-deep curbside gutters make parking
nerve-wracking. In addition, break-ins are frequent,
and leaving a car – even in a guarded lot – might
result in a smashed window and stolen belongings.

If you are renting a car to travel throughout
Costa Rica, there are more than 50 car-rental
agencies – including many of the global brands –
in and around San José. Travel agencies and upmarket hotels can arrange rentals; you can also
arrange rentals online and at the airport. Note:
If you book a rental car online and the low cost
seems too good to be true, it is. Rental agencies
are notorious for tacking on hundreds of dollars
in mandatory insurance when you arrive. They
are also known to lie about this over the phone.

One excellent local option is **Wild Rider**
(☏2258-4604; Paseo Colón btwn Calles 30 & 32;
⏰8am-6pm). It has a fleet of more than 60 very
reasonably priced 4WD vehicles (from US$380
per week in high season, including all mandatory
insurance coverage). Long-term rentals (four
weeks or more) allow a discount of up to 40%.
Reserve well in advance.

TAXI

Red taxis can be hailed on the street day or
night, or you can have your hotel call one for you.

Marías (meters) are generally used, though a
few drivers will tell you they're broken and try to
charge you more – especially if you don't speak
Spanish. Not using a meter is illegal. The rate for
the first kilometer should automatically appear
when the meter starts up (at the time of research,
the correct starting amount was 610 colones).
Make sure the *maría* is operating when you get in,
or negotiate the fare up front. Short rides downtown cost US$2 to US$4. There's a 20% surcharge
after 10pm that may not appear on the *maría*.

You can hire a taxi and a driver for half a day
or longer if you want to do some touring around
the area; for such trips, it is best to negotiate
a flat fee in advance. Uber has also become a
popular form of transport in the city.

Where to Stay

Reservations are recommended in the high season (December through April), in particular the two weeks around Christmas and Semana Santa (Holy Week, the week preceding Easter).

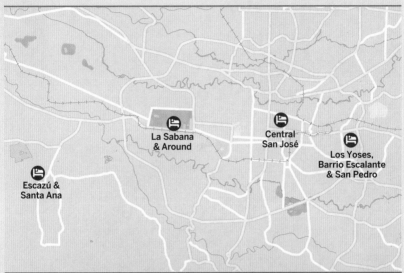

Neighborhood	Atmosphere
Central San José	The best hotels are east of Calle Central, many of which are housed in historic Victorian and art-deco mansions; close to sights, restaurants and nightlife; non-stop traffic jams and street noise.
La Sabana & Around	West of the city center; great variety of accommodations, from hostels to vintage B&Bs; pleasant setting around Parque Metropolitano La Sabana; some good dining venues, though budget options are limited.
Los Yoses, Barrio Escalante & San Pedro	Lively university area, with restaurants and nightlife; walking distance to city center; excellent choices for budget travelers.
Escazú & Santa Ana	Affluent suburbs with accommodations ranging from sleek boutique inns to homey B&Bs, mostly upscale; innovative dining scene; 20-minute drive or bus ride from city center; challenging to navigate.

TORTUGUERO

Tortuguero at a Glance...

Located within the confines of Parque Nacional Tortuguero (p72), accessible only by air or water, this bustling little village with strong Afro-Caribbean roots is best known for attracting hordes of sea turtles (tortuguero means 'turtle catcher') — and the hordes of tourists who want to see them. While peak turtle season is in July and August, the park and village have begun to attract travelers year-round. Even in October, when the turtles have pretty much returned to the sea, families and adventure travelers arrive to go on jungle hikes, take in the wild national park, and canoe the area's lush canals.

One Day in Tortuguero

If you only have one day in Tortuguero, it's going to be a busy one. Start early with breakfast from **Dorling Bakery** (p75), then hit the aquatic trails on a **boat tour**, keeping your eyes peeled for wildlife. Rest up in the afternoon so you're ready for a (seasonal) **turtle tour** (p66) at sunset.

Two Days in Tortuguero

With an extra day, you can spread out the action. On the first day, take a **boat tour** (p70), followed by a few hours relaxing at the lodge or grabbing a beer at **La Taberna Punto de Encuentro** (p77).

On day two, follow the short **hiking trail** (p72) behind Cuatro Esquinas ranger station.

20 km
10 miles

NICARAGUA

San Juan River

Trinidad

COSTA RICA

Refugio Nacional
de Vida Silvestre
Barra del Colorado

Canadian Organization
for Tropical Education &
Rainforest Conservation

*CARIBBEAN
SEA*

Airstrip ✈ Sea Turtle
Conservancy

Río Suerte

Tortuguero

Río Chirripo

Río Tortuguero

Parque
Nacional
Tortuguero

Santa
Rosa   Cariari

Horquetas

Río Frio

Parismina

Caño
Blanco

Río Parismina

Santa
Clara

Guápiles   Guácimo

Punta
del Riel

San Rafael

↙ *San José (30km)*

Tortuguero Village Map (p73)

Caption

Arriving in Tortuguero

If you're coming from San José, the
two most convenient ways to get to
Tortuguero are by air or all-inclusive
bus-boat shuttles – though budget travelers can save money by taking public
transportation.

If you're coming from the southern Caribbean, your best bets are with private
boat operators from Moín or shuttle
deals from Cahuita and Puerto Viejo.

Sleeping

There are two main areas of Tortuguero
where travelers stay. The village itself
has the largest variety and selection of
accommodation options, catering especially to budget and midrange travelers.
The higher-end lodges are north of the
village (and across a canal, meaning
that guests can only access the village
by water taxi).

Sea turtle, Parque Nacional Tortuguero (p72)

Turtle Tours

One of the most moving experiences is turtle-watching on these wild beaches. Witnessing a massive turtle return to its natal beach and perform its laborious nesting ritual feels both solemn and magical.

Great For...

☑ **Don't Miss**

The scurrying hatchlings as they set off on their journey to the sea.

ⓘ Need to Know

The most convenient places to arrange tours are at local hotels and at the official Asociación de Guías de Tortuguero (p74) kiosk.

JARNO GONZALEZ ZARRAONANDIA/SHUTTERSTOCK ©

Turtle Nesting

Most female turtles share a nesting instinct that drives them to return to the beach of their birth (their natal beach) in order to lay their eggs. (Only the leatherback returns to a more general region instead of a specific beach.) During their lifetimes, they will usually nest every two to three years and, depending on the species, may come ashore to lay eggs 10 times in one season. Often, a turtle's ability to reproduce depends on the ecological health of this original habitat.

The female turtle digs a perfect cylindrical cavity in the sand using her flippers, and then lays 80 to 120 eggs. She diligently covers the nest with sand to protect the eggs, and she may even create a false nest in another location in an attempt to confuse predators. She then makes her way back to sea – after which the eggs are on their own.

Incubation ranges from 45 to 70 days, after which hatchlings – no bigger than the size of your palm – break out of their shells using a caruncle, a temporary tooth. They crawl to the ocean in small groups, moving as quickly as possible to avoid dehydration and predators. Once they reach the surf, they must swim for at least 24 hours to get to deeper water, away from land-based predators.

Tours

Because of the sensitive nature of the habitat and the critically endangered status of some species, tours to see this activity are highly regulated. It is important not to alarm turtles as they come to shore (a frightened turtle will return to the ocean and dump her eggs). In high season, tour groups gather in shelter sites close to the beach and a spotter relays a turtle's

Hatchling heading to the sea

location via radio once she has safely crossed the high-tide mark and built her nest. At this time, visitors can then go to the beach and watch the turtle lay her eggs, cover her nest and return to the ocean. Seeing a turtle is not guaranteed, but licensed guides will still make your tour worthwhile with the wealth of turtle information they'll share. By law, tours can only take place between 8am and midnight. Some guides will offer tours after midnight; these are illegal.

Visitors should wear closed-toe shoes and rain gear. Tours cost US$25. Nesting season runs from March to October, with July and August being prime time. The

---

★ Top Tip

Four species of sea turtle nest in Tortuguero – green, leatherback, hawksbill and loggerhead.

STEPHAN DE PROUW/GETTY IMAGES ©

---

next best time is April, when leatherback turtles nest in small numbers. Flashlights and cameras are not allowed on the beach. Wear nonreflective, dark clothing.

Save the Turtles

The area attracts four of the world's eight species of sea turtle, making it a crucial habitat for these massive reptiles. It will come as little surprise, then, that these hatching grounds gave birth to the sea-turtle conservation movement. The Caribbean Conservation Corporation, the first program of its kind in the world, has continuously monitored turtle populations here since 1955. Today green sea turtles are increasing in numbers along this coast, but the leatherback, hawksbill and loggerhead are in decline.

Canadian Organization for Tropical Education & Rainforest Conservation (COTERC; ☎2709-8052; www.coterc.org; dm per week incl 3 meals per day US$275) is a not-for-profit organization operating the Estación Biológica Caño Palma, 8km north of Tortuguero village. This small biological research station runs a volunteer program in which visitors can assist with upkeep of the station and ongoing research projects, including sea-turtle and bird monitoring, mammal, caiman and snake monitoring, and also a community program.

About 200m north of the village, **Sea Turtle Conservancy** (☎2297-5510, in USA 352-373-6441; www.conserveturtles.org; museum US$2; ◷10am-noon & 2-5pm), Tortuguero's original turtle-conservation organization (founded in 1959), operates a research station, visitor center and museum. Exhibits focus on all things turtle-related, including a video about the local history of turtle conservation. STC also runs a highly reputable volunteer program. During nesting season volunteers can observe turtle-tagging and assist with egg counts and biometric-data collection.

✕ Take a Break

Serving until 9pm, Taylor's Place (p75) will set you up if watching turtles has made you hungry.

Parque Nacional Tortuguero (p72)

GONZALO AZUMENDI/GETTY IMAGES ©

Boat Tours

Tortuguero teems with wildlife. You'll find howler monkeys in the treetops, green iguanas scurrying among buttress roots, and endangered manatees swimming in the canals – all visible from the seat of a canoe or kayak.

Great For...

☑ **Don't Miss**

The great green macaw (though you'll need a good guide and some luck).

Aquatic Trails

Four aquatic trails wind their way through Parque Nacional Tortuguero, inviting waterborne exploration. **Río Tortuguero** acts as the entranceway to the network of trails. This wide, beautiful river is often covered with water lilies and is frequented by aquatic birds such as herons, kingfishers and anhingas – the latter is known as the snakebird for the way its slim, winding neck pokes out of the water when it swims.

Caño Chiquero and **Canõ Mora** are two narrower waterways with good wildlife-spotting opportunities. According to park regulations, only kayaks, canoes and silent electric boats are allowed in these areas. Caño Chiquero is thick with vegetation, especially red *guácimo* trees and epiphytes. Black turtles and green iguanas like to hang out here. Caño Mora is about 3km long but

Eyelash viper

KEVIN WELLS PHOTOGRAPHY/SHUTTERSTOCK ©

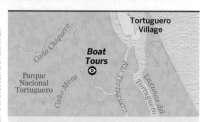

ⓘ Need to Know

To see the most wildlife, be on the water early or go out following a heavy rain.

✕ Take a Break

Grab a yummy breakfast from Dorling Bakery (p75) before you set out.

★ Top Tip

Small, silent watercraft, like canoes and kayaks, will allow you to get into less-trafficked areas.

only 10m wide, so it feels as if it's straight out of *The Jungle Book*. **Caño Haroldas** is actually an artificially constructed canal, but that doesn't stop the creatures – such as Jesus Christ lizards and caimans – from inhabiting its tranquil waters.

Tour Guides

Leonardo Tours (p74) and Tinamon Tours (p74) are recommended for their canoeing and kayaking tours.

Wildlife-Watching

More than 400 bird species, both resident and migratory, have been recorded in Tortuguero – it's a bird-watchers paradise. Due to the wet habitat, the park is especially rich in waders, including egrets, jacanas and 14 types of heron, as well as species such as kingfishers, toucans and the great

curassow (a type of jungle peacock known locally as the *pavón*). The great green macaw is a highlight, most common from December to April, when the almond trees are fruiting. In September and October, look for flocks of migratory species such as eastern kingbirds, barn swallows and purple martins. The Sea Turtle Conservancy conducts a biannual monitoring program in which volunteers can help scientists take inventory of local and migratory species.

Certain species of mammal are particularly evident in Tortuguero, especially mantled howler monkeys, the Central American spider monkey and the white-faced capuchin. If you've got a reliable pair of binoculars and a good guide, you can usually see both two- and three-toed sloths. In addition, normally shy neotropical river otters are reasonably habituated to boats. Harder to spot are timid West Indian manatees and dolphins, which swim into the brackish canals looking for food. The park is also home to big cats such as jaguars and ocelots, but these are savvy, nocturnal animals – sightings are very rare.

Tortuguero Village

◎ SIGHTS

Parque Nacional Tortuguero
National Park

(☏2709-8086; www.acto.go.cr; US$15; ◷6am-6pm, last entry 4pm) This misty, green coastal park sits on a broad floodplain parted by a jigsaw of canals. Referred to as the 'mini-Amazon,' Parque Nacional Tortuguero is a place of intense biodiversity that includes more than 400 bird species, 60 known species of frog, 30 species of freshwater fish and three monkey species, as well as the threatened West Indian manatee. Caimans and crocodiles can be seen lounging on riverbanks, while freshwater turtles bask on logs.

More than 150,000 visitors a year come to boat the canals and see the wildlife, particularly to watch turtles lay eggs. This is the most important Caribbean breeding site of the green sea turtle, 40,000 of which arrive every season to nest. Of the eight species of marine turtle in the world, six nest in Costa Rica, and four nest in

Tortuguero. Various volunteer organizations address the problem of poaching with vigilant turtle patrols.

Park headquarters is at **Cuatro Esquinas** (☏2709-8086; www.acto.go.cr; ◷6am-4pm), just south of Tortuguero village.

Strong currents make the beaches unsuitable for swimming.

✪ ACTIVITIES

Most visitors come to watch sea turtles lay eggs on the wild beaches. The area is about more than just turtles, though: Tortuguero teems with wildlife. You'll find sloths and howler monkeys in the treetops, tiny frogs and green iguanas scurrying among buttress roots, plus mighty tarpons, alligators and endangered manatees swimming in the waters.

⊛ Hiking

Behind **Cuatro Esquinas ranger station** (admission US$15), the main well-trodden trail is a muddy, 2km out-and-back hike that traverses the tropical humid forest

Caiman crocodile

Tortuguero Village

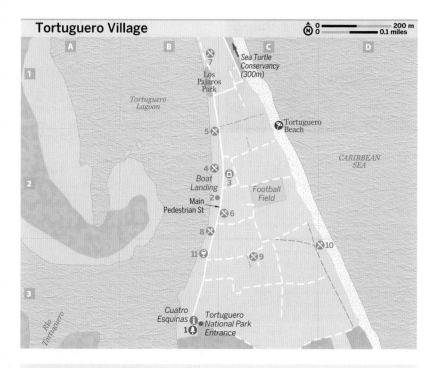

Ⓝ 0 ┃━━━━━━━┃ 200 m
   0 ┃━━━━━━━┃ 0.1 miles

Tortuguero Village

and parallels a stretch of beach. Green parrots and several species of monkey are commonly sighted here. The short trail is well marked. Rubber boots are required and can be rented at hotels and near the park entrance.

A second hiking option, Cerro Tortuguero Trail, is also worth considering. To reach the trailhead, guests have to take a boat to the town of San Francisco, north of Tortuguero village, where they will disembark at another ranger station and buy a ticket (US$7, plus US$4 for the 15- to 20-minute round-trip boat ride). The trail then takes visitors 1.8km up a hill for a view of the surrounding lagoon, forest and ocean. **Casa Marbella** in Tortuguero village can help guests organize the details and even arrange a local guide (from US$35) to take you on the trip.

🍴 Afro-Caribbean Cuisine

Thanks to the Afro-Caribbean influence, the food here has more of a kick than that of other regions. Even rice-and-beans becomes something special in the southern Caribbean, with the simple additions of coconut milk, Panamanian peppers, thyme and ginger. Mouthwatering lobster and whole fish are ubiquitous, as is the staple *pollo caribeño* (Caribbean chicken). Pair these delights with *agua de sapo* (lemonade with ginger and sugarcane juice).

Fried fish with plantains and salad
AYOTOGRAPHY/SHUTTERSTOCK ©

🅖 TOURS

Leonardo Tours   Outdoors

(📱8577-1685; www.leonardotours.wordpress. com; nature walks from US$20; ⊘9am-7pm) With nine years of experience guiding tours in the area, Leonardo Estrada brings extensive knowledge and infectious enthusiasm to his turtle, canoeing, kayaking and hiking tours.

Tinamon Tours   Tours

(📱8842-6561; www.tinamontours.de; 2½hr hikes from US$25, 2-night tour packages per person from US$100) Zoologist and 20-plus-year Tortuguero resident Barbara Hartung offers hiking, canoeing, cultural and turtle tours in German, English, French or Spanish. Tour packages, including two nights' accommodation, breakfast, a canoe tour and a hike, start at US$100 per person.

Note that you'll need to pay the US$15 entrance fee for park (p72) hikes.

Castor Hunter Thomas   Tours

(📱8870-8634; www.castorhunter.blogspot. com; nature tours per person from US$35) Excellent local guide and 44-year Tortuguero resident Castor has led hikes, turtle tours and canoe tours for more than 20 years.

Riverboat Francesca Nature Tours   Fishing

(📱2226-0986; www.tortuguerocanals.com; 2-day sportfishing packages from US$200) A highly recommended company run by Modesto and Fran Watson, Riverboat Francesca offers sportfishing.

Asociación de Guías de Tortuguero   Tours

(📱2767-0836; www.asoprotur.com; ⊘6am-7pm) The most convenient place to arrange tours is at the official Asociación de Guías de Tortuguero kiosk by the boat landing. Made up of scores of local guides, the association offers tours in English, French, German and other languages. Although guides are all certified to lead tours in the park, the quality of the tours can vary.

Rates at the time of research were US$25 per person for a two-hour turtle tour and US$20 for a canoe tour. Other options include two-hour walking (US$20), birdwatching (US$35) and fishing (US$80, minimum two people) tours. Tours also involve an extra US$15 admission fee to the park (not required for the fishing tour).

Tortuguero Keysi Tours   Tours

(📱8579-9414; ⊘5:30am-6pm) Opposite and slightly to the right of the boat landing, this family-run outfit offers day and night walking tours with naturalist guides (from US$20), canoe tours (from US$20), boat tours (from US$35) and turtle-observation tours (from US$25). It can also arrange transfers to Moín, Cahuita, San José and Puerto Viejo, as well as to local towns and canal hotels.

🔒 SHOPPING

Kolibri Design
(📞2767-0010; tiendakolibri@hotmail.com; small art pieces from US$40; ⏰11am-1pm & 3-6pm) Colorful artworks made of recycled driftwood, jicaro fruit and the flower pods of coconut trees are housed in this sleek white gallery space on Tortuguero's main street. Most creations are by Austrian resident Tina Lindner, but other pieces are made by locals. Find handmade jewelry here, too.

✖ EATING

One of Tortuguero's unsung pleasures is its cuisine: the homey restaurants lure you in with steaming platters of Caribbean-style food, plus international options like pizza and pasta. Most use local produce.

Taylor's Place  Caribbean $
(📞8319-5627; mains US$7-14; ⏰6-9pm) Low-key atmosphere and high-quality cooking come together beautifully at this back-street restaurant southwest of the soccer field. The inviting garden setting, with chirping insects and picnic benches spread under colorful paper lanterns, is rivaled only by friendly chef Ray Taylor's culinary artistry. House specialties include beef in tamarind sauce, grilled fish in garlic sauce, and avocado and chicken salad.

Fresh Foods Caribbean $
(📞2767-1063; mains US$3.50-9, smoothies US$3-4; ⏰7:30am-9:30pm) In the commercial center of the village, this family-owned restaurant offers breakfasts (omelets, juice, fruit, toast), solid Caribbean meals (chicken and rice) and giant, delicious smoothies in fishbowl glasses. After a long day on the canals, a tasty Caribbean-style filet and a passion-fruit drink really nail it.

Dorling Bakery Bakery $
(📞2767-0444; pastries US$2, breakfast US$4-5; ⏰5am-8:30pm Mon-Sat, to noon Sun) Thanks to its predawn opening time, this is a good spot to pick up homemade banana bread, lemon and orange cake or cinnamon rolls before an early-morning flight or canal tour.

Ladybug, Parque Nacional Tortuguero (p72)

Dragonfly, Parque Nacional Tortuguero (p72)

KEVIN WELLS PHOTOGRAPHY/SHUTTERSTOCK ©

Sunrise Restaurant   Caribbean $

(mains US$6.50-8; ⊙9:30am-9pm Wed-Mon, from 11am low season) Between the dock and the national park, this cozy log cabin–like place will lure you in with the delicious smoky aroma of its grilled chicken and pork ribs. It also serves seafood pasta, fajitas, salad, breakfast and a full Caribbean menu at lunch and dinnertime, with some of the best prices in town.

Soda Doña María   Soda $

(☑8928-8424; dishes US$5-8; ⊙11am-8:30pm) Recover from a hike in the park at this riverside *soda*, serving *jugos* (juices), burgers and *casados*. It's about 200m north of the park entrance.

Miss Junie's   Caribbean $$

(☑2709-8029; mains US$9-16; ⊙7-9am, noon-2:30pm & 6-9pm) Over the years, Tortuguero's best-known and most delicious Caribbean eatery has grown from a personal kitchen to a full-blown restaurant. Prices have climbed accordingly, but the menu remains true to its roots: jerk chicken, filet mignon, whole snapper and coconut-curry

mackerel with rice and beans. It's at the northern end of the main street.

Tutti's Restaurant   Italian $

(☑2709-8117; mains $5.50-9; ⊙noon-9pm) The place to come for an Italian fix, Tutti's serves lasagna, penne and spaghetti dishes, and focaccia with cheese. There are also plenty of pizza varieties and loaded calzones – the Caribbean flavor comes with tomato sauce infused with coconut and shrimps, onion and mozzarella. Happy hour (two selected drinks for $10) runs between 3.30pm and 5.30pm.

Budda Cafe   European $$

(☑2709-8084; www.buddacafe.com; mains US$10-18, pizzas US$7-9; ⊙1-9pm; 🛜🍴) Ambient club music, Tibetan prayer flags and a river view give this trendy cafe a tranquil vibe. It's a pleasant setting for pizzas, salads, cocktails and crepes (savory and sweet). Grab a table outside for a prime view of the boats going by and, if you're lucky, the yellow-bellied flycatchers zipping across the water.

DRINKING & NIGHTLIFE

La Taberna Punto de Encuentro
Bar

(📞8877-6515; ⏰11am-2am) This popular tavern is mellow in the afternoons but draws the party people after dark with cold beer and blaring reggaetón. The main dance floor has a beautiful open-air view of the river.

INFORMATION

There's one new ATM in town, but bring backup cash as it may run out of money in high season.

🛈 GETTING THERE & AWAY

The small airstrip is 4km north of Tortuguero village. **NatureAir** (📞2299-6000; www.natureair. com) has early-morning flights to/from San José daily during high season. Charter flights land here regularly as well.

The classic public-transit route to Tortuguero is a bit of a faff, taking four to six hours, but is by far the cheapest option. You'll travel by bus from San José to Cariari and then La Pavona, and then by boat from La Pavona to Tortuguero. Alternatively, Tortuguero is easily accessible by private boat from Moín (three to four hours).

SHUTTLE TRIPS

If you prefer to leave the planning to someone else, convenient shuttle services can whisk you to Tortuguero from San José, Arenal-La Fortuna or the southern Caribbean coast in just a few hours. Shuttle companies typically offer minivan service to La Pavona or Moín, where waiting boats take you the rest of the way to Tortuguero. This is a relatively inexpensive, hassle-free option, as you only have to buy a single ticket, and guides help you negotiate the van-to-boat transfer.

Caribe Shuttle (📞2750-0626; www.caribeshuttle.com) Shuttles from Puerto Viejo (US$75, five hours) and Arenal-La Fortuna (US$60, six hours).

Exploradores Outdoors (📞2222-6262; www.exploradoresoutdoors.com; 1-day rafting trips incl lunch & transportation from US$99) More-expensive package deals that include transport from San José, Puerto Viejo or Arenal-La Fortuna, a mid-journey Río Pacuare rafting trip, and accommodation in Tortuguero.

Pleasure Ride (📞2750-2113, 2750-0290; www.pleasureridecr.com) Shuttles from Puerto Viejo (from US$75, around 1½ hours) and Cahuita (from US$70, around one hour).

Jungle Tom Safaris (📞2221-7878; www.jungletomsafaris.com) Offers one-way shuttles between Tortuguero and San José (US$45). All-inclusive one- and two-night packages (US$99 to US$152) can also include shuttles from Cahuita (US$60), Puerto Viejo (US$60) and Arenal-La Fortuna (US$60), as well as optional tours.

Ride CR (📞2469-2525; www.ridecr.com) Shuttles from Arenal-La Fortuna (US$55). Minimum two passengers.

Riverboat Francesca Nature Tours (p74) Shuttles from San José to Tortuguero via Moín (from US$75, including lunch) as well as package deals including accommodations.

Terraventuras (p86) Overnight shuttle packages from Puerto Viejo (US$99).

Willie's Tours (📞2755-1024, 8917-6982; www.williestourscostarica.com; tours from US$20; ⏰8am-6pm Mon-Sat) Shuttles from Cahuita (from US$70).

All Rankin's Tours (📞2709-8101, 2758-4160; www.greencoast.com/allrankin; return trips to Tortuguero from US$70) Round-trip shuttles to Tortuguero from Moín, including excellent nature guides (from US$70).

SOUTHERN CARIBBEAN

Southern Caribbean at a Glance...

The southern coast is the heart and soul of Costa Rica's Afro-Caribbean community. Jamaican workers arrived in the middle of the 19th century, and stayed to build the railroad and work for the United Fruit corporation. Then in the 1980s the southern coast began to welcome surfers, backpackers and adventurous families on holiday – many of whom have stayed, adding Italian, German and North American flavors to the cultural stew. For the traveler, it's a rich and rewarding experience – with lovely beaches to boot.

Two Days in the Southern Caribbean

When in the southern Caribbean, go **surfing** (p82)! Remember that Salsa Brava is for experts only; otherwise, head to Playa Cocles. After riding the waves, enjoy a seafood feast at **Laszlo's** (p92). On day two, explore **REGAMA** (p84) with an early-morning hike, followed by lunch at the **Cool & Calm Cafe** (p95), and an afternoon of swimming and snorkeling at Manzanillo beach.

Four Days in the Southern Caribbean

Rent a bicycle and spend a day beach-hopping from Playa Cocles to Playa Chiquita to Punta Uva, with a stop at the **Jaguar Centro de Rescate** (p86). Have dinner at one of the southern Caribbean's phenomenal restaurants, such as **La Pecora Nera** (p89) or **Selvin's** (p89). Your final day is free for the **Chocolate Forest Experience** (p86). How's that for dessert?

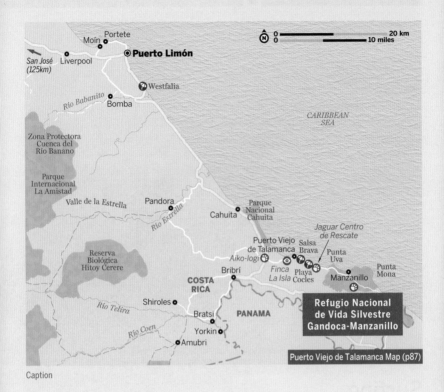

Caption

Arriving in the Southern Caribbean

It's about a four-hour drive from San José to Puerto Viejo de Talamanca, on paved (but not always well-maintained) roads. Shuttle companies like **Grayline** and **Interbus** make this run, as do the public buses.

Sleeping

Here you'll find everything from inventive tree houses to laid-back B&Bs and raucous hostels. What you won't find are chain hotels: the southern Caribbean prides itself on inspired and independent lodgings.

In Puerto Viejo, many budget spots have private hot-water bathrooms and internet access. Rates are generally discounted slightly if you pay in cash.

Surfing at Salsa Brava

TROPICALPIXSINGAPORE/GETTY IMAGES ©

Surfing

This town was built on waves –
specifically, the infamous 'Salsa
Brava' that breaks on the sharp,
shallow reef offshore. But there
are other, more forgiving places to
surf, even for beginners.

Great For...

☑ Don't Miss

Riding one of the most celebrated (and
feared) waves in the country.

Where to Surf

Find one of the country's most notorious
waves at **Salsa Brava** – a shallow reef
break that's most definitely for experts
only. It's a tricky but thrilling ride over sharp
coral. Salsa Brava offers both rights and
lefts, although the right is usually faster.
Conditions are best with a southeasterly
swell.

For a softer landing, try the beach break
at **Playa Cocles**, where the waves are
consistent, the white water is abundant
for beginners, and the wipeouts are more
forgiving. Cocles is about 2km east of town.
Conditions are usually best early in the day,
before the wind picks up.

Playa Cocles

CARIBBEAN SEA

Salsa Brava

Puerto Viejo de Talamanca

Playa Cocles

❶ Need to Know

Waves peak from November to March, with a surfing miniseason from June to July.

✕ Take a Break

Sip a cold one and enjoy the view of the namesake break at Salsa Brava (p93).

★ Top Tip

The nearest medical facility is **Hospital Tony Facio** (☏ 2758-2222) in Puerto Limón.

Salsa Brava

One of the best breaks in Costa Rica, Salsa Brava is named for the heaping helping of 'spicy sauce' it serves up on the sharp, shallow reef, continually collecting its debt of fun in broken skin, boards and bones. The wave makes its regular, dramatic appearance when the swells pull in from the east, pushing a wall of water against the reef and in the process generating a thick and powerful curl. There's no gradual build-up here: the water is transformed from swell to wave in a matter of seconds. Ride it out and you're golden. Wipe out and you may rocket into the reef. Some mordant locals have dubbed it 'the cheese grater.'

Surf Lessons

Several surf schools around town charge US$40 to US$50 for two-hour lessons. Locals on Playa Cocles rent boards from about US$20 per day.

Caribbean Surf School (☏ 8357-7703; 2hr lesson US$50) Lessons by super-smiley surf instructor Hershel Lewis are widely considered the best in town. Recently he also started teaching paddle boarding.

One Love Surf School (☏ 8719-4654; https://onelovecostarica.wordpress.com/about; 2hr surf lessons US$50, 1hr reiki US$50) Julie Hickey and her surfing sons, Cedric and Solomon, specialize in beginners surf lessons, reiki and Thai massage.

Refugio Nacional de Vida Silvestre Gandoca-Manzanillo

This little-explored refuge protects nearly 70% of the southern Caribbean coast, extending from Manzanillo all the way to the Panamanian border.

Great For...

☑ Don't Miss

Swimming and snorkeling off the gorgeous beach in Manzanillo village.

REGAMA encompasses 50 sq km of land plus 44 sq km of marine environment. The peaceful, pristine stretch of sandy white beach – one of the area's main attractions and the center of village life in Manzanillo – stretches from Punta Uva in the west to Punta Mona in the east. Offshore, a 5-sq-km coral reef is a teeming habitat for lobsters, sea fans and long-spined urchins.

Hiking

A coastal trail heads 5.5km east out of Manzanillo to **Punta Mona**. The first part of this path, which leads from Manzanillo to Tom Bay (about a 40-minute walk), is well trammeled, clearly marked and doesn't require a guide. Once you pass Tom Bay, however, the path gets murky and it's easy to get lost, so ask about conditions before you set out, or hire a local guide. It's a

Mantled howler monkey

ⓘ Need to Know

☎2755-0302, 2759-9100; ⏱8am-4pm Fri & Sat

✕ Take a Break

Enjoy the hot food and cool vibe at Cool & Calm Cafe (p95).

★ Top Tip

Refugio Nacional de Vida Silvestre Gandoca-Manzanillo is an excellent photo book by Juan José Pucci.

rewarding walk with amazing scenery, as well as excellent (and safe) swimming and snorkeling at the end.

Recommended Guides

Local guide and former park ranger **Florentino Grenald (Tino)** (☎8841-2732; 4hr tours per person from US$40) is one of the most knowledgeable naturalists on the Caribbean. Since 1992 he's been handing out rubber boots and escorting guests through his yard, a veritable tropical Eden, before taking them into the Gandoca-Manzanillo reserve, where he quickly spots caimans, frogs, snakes and whatever else happens to be nearby. Other recommended guides include **Omar** and **Abel Bustamante**.

Snorkeling & Diving

The undersea portion of the park cradles one of the two accessible living coral reefs in the country. Comprising five types of coral, the reefs begin in about 1m of water and extend 5km offshore to a barrier reef. **Punta Mona** is a popular destination for snorkeling, though it's a trek so you may wish to hire a boat. Otherwise, you can snorkel offshore at **Manzanillo** at the eastern end of the beach (the riptide can be dangerous here; inquire about conditions before setting out). Also check out the Coral Reef Information Center at Bad Barts (p95) in Manzanillo. Bad Barts also rents kayaks, in case you wish to kayak out to the reef.

Dolphin-Watching

In 1997 a group of local guides in Manzanillo identified tucuxi dolphins, a little-known species previously not found in Costa Rica, and began to observe their interactions with bottlenose dolphins. A third species – the Atlantic spotted dolphin – is also common in this area. For dolphin-watching trips in the reserve (from US$50 for three hours), contact Bad Barts (p95), and keep in mind that it is illegal to swim with dolphins.

Puerto Viejo de Talamanca

This burgeoning party town is no longer a destination for intrepid surfers only; it's bustling with tourist activity. Street vendors tout Rasta trinkets and Bob Marley T-shirts, stylish eateries serve global fusion, and intentionally rustic bamboo bars pump dancehall and reggaetón. It can get downright hedonistic, attracting revelers wanting to marinate in ganja and *guaro*. Despite that reputation, Puerto Viejo manages to hold onto an easy charm. If you're looking to chill a little, party a little and eat a little, you've come to the right place.

◎ SIGHTS

Jaguar Centro de Rescate
Wildlife Reserve

(📱2750-0710; www.jaguarrescue.foundation; Playa Chiquita; 1½hr tours adult/child under 10yr US$20/free; ⏱tours 9:30am & 11:30am Mon-Sat; 👪) 🖉 Named in honor of its original resident, a jaguar, this well-run wildlife-rescue center in Playa Chiquita (just over 4km east of Puerto Viejo) now focuses mostly on other animals, including sloths, alligators, anteaters, snakes and monkeys. Founded by zoologist Encar and her partner, Sandro, a herpetologist, the center rehabilitates orphaned, injured and rescued animals, for reintroduction into the wild whenever possible. Volunteer opportunities (US$350 including accommodation) are available with a one-month minimum commitment.

Aiko-logi
Wildlife Reserve

(📱2750-2084, 8997-6869; www.aiko-logi-tours. com; day tours incl transport & lunch US$60, overnight stays per person incl meals US$120; 🅿) 🖉 Nestled into the Cordillera de Talamanca, 15km outside Puerto Viejo, this private 135-hectare reserve is centered on a former *finca* (farm), on land fringed with dense primary rainforest. It's ideal for birdwatching, hiking and splashing around in swimming holes. Day tours from Puerto Viejo (or Cahuita) can be arranged, as can overnight tent-platform stays and yoga classes. Reserve.

Finca La Isla
Gardens

(📱2750-0046, 8886-8530; self-guided/guided tours US$6/12; ⏱10am-4pm Fri-Mon; 🅿) 🖉 West of town, this farm and botanical garden has long produced organic pepper and cacao, along with more than 150 tropical fruits and ornamental plants. Birds and wildlife, including sloths, poison-dart frogs and toucans, abound. Informative guided tours (minimum three people) include admission, fruit tasting and a glass of fresh juice; alternatively, buy a booklet (US$1) and take a self-guided tour. The farm also makes its own chocolate.

ⓕ TOURS

Chocolate Forest Experience
Tours

(📱2750-0504, 8341-2034; www.caribeanscr.com; Playa Cocles; tours US$28; ⏱8:30am-6pm Mon-Sat, tours 10am Mon, 10am & 2pm Tue & Thu, 2pm Fri & Sat) 🖉 Playa Cocles–based chocolate producer Caribeans leads tours of its sustainable cacao forest and chocolate-creation lab, accompanied by gourmet chocolate tastings. There's also a shop with a refrigerated chocolate room where visitors can try several varieties of chocolate.

Terraventuras
Tours

(📱2750-0750; www.terraventuras.com; ⏱7am-7pm) Offers overnight stays in Tortuguero (US$99), a cultural tour to an indigenous reserve (US$80) and a Caribbean cooking class (US$50), along with the usual local tours. It also has its very own 23-platform, 2.1km-long canopy tour (US$58), complete with Tarzan swing.

Gecko Trail Costa Rica
Tours

(📱2756-8159, in USA & Canada 415-230-0298; www.geckotrail.com; ⏱tours from US$50) This full-service agency arranges local tours as well as transportation, accommodation and excursions throughout Costa Rica, including horseback riding, hikes, rafting, hot-spring visits and spa days. It has an administrative office in Puerto Viejo (inside the Pleasure Ride building), but bookings are made by phone and online.

Puerto Viejo de Talamanca

Ⓝ 0 ____ 200 m
0 ____ 0.1 miles

Puerto Viejo de Talamanca

🔒 SHOPPING

Lulu Berlu Gallery
Arts & Crafts

(📞2750-0394; ⊙9am-9pm) On a backstreet parallel to the main road, this gallery carries folk art, clothing, jewelry, ceramics, embroidered purses and mosaic mirrors, among many other locally made items.

Organic Market
Market

(⊙6am-noon Sat) Don't miss the weekly organic market, when local vendors and growers sell snacks typical of the region, particularly tropical produce and chocolate. Arrive before 9am or the best stuff will be long gone.

✖ EATING

With the most diverse restaurant scene on the Caribbean coast, Puerto Viejo has the cure for *casado* overkill. You'll find everything from sushi to homemade pizza.

Bread
& Chocolate   Breakfast $

(☑2750-0723; www.facebook.com/band cpuertoviejo; cakes US$3.50-4, meals US$6-9; ⊙6:30am-6:30pm Wed-Sat, to 2:30pm Sun; ☑) Ever had a completely homemade PB&J (with bread, peanut butter and jelly all made from scratch)? That and more can be yours at this dream of a cafe, serving sandwiches, soups and salads, and of course the treat that gives it its name: chocolate. It's served as truffles, bars, cakes, tarts and covered nuts, and in cookies (gluten free available).

Café Rico   Cafe $

(☑2750-0510; caferico.puertoviejo@yahoo. com; breakfast US$3-8, lunch from US$6; ⊙7am-12:45pm Sat-Wed; ☎) Home to some of Puerto Viejo's best house-roasted coffee,

and natural smoothies such as probiotic ginger ale, this cozy garden cafe serves breakfast (yogurt and strawberries, omelets) and early lunch (the Hawaiian pineapple sandwich with ham and cheese is tasty). A plethora of other services include wi-fi, a large book exchange, laundry, plus snorkel and bike rentals.

Soda
Riquisimo   Caribbean $

(☑2750-0367; US$4.50-9; ⊙7am-10pm; ☎) Typical Caribbean dishes, like jerk chicken served with salad, beans, rice and plantain, are done well at this simple *soda* off the main strip. Reggae plays in the background and the atmosphere is friendly enough, but in this touristy town you can't beat these prices. At weekends the place is packed. It also serves toast, omelets and fruit for breakfast.

Como en mi
Casa Art Café   Cafe $

(☑6069-6337; www.comoenmicasacostarica. wordpress.com; mains US$3.50-6; ⊙8am-4pm Wed-Mon, kitchen to 2:30pm; ☑) Owned by

Rainforest, Puerto Viejo

DAMSEA/SHUTTERSTOCK ©

a friendly bohemian expat couple, this charming vegetarian cafe champions the 'slow food' movement and makes everything from scratch, from the jams and the hot sauces to the gluten-free pancakes. Popular items include raw cakes, homemade lentil-bean burgers, and gluten-free avocado wraps, smoothies and chocolate brownies. The walls are covered in local art.

De Gustibus   Bakery $
(☑2756-8397; www.facebook.com/degustibus bakery; baked goods from US$1; ⊘6.45am-6pm) This bakery on Puerto Viejo's main drag draws a devoted following with its fabulous focaccia, along with slices of pizza, apple strudels, profiteroles and all sorts of other sweet and savory goodies. Eat in or grab a snack for the beach.

Sel & Sucre   French $
(☑2750-0636; meals US$4-10; ⊘noon-9:30pm Tue-Sun; ✐) Dark coffee and fresh-fruit smoothies offer a nice complement to the menu of crepes, both savory and sweet. These delights are all prepared by the one and only chef Sebastien Flageul, who also owns the hostel next door. Service can be slow, but it's worth the wait.

Soda
Shekiná   Caribbean $
(☑2750-0549; mains US$6-10; ⊘breakfast 7:30-11:30am, lunch & dinner 11:30am-9pm Thu-Sun) Delicious pancake and fruit breakfasts and Caribbean home cooking can be found at this backstreet *soda* with wooden slab tables on an open-air terrace. Lunch and dinner mains are served with coconut rice and beans, salad and caramelized fried bananas. It's just northwest of the soccer field.

Mopri   Seafood $$
(☑2756-8411; mains US$9-20; ⊘noon-10pm) You'd never know it from Mopri's dingy facade and cheap plastic tables, but this place serves some of the best seafood in Puerto Viejo. Choose your star ingredient – whole snapper, calamari, lobster or prawns. Then choose your sauce – Caribbean,

🍽️ Out of Town Eating

Pita Bonita (☑2756-8173; Playa Chiquita; US$7.50-13.50; ⊘1-9pm Mon-Sat) For Turkish coffee, hummus and the best pita bread in the Caribbean, this Israeli-owned spot is the place. There's also spicy *shakshuka* (a Middle Eastern dish with poached eggs and tomato sauce) and fresh tabouli (tomatoes, parsley, mint, bulgur, lemon juice and onion). Find the open-air restaurant across from Tree House Lodge.

Selvin's Restaurant (☑2750-0664; www.selvinpuntauva.com; Punta Uva; mains US$12-18; ⊘noon-8pm Thu-Sun) Selvin has been serving Caribbean food since 1982 and his place is considered one of the region's best, specializing in shrimp, sautéed lobster in butter, garlic and onion, T-bone steak and a terrific *rondón* (seafood gumbo). Those with a sweet tooth will enjoy the organic chocolate bar and coconut candy.

El Refugio (☑2759-9007; Punta Uva; mains US$12-25; ⊘5-9pm Thu-Tue) This Argentine-owned restaurant with only five tables is renowned for its rotating menu of three appetizers, five main dishes and three desserts. New offerings get chalked up on the board daily, anchored by perennial favorites such as red tuna in garlic, *bife de entraña* with chimichurri (beef in a marinade of parsley, garlic and spices). Reserve ahead.

La Pecora Nera (☑2750-0490; Playa Cocles; mains US$15-30; ⊘5:30-10pm Tue-Sun; ✐) If you're looking to splurge on a fancy meal during your trip, do it at this romantic eatery run by Ilario Giannoni. On a lovely, candlelit patio, deftly prepared Italian seafood and pasta dishes are served alongside unusual offerings such as the delicate *carpaccio di carambola:* transparent slices of starfruit topped with shrimp, tomatoes and balsamic vinaigrette.

Mopri's garlic butter, curry, jalapeño or a lip-smacking salsa. Last, pile on the sides – rice, fried potatoes, plantains, salad, veggies or beans.

Stashu's con Fusion
Fusion $$

(☎2750-0530; mains US$10-14; ⏰5-10pm Thu-Tue; 🖋) Stroll 250m out of town toward Playa Cocles to this romantic low-lit patio cafe serving creative cuisine that combines elements of Caribbean, Indian, Mexican and Thai cooking. Macadamia- and coconut-encrusted tilapia and tandoori chicken are just a couple of standouts. Excellent vegetarian and vegan items. Owner-chef Stash Golas is an artist in the kitchen and out.

Miss Lidia's Place
Caribbean $$

(☎2750-0598; dishes US$7-20; ⏰1-9pm Tue-Sat, 11:30am-8pm Sun) A long-standing favorite for classic Caribbean flavors, Miss Lidia's has been around for years, pleasing the palates and satisfying the stomachs of locals and tourists alike. Fruit-and-veggie lovers will appreciate the ice-cold *batidos* (fresh-fruit drinks) and the delicious assortment of broccoli, green beans, cauliflower, corn-on-the-cob, carrots and mushrooms accompanying most dishes (red snapper, shrimp, chicken etc).

Bikini Restaurant & Bar
Fusion $$

(☎2750-3061; mojitos US$3.50, mains US$5.50-14; ⏰5.30-11pm; 🖋) If frozen mojitos are your thing, get thee to Bikini. This hip restaurant and bar attracts a crowd of revelers with its affordable cocktails and varied menu. Caribbean dishes, pasta,

★ Top Caribbean Cooking

Selvin's Restaurant (p89), Punta Uva

Miss Lidia's Place, Puerto Viejo

Mopri (p89), Puerto Viejo

Cool & Calm Cafe (p95), Manzanillo

Soda Riquisimo (p88), Puerto Viejo

Clockwise from top left: Guacamole and banana strips; Cafe in Puerto Viejo de Talamanca; Fruit shop; Soda Shekiná (p89)

⚠ Safety First

Be aware that though the use of marijuana (and harder stuff) is common in Puerto Viejo, it is nonetheless illegal.

As in other popular tourist centers, theft can be an issue. Stay aware, use your hotel safe, and if staying outside of town avoid walking alone late at night.

salads, curries and sushi all pair well with strong drinks and a convivial atmosphere. There are also 32 vegan and vegetarian options.

Laszlo's　　　　Seafood **$$$**

(☑8730-6185; mains US$16; ☺6-9pm) Whaddya get when you take a champion sport fisherman, born and raised in Transylvania, and transplant him to Puerto Viejo by way of New Jersey? Answer: an amazing, eclectic restaurant with no sign and no menu that only opens when owner Laszlo catches enough fish. The day's catch

comes with garlic and parsley, homemade French fries and grilled veggies. Yum.

Koki Beach　　　Latin American **$$$**

(☑2750-0902; http://kokibeach.blogspot.com.au; mains US$10-43; ☺5-11pm Tue-Sun, sometimes closed low season;) ⚓ A high-end favorite for drinks and dinner, this sleek place at the eastern end of town cranks up the lounge music and sports colorful Adirondack chairs that face the ocean from an elevated platform. There's a decent selection of Peruvian-inflected *ceviches,* plus meat and other seafood dishes. Produce comes from local organic suppliers, but there are slim pickings for vegetarians.

🍷 DRINKING & NIGHTLIFE

Restaurants often metamorphose into rollicking bar scenes after the tables are cleared.

Lazy Mon　　　　　　Club

(☑2750-2116; www.thelazymon.com; signature cocktails from US$5; ☺noon-2:30am) Run by brothers Khalil and Abasi and their friend

From left: Banana plantation; Playa Chiquita; Outback Jack's

Rocky, Puerto Viejo's most dependable spot for live music opened in 2010. Lazy Mon draws big crowds, plays reggae, and serves two-for-one cocktails (4pm to 7pm); sometimes there's even a 'crappy hour' (10pm to midnight). Try Jamakin' Me Crzy, a potent mix of vanilla vodka, orange liquor, mango and coconut cream.

Johnny's Place   Club

(📞2750-2000; meals US$5-18; ⏱11am-8pm Mon, Thu & Sun, to 3am Wed, Fri & Sat) Once a beachside clubbing institution, Johnny's slowed after the party started getting out of control in 2015. The place shut down briefly and reopened under new ownership as a classy restaurant (selling *ceviche*, salads, mixed rice and grilled fish) and bar with fancy cocktails. There are still DJs, dancing and occasional revelry on weekends, though.

Outback Jack's   Bar

(📞8554-4903; ⏱11am-11pm; 🛜) This Aussie-owned, junk-shop-style bar and grill is decorated with colorful refuse sculptures, bent pieces of metal, painted bikes and other recycled bits. Boards behind the outdoor bar read 'moonshine,' and they ain't kid-ding: it comes in many varieties, including chocolate, coconut, mango and banana. A daily two-for-one happy hour runs from 11am to 5.30pm, and there's live music in high season.

Point Bar
& Grill   Sports Bar

(📞2756-8491; www.thepointcostarica.com; Playa Negra; ⏱10:30am-11:30pm; 🛜) If you happen to be traveling during football season (or any other sport season, for that matter), you don't have to miss the big game. Just head to this convivial spot on the beach northwest of town. Decent food, big screens, craft beer and daily drink deals – 'nuff said.

Salsa Brava   Bar

(www.facebook.com/SalsaBravaBeachBar; cocktails from US$5; ⏱11am-2am) Specializing in tacos, Caribbean bowls and sweet plantain fries, this popular spot is the perfect end-of-day cocktail stop. Hit happy hour from 4pm to 6pm and you'll also catch two-for-one mojitos to enjoy while taking in the sunset over the Salsa Brava surf break. On Friday and Sunday the bar brings in DJs for popular reggae nights.

Parque Nacional Cahuita

This small but beautiful **park** (☎2755-0302, 2755-0461; US$5; ⏰Kelly Creek entrance 6am-5pm, Puerto Vargas entrance 8am-4pm) just 10 sq km is one of the more frequently visited national parks in Costa Rica. The reasons are simple: it's bursting with wildlife and easily walkable from the nearby town of Cahuita, which provides attractive accommodation. It also has the unusual combination of white-sand beach, coral reef and coastal rainforest, so you can spot an abundance of exotic species on land and underwater all in one day.

Declared a national park in 1978, Cahuita is meteorologically typical of the entire coast (that is to say, very humid), which results in dense tropical foliage, as well as coconut palms and sea grapes. The area includes the swampy Punta Cahuita, which juts into the sea between two stretches of sandy beach. Often flooded, the point is covered with cativo and mango trees and is a popular hangout for birds such as the green ibis, the yellow-crowned night heron, the boat-billed heron and the rare green-and-rufous kingfisher.

Red land and fiddler crabs live along the beaches, attracting mammals such as crab-eating raccoons and white-nosed pizotes (coatis). White-faced capuchins, southern opossums and three-toed sloths also live in these parts. The mammal you are most likely to see (and hear) is the mantled howler monkey, which makes its bellowing presence known. The coral reef represents another rich ecosystem, abounding with sea life.

😃 ENTERTAINMENT

Live music happens almost nightly during high season at Lazy Mon (p92). Pop by during the day to find out who's performing.

ℹ️ GETTING THERE & AWAY

If you're driving your own vehicle, Puerto Viejo de Talamanca is a straight shot down the paved coastal highway from Puerto Limón.

An ever-growing number of companies offer convenient van shuttles from Puerto Viejo to other tourist hot spots around Costa Rica and down the coast to Bocas del Toro (Panama). For an exhaustive list, see Gecko Trail's very helpful website (www.geckotrail.com). The following companies operate out of Puerto Viejo.

Caribe Shuttle (☎2750-0626; www.caribeshuttle.com/puerto-viejo-tours; tours from US$45) Serves Bocas del Toro (Panama), San José and Tortuguero.

Gecko Trail Costa Rica (p86) Standard shuttle service to San José and Tortuguero; also offers good-value Adventure Connection packages.

Interbus (☎2750-2145, 4100-0888; www.interbusonline.com; ⏰Mon-Sat) Serves Arenal-La Fortuna, San José, Siquirres and Puerto Viejo de Sarapiquí.

Pleasure Ride (p77) Operates tours and transportation in the Caribbean, as well as reliable private vans to the rest of the country. It also runs an Airport Express to and from San José.

ℹ️ GETTING AROUND

A bicycle is a fine way to get around town, and pedaling out to beaches east of Puerto Viejo is one of the highlights of this corner of Costa Rica. You'll find rentals all over town for about US$10 per day.

Manzanillo

The chilled-out village of Manzanillo has long been off the beaten track, even after the paved road arrived in 2003. This little town is still a vibrant outpost of Afro-Caribbean culture and has also remained pristine, thanks to the 1985 establishment of the Refugio Nacional de Vida Silvestre Gandoca-Manzanillo, which includes the village and imposes strict regulations on regional development. Activities are of a simple nature, in nature: hiking, snorkeling and kayaking reign supreme. As elsewhere, ask about riptides before heading out.

ACTIVITIES

Bad Barts   Snorkeling
(☑8650-2860, 2759-9012; www.badbartsman zanillo.com; per hour bike/snorkel/kayak rental US$2/4/6; ⊗8am-5pm Tue-Sun) Near the bus stop in Manzanillo, this outfit rents snorkel and scuba gear, kayaks, boogie boards and bicycles. Hours can vary; call ahead.

EATING

**Maxi's
Restaurant**   Caribbean $$
(☑2759-9086; mains US$7-14, lobster US$45-70; ⊗noon-10pm; 🛜🍴) Manzanillo's most famous restaurant draws a tourist crowd with large platters of grilled seafood, *pargo rojo* (whole red snapper), *ceviche*, pork and rice, steak, and pricey Caribbean-style lobster. Service can be slow, but the open-air upstairs dining area is a wonderful seaside setting for a meal and a beer with views of the beach and the street below.

Cool & Calm Cafe   Caribbean $$$
(mains US$12-26; ⊗11am-9pm Wed-Mon) Directly across from Manzanillo's western beachfront, this front-porch eatery plies visitors with fine Caribbean cooking – from snapper to shrimp to chicken to lobster – with a few extras like guacamole, tacos and veggie curry thrown in for good measure. Owner Andy offers Caribbean cooking classes and a 'reef-to-plate' tour where, in certain seasons, you can dive for your own lobster or fish. Andy catches the lobster and prepares his outrageous lobster *caribeño* daily.

DRINKING & NIGHTLIFE

You may find the occasional party at Maxi's Restaurant.

 **Crazy Monkey
Canopy Tour**

The region's only **canopy tour** (☑2271-3000, in USA 800-253-6591; www.almonds andcorals.com/activities/crazy-monkey -canopy-ride; per person US$60; ⊗10am-2pm) has 13 cables and platforms among the trees, with treetop views of nature and a thatched indigenous village. The 1¼-hour tour finishes on the beach. Located between Punta Uva and Manzanillo, it's operated by **Almonds & Corals Lodge** (☑2759-9031, 2271-3000, in USA 1-888-373-9042; www.almondsand corals.com; ste incl breakfast US$145-245, additional person from US$20; 🅿@🛜🌊) 🐾.

Mantled howler monkey
KRYSSIA CAMPOS/GETTY IMAGES ©

GETTING THERE & AWAY

A 13km road winds east from Puerto Viejo, through rows of coconut palms, alongside coastal lodges and through lush lowland rainforest before coming to a dead end at the sleepy town of Manzanillo. The road was paved for the first time in 2003, dramatically shortening the amount of time it takes to travel this route. The roadway is narrow, however; so if you're driving, take your time and be alert for cyclists and one-lane bridges.

RÍO PACUARE

Río Pacuare at a Glance...

World-class white water awaits on the Río Pacuare, which is well worth a run for its cascade of thrilling rapids through a stunningly beauteous jungle gorge. Rapids range from Class II to IV and the calmer parts offer some of Central America's most scenic rafting, with plenty of wildlife sightings and ideally a dip in the refreshingly icy river. The lesser-explored mountain town of Turrialba and the steamy lowlands of Siquirres are the best bases for taking on the river, with some surprising attractions of their own.

One Day on the Río Pacuare

If you've only got one day for the river, base yourself at one of the charming mountain lodges in Turrialba and plop into the river early, with help from one of the **local tour companies** (p102). After the thrills, replenish yourself at **Maracuyá** (p104), a fantastic little cafe, or celebrate river domination with beers at **Loco's Bar and Restaurant** (p106).

Two Days on the Río Pacuare

Multiday trips on the Pacuare are nothing short of exhilarating, and you can break up the wet and wild ride with a stay at one of the country's dreamiest digs, **Pacuare Lodge** (p106). Some of the tour companies offer good package deals, and for a fascinating glimpse into the nearby town of Siquirres and its eccentric residents, visit the **Centro Turístico Las Tilapias** (p106) before or after you raft.

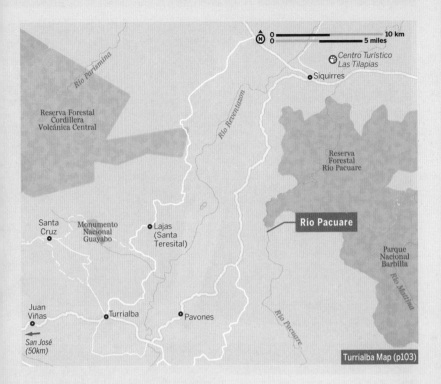

Turrialba Map (p103)

Arriving at Río Pacuare

All of the river-rafting companies will arrange transport for you to and from the river, be it from the southern Caribbean, San José or anywhere in between. To save a few bucks, base yourself in Siquirres or Turrialba, which are the closest towns to the river, and take your own wheels to your chosen operators headquarters on the river.

Sleeping

The posh, riverfront Pacuare Lodge transcends the need for electricity with high style and adventure. Those with shallower pockets will want to grab a room in the mountains of Turrialba or the fascinating Centro Las Tilapias in Siquirres. It's also feasible to travel from San José or the southern Caribbean, but you'll be rising early in the morning.

KEVIN SCHAFER/GETTY IMAGES ©

Rafting the River

Ranging from family-friendly riffles to nearly unnavigable rapids, this river offers highly varied but always thrilling experiences. All white-water rafting requires a certified guide, so you need to book trips through a reputable tour agency. No matter the run, you'll get totally soaked and tossed about, so pack a sense of humor.

Traditionally the two most popular rafting rivers have been Río Reventazón and Río Pacuare, but the former has been dramatically impacted by a series of hydroelectric projects, including a huge 305-megawatt dam currently under construction.

As a result, most organized expeditions from Turrialba now head for the Río Pacuare, which arguably offers the most scenic rafting in Central America. The river plunges down the Caribbean slope through a series of spectacular canyons clothed in virgin rainforest, through runs named for their fury and separated by calm stretches that enable you to stare at near-vertical green walls towering hundreds of meters above.

Great For...

☑ **Don't Miss**

A cool, invigorating dip in the river during one of the calmer stretches.

❶ Need to Know

If you have your own vehicle, you can base yourself in Turrialba (p102) or Siquirres (p106), the closest towns to the river. Alternatively, river-rafting companies can arrange transportation to the river, even from San José.

✕ Take a Break

After braving the rapids, reward yourself with a passion-fruit coffee drink at Maracuyá (p104).

★ Top Tip

When the guide says paddle hard, just do it.

○ **Lower Pacuare** With Class II to IV rapids, this is the more accessible run: 28km through rocky gorges, past an indigenous village and untamed jungle.

○ **Upper Pacuare** Classified as Class III to IV, but a few sections can go to Class V, depending on conditions. It's about a two-hour drive to the put-in, after which you'll have the prettiest jungle cruise on earth all to yourself.

When to Go

The Pacuare can be run year-round, though June to October are considered the best months. The highest water is from October to December, when the river runs fast with huge waves. March and April are when the river is at its lowest, although it's still challenging.

Trips & Prices

Rafting trips are offered by several Turri-alba-based agencies as well as reputable national companies such as Exploradores Outdoors (p77) and **Ríos Tropicales** (☑2233-6455, in USA 866-722-8273; www. riostropicales.com).

Day trips usually raft the Class II to IV Lower Pacuare, thanks to its relative ease of access. A tamer alternative for beginners and families is the Class I to II Río Pejibaye. Other runs – such as the Upper Pacuare and/or remaining navigable segments of Río Reventazón – require more time spent in a van and tend to be more expensive.

For day trips (many of which originate in San José), expect to pay from US$100 to US$150 depending on transportation, accessibility and amenities. It is generally less expensive to leave from Turrialba (day trips around US$80). Multiday excursions with camping or lodge accommodation are also offered by numerous companies. For two-day trips, prices vary widely depending on accommodation, but expect to pay US$200 to US$350 per person. Children must be at least nine years old for most trips, and older for tougher runs.

Turrialba

When the railway shut down in 1991, commerce slowed, but Turrialba nonetheless remained a regional agricultural center where local coffee growers could bring their crops to market. And with tourism on the rise in Costa Rica in the 1990s, this modest mountain town soon became known as the gateway to some of the best white-water rafting on the planet. By the early 2000s Turrialba was a hotbed of international rafters looking for Class V thrills. For now, the Río Pacuare runs on, but its future is uncertain.

 ACTIVITIES

There are several local companies that run multiday rafting trips on the Pacuare, as well as trips to other rivers and ziplining courses, and horseback-riding sites.

> *some of the best white-water rafting on the planet*

Ecoaventuras   Outdoors

(☏2556-7171, 8868-3938; www.ecoaventuras.co.cr; white-water rafting packages per person from US$70) Ecoaventuras offers white-water rafting on the Ríos Pacuare and Pejibaye, along with horseback riding (from US$50) and mountain biking (prices depend on tour length and rider experience). Three-day rafting experiences include all meals, accommodation, equipment and a zipline tour (inquire for prices). It's 100m north and 100m west of the Rawlings Factory.

Costa Rica Ríos   Rafting

(☏2556-8664, in USA & Canada 888-434-0776; www.costaricarios.com; Calle 1) Offers week-long rafting trips that must be booked in advance. An eight-day kayaking and canoeing trip costs US$1699 per person (based on double occupancy), while the adventure-tour package, including rafting, ziplining, snorkeling, surfing and mountain biking, costs US$2899 per person (also based on double occupancy). The office is located near Av 6.

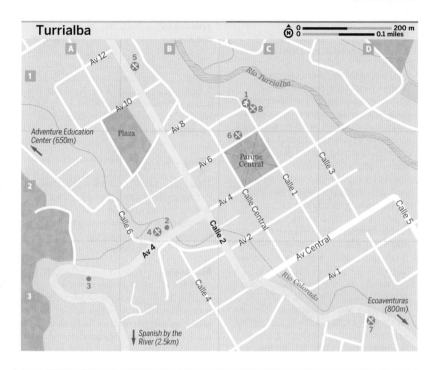

Turrialba

Explornatura   Rafting
(☎2556-0111, in USA & Canada 866-571-2443; www.explornatura.com/en/; Av 4 btwn Calles 2 & 4) Offers rafting, mountain-biking and horseback-riding tours. A rafting day trip on the Pacuare is US$85 per person, a canyoneering and canopy tour is US$75 per person.

Loco's   Rafting
(☎8704-3535, 2556-6035, in USA 707-703-5935; www.whiteh2o.com) Loco's takes guests on wild rides of varying difficulty down the Ríos Pacuare and Reventazón. The outfit also runs camping trips on the Pacuare,

plus canyoning and rappelling adventures. A day of rafting starts at around US$70 per person, depending on group size; prices include lunch and transport.

**Adventure
Education
Center**   Rafting, Language
(☎in USA 800-237-2730; www.facebook.com/AECSpanishInstitute/; 1 week with/without homestay US$490/325) Combine Spanish classes and white-water rafting at this Turrialba school that also offers medical Spanish. A week's group language instruction entails 20 hours of lessons.

Segregated Costa Rica

Even before the highways bisecting the town were built, Siquirres was a significant location, for it was here in the early 20th century that the lines of segregation were drawn. At the time, black people were barred from traveling west of the town without special permission. Accordingly, any train making its way from Limón to San José was required to stop here and change its crew: black people working as conductors and engineers would change places with their Spanish counterparts and the train would continue on its route to the capital. This ended in 1949, when a new constitution outlawed racial discrimination.

Today Siquirres still marks the place where Costa Rica takes a dip into the Caribbean – and not just geographically. This is where Costa Rican *casados* give way to West Indian *rondón* and where Spanish guitar is replaced with the strains of calypso.

Spanish by the River Language
(2556-7380, in USA 1-877-268-3730; www.spanishatlocations.com; 10/30hr per week US$160/300, homestay/hostel bed US$22/12) A five-minute bus ride from Turrialba, this school offers accommodation along with weekly Spanish classes for students at varying levels of fluency.

⊗ EATING

Those on a budget will have no problem finding cheap meals in Turrialba; if you're looking to make an evening of it, there's the choice of Asian, fusion, Costa Rican or barbecue food. There are plenty of supermarkets for self-caterers, too.

Maracuyá Cafe $
(☑2556-2021; www.facebook.com/maracuya2012; Calle 2; frozen coffee around US$4, mains US$5-7; ☺2-9:30pm Wed-Mon; ✍) This bright-walled cafe north of Av 10 serves up one of the best coffee treats in the country – a frozen caffeine concoction with gooey *maracuyá* (passion fruit) syrup

River guides preparing lunch

and crunchy seeds. Dishes include veggie wraps, creative salads, fried chicken and chips, and Latin American favorites such as *patacones* (fried plantains).

La Feria
Costa Rican $

(☎8378-7979, 2556-0386, 2556-5550; www. facebook.com/RestauranteLaFeria; Calle 6; mains US$5-14; ◎11am-9:30pm Wed-Mon, to 2:30pm Tue; 🖉) This unremarkable-looking restaurant has friendly service and excellent, reasonably priced home cooking. Sometimes the kitchen gets a bit backed up, but the hearty *casados* (typical dishes with beans, rice, a small salad and a choice of protein) are well worth the wait. Caribbean chicken, salads, pasta and red snapper are also available. Find the place north of Av 4.

Restaurant Betico Mata
Barbecue $

(☎2556-8640; Hwy 10; gallos US$2, mains US$6; ◎11am-midnight Mon-Fri, to late Sat & Sun) This carnivores' delight is at the southern end of town. Its cafeteria style isn't pretty, but you can't beat the good-value *gallos* (open-face tacos on corn tortillas) piled with succulent, fresh-grilled meats including beef, chicken, sausage or pork, all soaked in the special house marinade. It all goes smashingly well with an ice-cold beer.

Wok & Roll
Asian $$

(☎2556-6756; www.facebook.com/Wok-Roll-489594887746705; Calle 1; mains US$9-16; ◎11am-10pm Wed-Mon) Pan-Asian cuisine fills the menu at this place near the main square. Enjoy sushi rolls and sashimi, teriyaki or sweet-and-sour chicken, Thai curry, wontons and other Asian favorites, plus tempura ice cream for dessert. Wash it all down with homemade mint lemonade and honey-sweetened jasmine tea.

More Than Words
Thai, Italian $$

(☎2556-1362; www.facebook.com/morethan-words888/; small/large pizzas from US$8/15, mains from US$10; ◎11am-10pm Tue-Thu, to

 Damning the River?

Considered one of the most beautiful white-water-rafting rivers in the world, wild Río Pacuare became the first federally protected river in Central America in 1985. Within two years, however, the national power company, Instituto Costarricense de Electricidad (ICE), unveiled plans to build a 200m gravity dam at the conveniently narrow and screamingly scenic ravine of Dos Montañas.

The dam would be the cornerstone of the massive Siquirres hydroelectric project, which would include four dams in total, linked by a 10km-long tunnel. If built, rising waters on the lower Pacuare would not only flood 12km of rapids up to the Tres Equis put-in, but also parts of Reserva Indígena Awari and a huge swath of primary rainforest where some 800 animal species have been recorded. The project was intended to help ICE keep up with the country's rapidly increasing power demands, but as the proposal moved from specu-lation to construction, a coalition of local landowners, indigenous leaders, conservation groups and, yep, white-water-rafting outfits fought against it, and won.

On August 29, 2015, former President Luis Guillermo Solís signed a decree banning hydroelectric projects of 500 kilowatts or more from the river for the next 25 years. Although the Pacuare seems safe for now, another decree by a future president could again leave it unprotected.

11pm Fri, noon-11pm Sat & Sun) With a large bar at its center, this restaurant oppo-site the church in the main square is the new venture from the owners of Wok & Roll. Service can be slow, but the dishes are satisfying. The diverse menu has

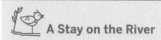

A Stay on the River

There are two ways into **Pacuare Lodge** (4033-0060, in USA & Canada 1-800-963-1195; www.pacuarelodge.com; 3-day, 2-night all-inclusive packages s/d from US$1348/1866;), a dream of an ecolodge, both equally adventurous. Most visitors arrive at its remote location on the Río Pacuare by raft, via a thrilling 45-minute guided paddle. Others take a 7km dirt path (only accessible via the hotel's 4WD) to the river, and then climb into a rickety cable car that crosses the water to the lodge.

Outdoor enthusiasts will love the elegant private bungalows overlooking the river, with solar-heated showers and thatched roofs; some bungalows have infinity pools. Most (aside from family rooms) have no electricity or walls, only screens – all the better to unplug from city life and immerse yourself in nature. Activities include guided hikes in rainforest, ziplining, canyoning and meeting nearby indigenous communities. Unwind at the spa or eat dinner in the treetops on an elevated canopy terrace.

The lodge is currently participating in a panther program: 40 motion-sensor cameras are set up around the reserve to capture wild-cat activity, and there's a learning center with video footage of recent sightings.

Package deals include transportation to and from San José, a bilingual guide, a rafting tour or ground transportation to the lodge, equipment, meals, most drinks and a hike.

freshly made pizzas, pasta dishes, New York steaks and interesting creations like *wantacos* (a hybrid wanton-taco stuffed with marinated chicken and salad). Ask about upcoming live events, from music to comedy.

DRINKING & NIGHTLIFE

Loco's Bar and Restaurant
Bar

(2556-3500; www.facebook.com/locos restauranteybar; drinks from US$2, dishes from US$4; 2pm-midnight Sun-Thu, to 2am Fri, noon-2am Sat) This new bar, from the owners of the Loco's adventure outfit, is where rafters end up after an adrenaline-fueled day on the rivers. Things might get lively with brightly colored cocktails, Jägermeister, B-52s and tequila shots, but it's a decent late-lunch and dinner spot, too. Bites include guacamole and nachos, mozzarella sticks, fajitas, *ceviche* and mixed plates.

GETTING THERE & AWAY

Regular and reliable buses serve the Turrialba area. But if you'd like the freedom to explore these twisting mountain roads, renting a car is a great idea.

Siquirres

The steamy lowland town of Siquirres has long served as an important transportation hub. It sits at the intersection of Hwy 32 (the main road that crosses the Atlantic slope to Puerto Limón) and Hwy 10, the old road that connects San José with Puerto Limón via Turrialba.

There is little reason to stop in Siquirres, unless you're heading to Parismina – in which case this is a good spot to find banking, internet and telephone services. Tip: buy phonecards here; they aren't sold in Parismina. For the purposes of orientation, Siquirres' church – a highly recognizable round, red-domed building – is located west of the soccer field.

SIGHTS

Centro Turístico Las Tilapias
Wildlife Reserve

(2768-9293; 30min canal tours from US$10, cabinas d with fan/air-con US$45/50;

Pacuare Lodge

⊙9am-7pm; P) Enthusiastic owner Chito is a passionate naturalist who spent 20 years building and introducing wildlife into a 5km canal system just outside Siquirres. It's now teeming with exotic nature, from birds, turtles and sloths to monkeys, frogs and more, and Chito runs tours around his thriving canal network. There's also a tasty restaurant-bar here and some charming rustic *cabinas* perched above a lagoon and the canals. Take a taxi or ask locals for careful directions, as it's tricky to find.

Chito is locally famous for befriending, training and performing with a 12ft crocodile named Pocho who lived on the premises. Pocho died in 2011, and the government has since outlawed crocodile training.

 EATING

**Pacuare River
Bar & Grill** Costa Rican $

(☑7016-3147; www.facebook.com/pacuare riverbar; bar food US$2-8; ⊙11am-midnight)

" *a dream of an ecolodge* "

Run by bilingual local Johanna and her American partner, Kirk, this Colorado-style bar and restaurant is on Hwy 10 between Turrialba and Siquirres. Enter the laid-back roadhouse through swing doors, grab a drink at the bar, decorated with a snake skin and bull horns, and tuck into tangy *ceviche*, fresh beef fajitas or buffalo wings. It's a good place to stop on the way to the Caribbean coast. Look for the kayaks out front.

ℹ **GETTING THERE & AWAY**

An asphalt highway (Hwy 32) – through Parque Nacional Braulio Carrillo – links San José and Puerto Limón to Siquirres. It's easy and cheap to take a bus, but it's far more convenient to rent your own vehicle.

PARQUE NACIONAL CHIRRIPÓ

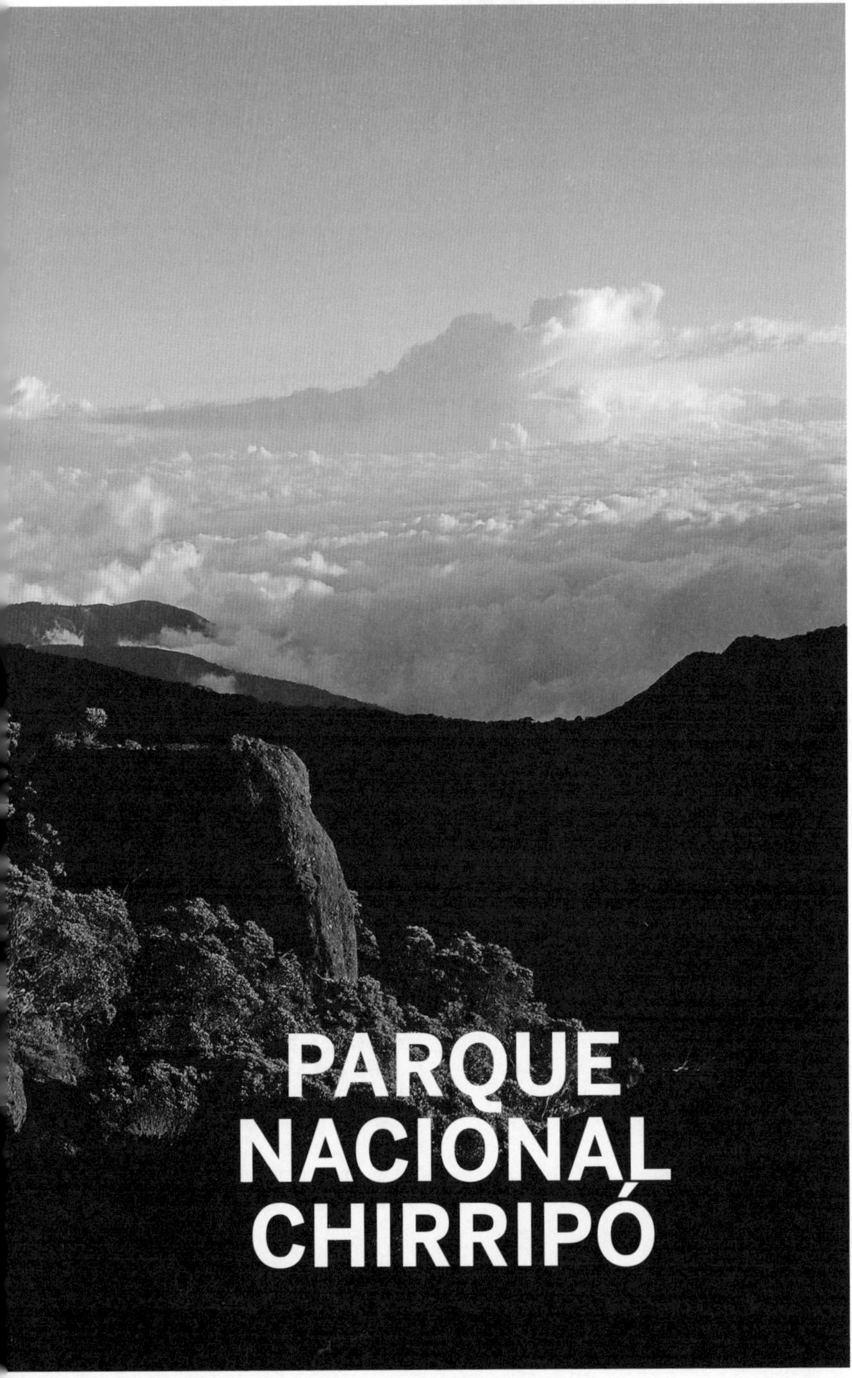

ADRIANA MARGARITA LARIOS ARELLANO/SHUTTERSTOCK ©

Parque Nacional Chirripó at a Glance...

Costa Rica's mountainous spine runs the length of the country in four distinct mountain ranges, of which the Cordillera de Talamanca is the highest, longest and most remote. The cordillera's highlight and the focus of the high-altitude Parque Nacional Chirripó is Costa Rica's highest peak, Cerro Chirripó (3820m). Above 3400m, the landscape is páramo, comprising scrubby trees and grasslands. The bare páramo contrasts with the lush cloud forest, which dominates the hillsides between 2500m and 3400m.

Two Days in Parque Nacional Chirripó

You certainly shouldn't plan for any less than two days to visit **Cerro Chirripó** (p112), as that's the bare minimum for the hike. Be sure to arrive early enough to check in at the ranger station the day before, and on your way in, grab a snack at **Antojos de Maíz** (p117).

Four Days in Parque Nacional Chirripó

You have the luxury of spending two nights at **Crestones Base Lodge** (p115), allowing two days to climb, plus an extra day to explore the trails around the summit and/or lodge. There would also be time to check out **Cloudbridge Nature Reserve** (p116), or to simply take advantage of the amenities on offer by some of the area's accommodations – **thermal hot springs** (p117), anyone?

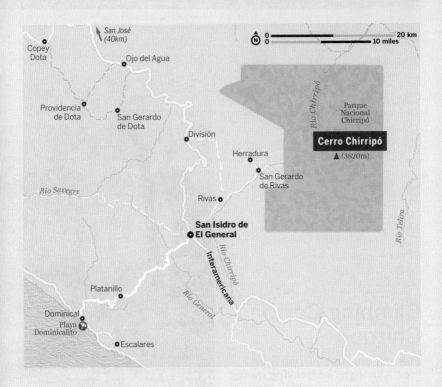

Arriving in Parque Nacional Chirripó

Traveling south from San José, the road to Chirripó passes through gorgeous countryside redolent of coffee plantations and cool, misty cloud forest. It's one of the most beautiful drives in the country, but it's also one of the most dangerous due to frequent mist and dangerous maneuvers by local drivers.

Sleeping

Even though San Isidro is the regional hub, few travelers stay there, moving on to San Gerardo de Rivas if they're hikers. Many accommodations in the Rivas area are geared toward backpackers in search of mountain adventure, although there are a few upscale mountain lodges and boutique hotels. Note that many accommodations close when Chirripó closes, during the last half of May and all of October.

Parque Nacional Chirripó

Climbing Cerro Chirripó

The only way up Chirripó is on foot. Although the trekking routes are challenging, watching the sun rise from such lofty heights is one of the country's undeniable highlights.

Great For...

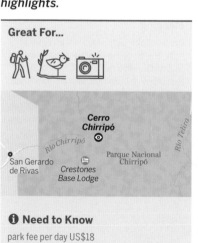

ℹ Need to Know

park fee per day US$18

★ Top Tip

You must register your permit with the ranger office before you hike.

Getting Started

The park entrance is at San Gerardo de Rivas, which lies 1219m above sea level; the altitude at the summit is 3820m, which makes it 2.6km straight up! A well-marked 19.6km trail leads all the way to the top, with trail markers every kilometer, and no technical climbing is required. It would be nearly impossible to get lost.

Altitude sickness can be an issue as you get higher up. Watch out for nausea, shortness of breath, headaches and exhaustion. If you start feeling unwell, rest for a little while; if the symptoms persist, descend immediately.

Permits

Hiking up Chirripó became significantly easier in 2016 when SINAC created an on-line booking system for park permits, which can be found at https://serviciosenlinea. sinac.go.cr. You can purchase your permits up to six months in advance and must also reserve a bed at Crestones Base Lodge.

Timing

The amount of time it takes to climb varies greatly – it can take as little as five and as many as 12 hours to cover the 14.5km from the start of the trail to the Crestones Base Lodge, depending on how fit you are; plan for at least seven hours. From the lodge it's another 5.1km to the summit, which takes around two hours one way.

For most people, a minimum of two days is needed to climb from the ranger station in San Gerardo to the summit and back, leaving no time for exploration. During peak season you're allowed to book a maximum

View from Cerro Chirripó

of two nights at the lodge, and at all other times the max is three nights. This gives you extra time to explore the trails around the summit and/or the Base Lodge.

The Route

Most hikers start between 4am and 5am, though there's nothing to stop you from leaving earlier. The actual entrance to the park is 4km from the start of the trail in San Gerardo, which is 70m beyond Hotel Urán (and about 4km from the ranger station).

The first 6km or so is mostly uphill, over uneven, rocky ground, with some relatively flat stretches. You pass through dense cloud forest, so keep an eye out for quetzals.

> ☑ **Don't Miss**
>
> Watching the sun rise over Costa Rica from the country's highest peak.

Then there's a gentle descent toward the shelter at Llano Bonito (7.5km), which is a good place for a break. Here you can stock up on water, use the toilets and buy snacks.

Just beyond begins the Cuesta de los Arrepentidos ('Hill of the Repentants') and boy, will you repent! It's a steep uphill slog until you reach the top of Monte Sin Fe (which translates as 'Mountain Without Faith'), a preliminary crest that reaches 3200m at around Km 10. By then you're on exposed ground, flanked by stunted tree growth, with gorgeous mountain views around you.

Reaching the lodge is the hardest part. From here the hike to the summit is 5.1km on relatively flatter terrain (although the last 100m is very steep). Carry a warm jacket, rain gear, water, snacks and a flashlight just in case, but leave anything you don't need at the lodge. From the summit on a clear day, the vista stretches to both the Caribbean Sea and the Pacific Ocean. The deep-blue lakes and the plush-green hills carpet the Valle de las Morenas in the foreground.

Most hikers reach the lodge around lunchtime and spend the rest of the day recuperating before leaving for the summit at around 3am to arrive in time to watch the sun rise – a spectacular experience.

Seasons & Weather

The dry season (from late December to April) is the most popular time to visit Chirripó. February and March are the driest months with the clearest skies, though it may still rain. On weekends, and especially during holidays, the trails can get a bit crowded with Tico hiking groups.

In any season, temperatures can drop below freezing at night, so warm clothes (including hat and gloves) and rainwear are necessary. Wear sturdy boots and bring good second-skin blister plasters.

> ✕ **Take a Break**
>
> Reservations are required to eat and sleep at **Crestones Base Lodge** (☏2742-5097; www.chirripo.org/hospedaje/; dm US$35; ☏).

Cloudbridge Nature Reserve

CHRISONTOURS4/SHUTTERSTOCK ©

San Gerardo de Rivas

If you have plans to climb Chirripó, you're in the right place – the tiny, tranquil, spread-out town of San Gerardo de Rivas is at the doorstep of the national park. This is a place to get supplies, a good night's rest and a hot shower before and after the trek.

With a new online reservation system, hiking permits recently became much easier to obtain. For those who don't have the time or energy to summit Chirripó, there are also lovely, less difficult hikes in private nature reserves, and rural tourism aplenty, from the local trout farm to local cheese- and chocolate-makers in nearby Canaán. San Gerardo's bird-filled alpine scenery certainly makes it a beautiful place to linger.

The road to San Gerardo de Rivas winds its way 22km up the valley of the Río Chirripó from San Isidro.

◎ SIGHTS

Cloudbridge Nature Reserve
Nature Reserve

(🖉in the USA 917-494-5408; www.cloudbridge.org; admission by donation, tours US$10-30; ⊘6am-6pm) About 2km past the trailhead to Cerro Chirripó you will find the entrance to the mystical, magical Cloudbridge Nature Reserve. Covering 283 hectares on the side of Cerro Chirripó, this private reserve is an ongoing reforestation and preservation project spearheaded by New Yorker Genevieve Giddy and her late husband Ian. A network of trails traverses the property, which is easy to explore independently. Even if you don't get far past the entrance, you'll find two waterfalls, including the magnificent Catarata Pacifica.

The trails range from the gentle Sendero Catarata Pacifica, leading to the waterfalls, to the steep uphill Sendero Montaña that joins the main trail up Cerro Chirripó. Guided tours including birdwatching, night hikes and strolls through old-growth forest have set times and English-speaking guides. They must be booked at least a full day in advance.

Volunteer reforestation and conservation opportunities are listed on the reserve's website.

Jardines Secretos — Gardens
(☑8451-3001, 2742-5086; US$5; ⏱7am-5pm) These not-so-secret gardens make for a tranquil pre- or post-Chirripó pastime as the owners talk you through their collection of orchids and other tropical plants. Find the turnoff just before the ranger station.

Talamanca Reserve — Nature Reserve
(☑2742-5080; www.talamancareserve.com) With over 4000 acres of primary and secondary cloud forest, this private reserve has numerous hiking trails, the longest being a seven-hour trek, and another leading to its 11 waterfalls. Talamanca is doing its best to promote itself as an alternative to Parque Nacional Chirripó, and nonguests are welcome to hike its trails for a day fee of US$25. ATV tours are available both to guests and nonguests.

✪ ACTIVITIES

Truchero Los Cocolisos — Fishing, Food
(☑2742-5054; ⏱9am-6pm Sat & Sun & by appointment) Down the left fork road just before the Quebrada Chispa bridge, uphill from the ranger station, is this lovely family-run trout farm. Catch your own fish from the trout pools or take in the celebrated orchid collection. Naturally, the fish is the best part; matronly Garita puts together a homemade feast of trout and home-cooked sides for US$7.

Thermal Hot Springs — Hot Springs
(Aguas Termales; ☑2742-5210; Herradura; US$7; ⏱7am-5:30pm) Between the ranger station and upper San Gerardo lies a bridge; before the bridge, a road forks to the left. Take this and walk for about 1km

 Birdwatching Around San Isidro de El General

Expat Pieter Westra runs highly recommended **Aratinga Tours** (☑2574-2319; www.aratinga-tours.com) ✈, and is fluent in English, Spanish and many dialects of bird. The website provides an excellent introduction to birdwatching in Costa Rica. Budget tours start at around US$1800, while the more luxurious trips start at around US$2700. Custom trips can also be arranged.

Small **Refugio de Aves Los Cusingos** (☑2738-2070; www.cct.or.cr; adult/child US$17/6; ⏱7am-4pm Mon-Sat, to 1pm Sun) was donated to Costa Rica by Alexander Skutch, co-author of *Birds of Costa Rica*. Expert birding guides are available (US$10) to help you make the most of the birding trails. It's south of San Isidro in Quizzara, on the opposite side of the Río General, signposted off the road to Santa Elena/ Quizarra valley. Call ahead.

Golden-hooded tanager
ONDREJ PROSICKY/SHUTTERSTOCK ©

on a paved road, then turn right and take the suspension bridge over the river. A switchback trail leads for 1km to a house with a *soda,* the entrance to the hot springs – two pools popular with soaking locals.

✖ EATING

Antojos de Maíz — Costa Rican $
(☑2772-4381; chorreadas US$3; ⏱8am-8pm Wed-Mon) For all things corn, stop at this traditional roadside restaurant on your way to

🔭 Finding the Quetzal

One of the best places to go birdwatching is Parque Nacional Los Quetzales, though you're just as likely to spot the elusive quetzal along the private trails in the grounds of Savegre Hotel de Montaña and Paraíso Quetzal Lodge, the latter a little way from San Gerardo (both allow access to nonguests for a fee). There's also a particular spot along the river (ask your lodgings where it is), which gets crowded with binocular-bearing twitchers at dawn. Your accommodations can arrange a birding guide for Parque Nacional Los Quetzales to maximize your chances of spotting the likes of collared trogons and emerald toucanets, as well as the quetzal. One particularly excellent local guide and quetzal expert who speaks perfect English is **Raul Chacón** (📱8920-9987; jrfc01@gmail.com; quetzal tour for up to 5 people US$70).

Quetzals are easily spotted every April and May (during breeding season) and are fairly common throughout the rest of the year. An especially nice place to photograph them and other birds is the lovely **Batsù Garden** (p120).

Male resplendent quetzal
MALLARDG500/GETTY IMAGES ©

or from the mountain. Our favorite here is the *chorreada*, a traditional sweet pancake made with fresh white or yellow corn and served with sour cream. Pairs very well with strong, organic coffee.

Restaurante Rio   Pizza $

(📱2742-5110; mains from US$8; ⊗11am-10pm; 🍴) Not far from the soccer field, this place serves surprisingly good pizzas; we particularly like the one topped with pepperoni, bacon and ham. Generous portions, and several pizza options are meat-free.

Restaurante
Roca Dura   International $

(📱2742-5071; mains from US$6; ⊗8am-9pm) The most happenin' place in town, right by the soccer field. The standard dishes won't set your tastebuds alight, but the french fries are excellent and it's a terrific place for people-watching.

ℹ️ INFORMATION

It is essential that you stop at the **ranger station** (Sinac; 📱905-244-7447, in the USA 506-2742-5348; ⊗8am-noon & 1-4:30pm) in San Gerardo de Rivas at least one day before you intend to climb Chirripó to confirm your park permit (bring your reservation and proof of payment). After you've done that, you have to confirm your Crestones Base Lodge reservation at the **consortium office** (📱2742-5097, 2742-5200; infochirriposervicios@gmail.com; ⊗8am-5pm Mon-Sat, from 9am Sun). Park fees are now US$18 per day. You can also make arrangements at the ranger station to hire a porter (a fixed fee of US$100 for up to 15kg of luggage), though it's now less necessary than ever. Since Crestones offers meals and includes bedding in the accommodations price, you can travel light, without cooking gear or a sleeping bag.

ℹ️ GETTING THERE & AWAY

The road to San Gerardo de Rivas winds its way 22km up the valley of the Río Chirripó from San Isidro.

Driving from San Isidro, head south on the Interamericana and cross Río San Isidro south of town. About 500m further on, cross the unsigned Río Jilguero and take the first, steep turn up to the left, about 300m beyond the Jilguero. Note that this turnoff is not marked

ADRIANA MARGARITA LARIOS ARELLANO/SHUTTERSTOCK ©

LEFT: JARIB GONZALEZ/ALAMY STOCK PHOTO; RIGHT: LOVETRAVELFLY/LOVETRAVELFLY/500PX ©

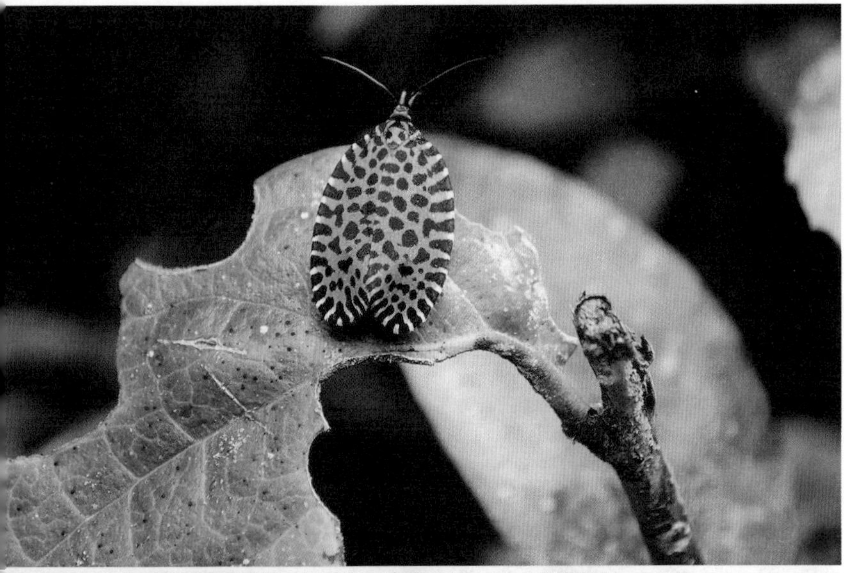

Clockwise from top: Insect, Parque Nacional Chirripó; Tree flower in bloom; Oyster mushroom

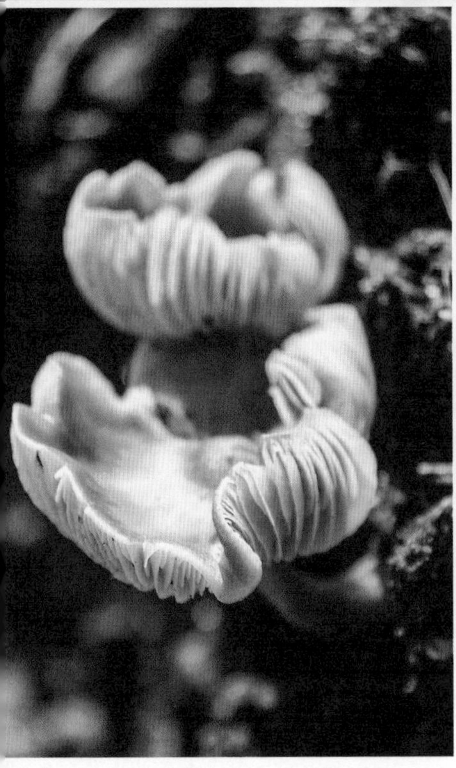

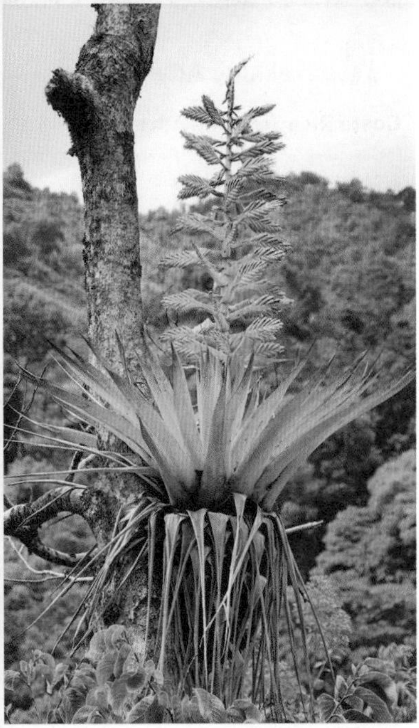

Trekking Adventures

Costa Rica Trekking Adventures
(☑2771-4582; www.chirripo.com) runs a couple of treks up Cerro Chirripó, including an alternative route for hardcore adventurers. This ascent is a guided three- or five-day loop that begins in the nearby village of Herradura and spends a day or two traversing cloud forest and *páramo* on the slopes of Fila Urán (which was closed at the time of research).

Hikers ascend Cerro Urán (3600m) before the final ascent of Chirripó and then descend through San Gerardo.

Parque Nacional Chirripó
ADRIANA MARGARITA LARIOS ARELLANO/SHUTTERSTOCK ©

(if you miss the turn, it is signed from the northbound side).

The ranger station is about 18km up this road from the Interamericana. The road passes through Rivas village and is paved as far as the entrance to San Gerardo de Rivas. It is passable for ordinary cars, but a 4WD is recommended if you are driving to Hotel Urán or to Cloudbridge Nature Reserve, as the unpaved road is steep and truly hideous.

San Gerardo de Dota

Off the road to Chirripó, San Gerardo de Dota is unlike any other place in Costa Rica – a bucolic mountain village run through by a clear, rushing river and surrounded by forested hills that more resemble the alps than the tropics. It's set deep within a mountain valley; the air is crisp and fresh, and chilly at night, and the orchard-lined Savegre basin hosts numerous high-altitude bird species, including the eye-catching and beloved resplendent quetzal, that draw birdwatchers from around the world.

◎ SIGHTS

Batsù Garden   Gardens
(☑8395-0115; www.batsucr.com; US$20; ◔5am-8pm) A garden designed specifically for birdwatching and photography, Batsù is a new attraction in a place where not much changes. The name of the garden comes from the Bribri indigenous tribes' word for 'small bird' and certainly there are a great many hummingbirds, parakeets, flycatchers, tanagers and more, along with some wonderfully natural backdrops.

✪ ACTIVITIES

For those interested in hiking, a challenging 9km trail runs up from San Gerardo to Cerro de la Muerte; the trailhead is in the Savegre Hotel grounds. It's easier to hike down (five hours), but best done with a guide as the trailhead down is not as easy to find as the one going up. Those who wish to do extensive hiking in the area are advised to collect maps before they arrive, and those less ambitious can enjoy an easy 1km trail that rambles along the Río Savegre to a pretty waterfall at the south end of the San Gerardo valley.

EATING

Most accommodations have their own dining facilities, but there are also a couple of *sodas* in the village, as well as a few good independent restaurants.

Café Kahawa   Cafe $
(☎2740-1081; mains US$5-10; ⊙7:30am-5:30pm; ℗) With alfresco tables sitting above the river, funky skull art and sparkling fish tanks filled with fingerling trout, this atmospheric spot prepares trout in many excellent ways (and there are a few non-fishy dishes). Variations on the theme – such as trout in coconut sauce and trout *ceviche* – can't be found just anywhere. Located toward the southern end of the valley.

Restaurante
Los Lagos   Costa Rican $
(☎2740-1009; mains US$7-10; ⊙7am-7pm Sun-Fri, to 8pm Sat) Set amid gardens, ponds and a splashing fountain, this is the place to catch your own trout and have it seasoned, lightly breaded and then deep-fried for lunch, alongside some french fries made from locally grown potatoes. The complimentary dessert, *papaya chilena* (sweet glacé papaya), is also a regional favorite and is served with a scoop of ice cream.

La Comida
Típica Miriam   Costa Rican $
(☎2740-1049; www.miriamquetzals.com/restaurant.html; meals US$6-10; ⊙7am-7pm; ℗) One of the first places you will pass in San Gerardo, about 6km from the Interamericana, is this cozy house advertising *comida típica* – regional specialties. Eating here is almost like receiving a personal invitation to dine in a Tico home: the food is delicious and abundant, and the hospitality even more so.

Miriam also rents a few cabins (US$40) in the woods behind the restaurant: a

 Racing up Chirripó

Carrera Chirripó (www.carrerachirripo.com; ⊙Feb), a grueling race from San Gerardo de Rivas to Crestones Base Lodge and back (34km), takes place at the end of February, with up to 225 participants. If you're trekking up the mountain you may be disheartened to know that the fastest man and woman have covered the distance in three hours four minutes, and four hours 19 minutes, respectively.

modest but comfortable place to spend a night or two.

Restaurant
Le Tapir   Costa Rican $$
(☎2740-1069; Dantica Cloud Forest Lodge; mains US$11-23; ⊙7am-9pm) With 270-degree views of the valley, this glass-encased restaurant specializes in homemade pasta, rainbow trout and mouthwatering steaks, all garnished with organic herbs fresh from the on-site garden. The breakfast is fabulous, and the blackberry tenderloin with ground pepper and rosemary is the kind of dish you continue thinking of a decade after you've eaten it.

ⓘ GETTING THERE & AWAY

The turnoff to San Gerardo de Dota is near Km 80 on the Interamericana. From here, the steep road down into the valley alternates between paved and dirt; it's best to have a 4WD. Take it slowly, as two-way traffic necessitates a bit of negotiation. Buses between San José and San Isidro de El General can drop you at the turnoff, but bear in mind that the village spreads along 9km of road, so you may have a fair hike ahead of you.

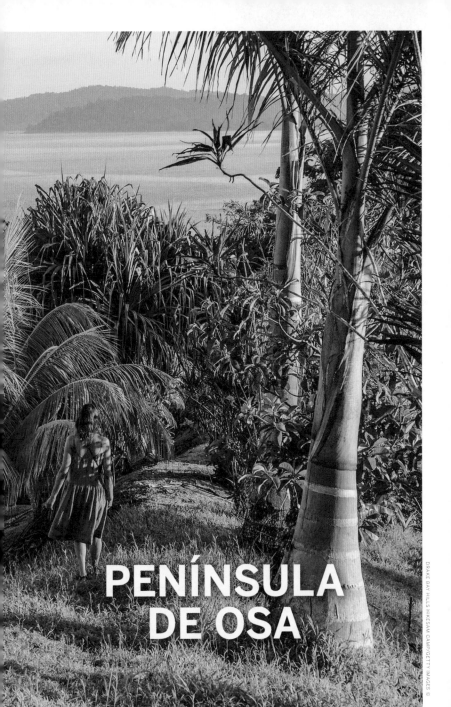

PENÍNSULA
DE OSA

Península de Osa at a Glance...

The steamy coastal jungles of the Península de Osa encompass some of the country's least-explored land. Monkeys, sloths and coatis roam the region's abundant parks and reserves, and in Parque Nacional Corcovado there's also the rare chance to spy on slumbering tapirs. Meanwhile, the rugged coast captivates travelers with abandoned wilderness beaches, world-class surf and opportunities for rugged exploration.

Two Days in Península de Osa

Hire a guide for a day of hiking and wildlife-watching in **Parque Nacional Corcovado** (p126) or explore the **Agujitas-Corcovado coastal trail** (p137) along Bahía Drake. Spend your second day watching cetaceans or scuba diving with **Drake Divers** (p141), or just swimming and snorkeling at the local beaches.

Four Days in Península de Osa

On day three, return to Jiménez for a celebratory breakfast at **Restaurante Monka** (p133) then retreat to **Playa Platanares** (p132) for recovery. Your fourth day is free to spend waterfall rappelling with **Psycho Tours** (p132) or learning about the cultivation of chocolate at **Finca Köbö** (p137).

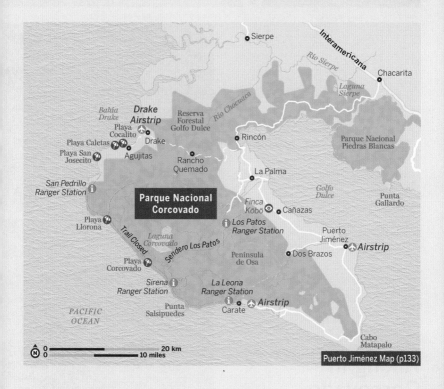

Sierpe

Interamericana

Río Sierpe

Chacarita

Laguna
Sierpe

Bahía
Drake

**Drake
Airstrip**

Reserva
Forestal
Golfo Dulce

Río Chocuaco

Rincón

Parque Nacional
Piedras Blancas

Playa
Cocalito

Drake

Playa Caletas

Agujitas

Rancho
Quemado

La Palma

Playa San
Josecito

San Pedrillo
Ranger Station

**Parque Nacional
Corcovado**

Golfo
Dulce

Punta
Gallardo

Finca
Köbö

Cañazas

Playa
Llorona

Trail Closed

Laguna
Corcovado

Sendero Los Patos

Los Patos
Ranger Station

Puerto
Jiménez

Airstrip

Península
de Osa

Dos Brazos

Playa
Corcovado

Sirena
Ranger Station

La Leona
Ranger Station

Airstrip

PACIFIC
OCEAN

Punta
Salsipuedes

Carate

Airstrip

Cabo
Matapalo

N

0   20 km
0   10 miles

Puerto Jiménez Map (p133)

Arriving in Península de Osa

Getting to Osa requires one of two things: lots of patience or flying in. Given the reasonable cost of flights, a good option for exploring the peninsula is to fly if your time is limited (you can then rent a vehicle in Puerto Jiménez). If you choose to drive, you'll need a 4WD and plenty of confidence: many roads in Osa are extremely poor and there are river crossings involved.

Sleeping

Jiménez has the best range of accommodations in the area, many geared toward Corcovado-bound backpackers. Top-end options tend to be located on the outskirts of town. Some of the best wilderness lodges are found in Bahía Drake, as well as Cabo Matapalo and Carate. This area is off the grid, so some places do not have electricity around the clock or hot water; top-end lodges have their own generators.

Parque Nacional Corcovado

Hiking in Corcovado

Corcovado's amazing biodiversity as well as the park's demanding, multiday hiking trails attract a stream of visitors who descend from Bahía Drake and Puerto Jiménez to experience a bona fide jungle adventure.

Great For...

ⓘ Need to Know

Área de Conservación Osa ACOSA; Osa Conservation Area Headquarters; ☎2735-5036; Corcovado park fee per person per day US$15; ☺8am-4pm Mon-Fri

☑ **Don't Miss**

The chance to see a rare Baird's tapir in its natural habitat near Sirena station.

Hiking Trails

There are three main trails in the park that are open to visitors, as well as shorter trails around the ranger stations. Trails are primitive and the hiking is hot, humid and insect-ridden, but the challenge of the trek and the interaction with wildlife at Corcovado are thrilling. Carry plenty of food, water and insect repellent.

One trail traverses the park from **Los Patos to Sirena**, then exits the park at La Leona (or vice versa). This allows hikers to begin and end their journey in or near Puerto Jiménez, offering easy access to La Leona and Los Patos. The most popular trail, however, is still **La Leona to Sirena**, with an additional trail section running parallel to the beach trail for those who don't want to expose themselves to the relentless sun.

The toughest day trek is from **La Tarde** to Sirena via Los Patos – a whopping 30km.

An **El Tigre** trail loop has been added that starts in Dos Brazos and dips into the park but doesn't join up with the rest of the trail network; you still have to pay the full park fee to hike it, though.

La Leona to Sirena

The largely flat 16km **hike** (five to seven hours) follows the shoreline through coastal forest and along deserted beaches. Take plenty of water, a hat and sunscreen. It involves one major river crossing at Río Claro, just south of Sirena, and there's an excellent chance of seeing monkeys, tapirs and scarlet macaws en route. La Leona is an additional 3.5km to Carate.

A trail running parallel to this trail allows you to avoid the tramp along the beach.

Sirena to Los Patos

This trail goes 18km through the heart of Corcovado, passing through primary and secondary forest, and is relatively flat for the first 12km. After you wade through two river tributaries before reaching the Laguna Corcovado, the route undulates steeply (mostly uphill!) for the remaining 6km. It's easier to do this trek in the opposite direction.

Sendero El Tigre

Part of this 8km loop trail passes through Parque Nacional Corcovado, so a guide is mandatory. It's a fairly rugged trail, part of which passes through an ancient indigenous burial ground; be prepared to spend the best

> ★ **Top Tip**
>
> Hiking is best in the dry season (from December to April), though still muddy.

SAM CAMP/GETTY IMAGES ©

part of a day hiking it. It's doable as a day trip yet gives you a good taste of the park.

Tour Guides

All visitors to Corcovado must be accompanied by an ICT-certified guide. Besides their intimate knowledge of the trails, local guides are amazingly informed about flora and fauna, including the best places to spot various species.

Osa Wild (☏8709-1083, 8376-1152, 2735-5848; www.osawildtravel.com; 80m west of Corcovado BM Supermarket; tours from US$30, 1-day Corcovado tour US$85; ☺8am-noon & 2-7pm Mon-Fri, 9am-noon &1-4pm Sat & Sun) connects with community-oriented initiatives, going to the heart of the real Osa through homestays, farm tours and sustainable cultural exchanges. It also offers kayaking tours and guided trips through Corcovado.

Run by Mike Boston, a biologist with a passion for nature, **Osa Aventura** (☏8372-6135, 2735-5670; www.osaaventura.com) aims to introduce travelers to the beauty of rainforest life and to raise awareness of the need to preserve Corcovado's unique environment. Adventures vary from three-day treks through Corcovado to a new tour that focuses on Golfo Dulce's rural communities. Custom tours are also available.

A trio of excellent guides makes **Surcos Tours** (☏8603-2387, 2237-4189; www.surcostours.com) the best into Osa for wildlife and bird-watching. Tours vary from day hikes in Corcovado and Matapalo to multiday experiences in Corcovado and specialized birding tours. Arrangements for tours are made through the website.

Leading tours into Corcovado and Isla del Caño, all guides with **Corcovado Info Center** (☏2775-0916, 8846-4734; www.corcovadoinfocenter.com; whale-watching/Corcovado day tours US$110/90) are local, bilingual and ICT-certified. It's at the beach end of the main road in Agujitas.

> ✕ **Take a Break**
>
> Make reservations in advance to camp and eat at Sirena ranger station (p131).

Jaguar

Wildlife-Watching

This bastion of biological diversity is home to half of Costa Rica's native species, including the largest population of scarlet macaws, as well as countless other endangered species.

The best wildlife-watching in Corcovado is around Sirena, but the coastal trails have two advantages: they are more open, and the constant crashing of waves covers the sound of noisy walkers. White-faced capuchins, red-tailed squirrels, collared peccaries, white-nosed coatis, tapirs and northern tamandua are regularly seen on all of these trails.

Coastal Trails

Besides the park trail between Sirena and La Leona ranger stations, there is an additional coastal trail that runs 17km – mostly outside the park – from Bahía Drake to San Pedrillo station. These coastal trails produce an endless pageant of birds. Sightings of scarlet macaws

Great For...

☑ **Don't Miss**

The hard-to-spot silky anteater frequents the beachside forests between the Río Claro and Sirena station.

Squirrel monkeys

ZORAN KOLUNDZIJA/GETTY IMAGES ©

are guaranteed, as the tropical almond trees lining the coast are a favorite food. The sections along the beach shelter mangrove black hawks by the dozens, and numerous waterbird species.

Los Patos–Sirena Trail

The Los Patos–Sirena trail attracts lowland rainforest birds such as great curassows, chestnut-mandibled toucans, fiery-billed aracaris and rufous piha. Encounters with mixed flocks are common.

All of the typical mammals get spotted here, but Los Patos is better for primates. Indeed, the Los Platos–Sirena trail is the best place to see the country's most endangered monkey, the Central American squirrel monkey. It's also excellent for other herbivores, particularly red brockets and both species of peccaries.

Sirena Station

For wildlife-watchers frustrated at the difficulty of seeing rainforest mammals, a stay at **Sirena ranger station** (dm US$30) is a must. Baird's tapirs are practically assured – a statement that can be made at few other places in the world. This endangered and distant relative of the rhinoceros is frequently spotted grazing along the airstrip after dusk. Agoutis and tayras are also common.

Jaguars are spotted extremely rarely, as their population in the Osa is suspected to be in the single digits. Ocelots represent your best chance for observing a cat, but again, don't get your hopes up. At night look for kinkajous and crab-eating skunks (especially at the mouth of the Río Sirena).

You might see any or all of the four monkey species, especially the more common species: Spider monkey, mantled howler and white-faced capuchin.

The Río Sirena is a popular spot for American crocodiles, three-toed sloths and bull sharks.

Puerto Jiménez

Sliced in half by the swampy, overgrown Quebrada Cacao, and flanked on one side by the emerald waters of the Golfo Dulce, the vaguely Wild West outpost of Puerto Jiménez is shared by local residents and wildlife. While walking through the dusty streets of Jiménez (as it's known to locals), it's not unusual to spot scarlet macaws roosting on the soccer field, or white-faced capuchins traversing the treetops along the main street.

On the edge of Parque Nacional Corcovado, Jiménez is the preferred jumping-off point for travelers heading to the famed Sirena ranger station, and a great place to organize an expedition, stock up on supplies, eat a hot meal and get a good night's rest before hitting the trails.

Despite the region's largest and most diverse offering of hotels, restaurants and other tourist services, this town, at its core, is a close-knit Tico community.

◎ SIGHTS

Playa Platanares   Beach
About 5km east of town, the long, secluded – and often deserted – Playa Platanares is excellent for swimming, sunning and recovering from too much adventure. The nearby mangroves of Río Platanares are a paradise for kayaking and birdwatching. Take the road that runs parallel to the airstrip.

⊕ TOURS

Psycho Tours   Adventure
(Everyday Adventures; ☑8428-3904; www.psychotours.com; tours US$55-130) Witty, energetic naturalist Andy Pruter runs Psycho Tours, which offers high-adrenaline adventures in Cabo Matapalo. His signature tour is tree climbing (US$65 per person): scaling a 60m ficus tree, aptly named 'Cathedral.' Also popular – and definitely adrenaline-inducing – is waterfall rappelling (US$95) down cascades ranging from 15m to 30m.

The best one? The tree-climbing/waterfall combo tour (US$130).

For the tamer of heart, excellent three-to four-hour guided nature walks (US$50) tap into the extensive knowledge base of Andy and his staff members.

**Aventuras
Tropicales**   Adventure
(☑2735-5195; www.aventurastropicales.com) Aventuras Tropicales is a professional, Tico-run operation that offers all sorts of active adventures. Some of its most popular excursions include kayaking tours of the mangroves, which cost US$45 per person. Located 2km east on the road to Platanares.

Osa Corcovado   Adventure
(☑8632-8150; www.soldeosa.com; Hwy 245; ⊙7am-4pm Mon-Fri) This operator offers anything from three-day Corcovado hikes to kayaking in the mangroves, sunset kayak dolphin-watching tours on the Golfo Dulce (US$75) and Matapalo day hikes.

⊕ SHOPPING

**Jagua Arts
& Crafts**   Arts & Crafts
(☑2735-5267; ⊙7am-3pm Mon-Sat) A terrific, well-stocked crafts shop, featuring local art and jewelry, a wonderful collection of high-quality, colorful Boruca masks and black-and-ocher Guaitil pottery, as well as woven goods by the Emberá and Wounaan people. Kuna weavings technically belong across the border in Panama, but they make excellent gifts.

Artes de Osa   Arts & Crafts
(☑2735-5317; ⊙7am-7pm) This locally run souvenir shop has interesting handmade carvings, furniture and other handicrafts, all made by Costa Rican artisans.

⊗ EATING

The restaurant scene in Puerto Jiménez is surprisingly subdued considering all the tourist traffic passing through, though

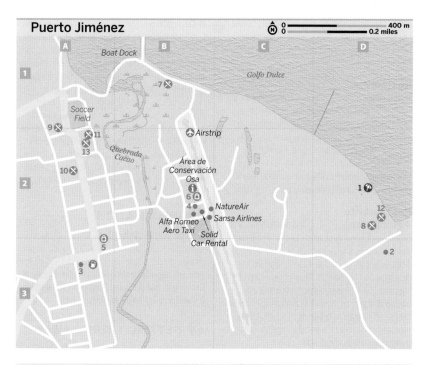

Puerto Jiménez

there are a couple of welcome newish additions to the scene, and seafood is big.

Restaurante Monka   Costa Rican $

(☏2735-5051; mains US$5-7; ☺6am-8pm; 🛜🅿) Bright and airy and the best breakfast spot in town, Monka does excellent cold coffee drinks, smoothies and extensive breakfast platters, from American-style, involving bacon and pancakes, to Mexican-style *huevos rancheros*. The

rest of the day you can fill up on good, inexpensive *casados*. Several breakfast options and *casados* are vegetarian.

Restaurant y Bar Lozaari   Costa Rican $

(☏8795-6861; mains US$3-10; ☺6am-9pm; 🛜) This adorable little Costa Rican restaurant is tucked back in a plaza, filled with plants and adorned with pretty paper lanterns. The breakfast is super cheap and delicious, and best taken at a picnic table in the lush garden out back. Favorites include *gallo pinto* (beans and rice) with eggs, fried plantains and natural fruit juices.

Restaurant Carolina
Costa Rican $

(☏2735-5185; dishes US$3-8; ⊗6am-10pm; 🛜) This local favorite on the main drag still attracts its share of expats, nature guides, tourists and locals. Expect Tico standards, fresh-fruit drinks, extensive breakfasts, good coffee and cold beers that go down pretty easily on a hot day.

Restaurante Agua Dulce
International $$

(www.aguadulcehotel.com; Agua Dulce Beach Resort; mains from US$8; ⊗7am-10pm; 🛜🅿) This breezy restaurant, on the premises of Agua Dulce Beach Resort on Playa Platanares, is a trusted spot for imaginative pasta dishes, grilled fish and ample breakfasts, although the service is positively languid. There are various vegetarian pasta dishes and salads.

La Perla de Osa
International $$

(☏8829-5865; mains US$10-17; ⊗11am-8pm; 🅿🛜🅿) On the grounds of Iguana Lodge, this jungle-fringed restaurant-bar is locally (and justifiably) famous for its cocktails, accompanied by such delectable nibbles as pulled-pork tacos, grilled Asian-style tuna and shrimp plates. Very popular with locals on weekends, and there are also vegetarian soups, salads and meat-free pasta mains.

Pizzamail.it
Pizza $$

(☏2735-5483; pizzas US$10-20; ⊗2-10:30pm; 🛜🅿) While this pizzeria's name sounds more like a website, all doubts will be cast aside when a server at Pizzamail.it brings out the pie: a thin-crust, wood-fired piece of Italy in the middle of the jungle. From its small patio diners can watch squawking macaws in the trees over the soccer pitch. Several pizza options are meat-free. *Bellissimo!*

Il Giardino
Italian $$

(☏2735-5129; www.ilgiardinoitalianrestaurant. com; meals US$11-16; ⊗7am-10pm) While the possibly overextended menu touts steaks and sushi as offerings, Il Giardino shines when it sticks to Italian specialties – homemade pasta, gnocchi and pizza. Although the service and cuisine can be somewhat inconsistent, there's a reliably romantic and candlelit waterfront ambience. The restaurant also contains three well-kept rooms (US$40 including breakfast) with views of a mangrove swamp.

ℹ INFORMATION

Área de Conservación Osa (ACOSA; Osa Conservation Area Headquarters; ☏2735-5036; Corcovado park fee per person per day US$15; ⊗8am-4pm Mon-Fri) has information about Parque Nacional Corcovado, Isla del Caño, Parque Nacional Marino Ballena and Golfito parks and reserves.

ℹ GETTING THERE & AWAY

The airstrip is to the east of town. During research it was closed for maintenance, but should have reopened by now.

NatureAir (☏2735-5062; www.natureair.com; ⊗6am-2pm) and **Sansa** (☏2735-5890; www. flysansa.com) have flights to/from San José (50 minutes, up to four daily); one-way flights are anywhere from US$59 to US$129. NatureAir also does the puddle jumper to Golfito (10 minutes, daily).

Alfa Romeo Aero Taxi (☏8632-8150, 2735-5353; www.alfaromeoair.com) has light aircraft (for three and five passengers) for charter flights to Golfito, Carate, Drake, Sirena, Palmar Sur, Quepos and Limón. Prices are dependent on the number of passengers, so it's best to try to organize a larger group if you're considering this option. Sometimes, if there's already a trip planned into the park, the cost can be as low as US$60 per person.

Puerto Jiménez is now connected to the rest of the country by a beautifully paved road. You can rent a vehicle from **Solid Car Rental** (☏2735-5777; www.solidcarrental.com; ⊗7am-4pm). If you're driving to Carate or Matapalo, you'll need a 4WD; be sure to fill up at the **gas station** in Jiménez.

Clockwise from top: Iguana; Harpy eagle; Spider monkey

ⓘ GETTING AROUND

If you're driving to Carate (the entrance to Corcovado) you'll need a 4WD, even in the dry season, as there are several streams to ford, as well as a river. Assuming you don't have valuables in sight, you can leave your car at the *pulpería* (corner store; per night US$5) and hike to La Leona station (1½ hours).

The *colectivo* (US$9) departs Puerto Jiménez for Carate at 6am and 1:30pm, returning at 8:30am and 3:30pm. Note that it often fills up on its return trip to Puerto Jiménez, especially during the dry season. Arrive at least 30 minutes ahead of time or you might find yourself stranded. Alternatively, catch a taxi from Puerto Jiménez (US$80).

Bahía Drake

One of Costa Rica's most isolated destinations, Bahía Drake *(drah-kay)* is a veritable Lost World, bordered by Parque Nacional Corcovado to the south. In the rainforest canopy, howlers greet the rising sun with their haunting bellows, while pairs of macaws soar between the treetops, filling the air with their cacophonous squawking. Offshore in the bay, pods of migrating dolphins glide through turquoise waters near the beautiful Isla del Caño marine reserve.

One of the reasons why Bahía Drake is brimming with wildlife is that it remains largely cut off from the rest of the country. Life is centered on the sedate village of Agujitas, the area's transport hub, which attracts increasing numbers of backpackers and nature-lovers with inexpensive digs and plenty of snorkeling, diving and wildlife-watching opportunities. The more remote corners of Bahía Drake are home to some of Costa Rica's best (and priciest) wilderness lodges.

◉ SIGHTS

Playa
Cocalito   Beach

Just west of Punta Agujitas, a short detour off the main trail leads to the picturesque Playa Cocalito, a secluded cove perfect for sunning, swimming and body surfing.

Bahía Drake

SAM CAMP/GETTY IMAGES ©

Playa Caletas — Beach

A recommended spot for snorkeling, situated in front of Las Caletas Lodge.

Playa San Josecito — Beach

South of Río Claro, Playa San Josecito is the longest stretch of white-sand beach on this side of the Península de Osa. It is popular with swimmers, snorkelers and sunbathers, though you'll only find it crowded at lunchtime since it's the favorite post-snorkeling picnic spot for tour companies coming back from Isla del Caño. Watch out for capuchin monkeys!

 ACTIVITIES

Agujitas–Corcovado Trail — Hiking

This 17km public trail follows the coastline from Agujitas to the San Pedrillo Ranger Station for the entire spectacular stretch, and it's excellent for wildlife-spotting (particularly early in the morning), beach-hopping and canoe tours with Río Claro Tours (p138). Tour operators can drop you off by boat at a point of your choosing and you can walk back to Agujitas.

Río Agujitas — Kayaking

The idyllic Río Agujitas attracts a huge variety of birdlife and lots of reptiles. The river conveniently empties out into the bay, which is surrounded by hidden coves and sandy beaches ideal for exploring in a sea kayak, best done at high tide. Some accommodations have kayaks and canoes for rent; kayaks can also be rented along Agujitas beach (around US$15 per hour).

TOURS

Pacheco Tours — Wildlife

(☑8906-2002; www.pachecotours.com) Very competent all-rounder organizing snorkeling tours to Isla del Caño, day trips to Corcovado, day-long tours combining jungle trekking with waterfall swimming (US$65), and whale-watching excursions.

🍴◎ Chocolate Farm

About 8km south of La Palma, **Finca Köbö** (☑8398-7604; www.fincakobo.com; 2hr tour US$32; Ⓟ) ✔ is a chocolate-lover's dream come true (in fact köbö means 'dream' in Ngöbere). The 20-hectare *finca* (farm) is dedicated to the organic cultivation of fruits and vegetables and – the product of choice – cacao. Tours in English give a comprehensive overview of the life cycle of cacao plants and the production of chocolate (with degustation!). More than half of the territory is dedicated to protecting and reforesting natural ecosystems.

To really experience the beauty and vision of this *finca*, you can stay in simple, comfortable teak cabins and bungalows (US$95 to US$155, including breakfast; dinner costs US$8 to US$15), with lovely open-air bathrooms and quality linens. Those who stay longer can hike the surrounding forest trails and speak with local farmers. The on-site gift store sells toasted cocoa nibs – great for energy! – and locally produced organic jam.

Cacao plant
KRISTEN BADALI/SHUTTERSTOCK ©

Tracie the Bug Lady — Wildlife

(☑8701-7462, 8701-7356; www.thenighttour.com; tours per person US$40; ⏱7:30-10:15pm) Tracie the 'Bug Lady' has created quite a name for herself with this fascinating nighttime walk in the jungle that takes in bugs, reptiles and birds. Tracie is a walking encyclopedia on bug facts – one of her fields of research is the military use of insects! Her naturalist-photographer husband Gian also leads the night tours; reserve in advance.

Río Claro Tours
Canoeing

(☑8931-1345; 1/2/3hr tour per person US$20/30/40) A 20-minute hike toward Agujitas from Playa San Josecito, a hermit called Ricardo ('Clavito') lives by the Río Claro and runs hugely entertaining canoeing tours. They start with a rope-swing plunge and continue to some waterfalls with refreshing plunge pools. Various tour operators can drop you off by boat, leaving you to walk back to Agujitas afterward.

Original Canopy Tour
Tours

(☑8371-1598, 2291-4465; www.jinetesdeosa.com/canopy_tour.htm; US$35; ☺8am-4pm) At Hotel Jinetes de Osa, the Original Canopy Tour has nine platforms, six cables and one 20m observation deck from where you can get a new perspective on the rainforest. Tours take two to three hours.

🍴 EATING

There are several local restaurants in the heart of Agujitas, as well as two supermarkets, while some accommodations, particularly the more remote ones, offer full board. Important: do not leave this place without ordering a milkshake at **Heladería Popis** (☺1-9pm).

Drake's Kitchen
Costa Rican $

(Casa el Tortugo; ☑6161-3193, 2775-1405; mains from US$7; ☺noon-9pm; ℗) Excellent, small local restaurant along the main dirt road from Agujitas to the airstrip. The casados, such as catch-of-the-day with fried plantains and avocado, are clearly prepared by a capable and passionate chef, the fresh juices are stellar and the ambience mellow.

Soda Mar y Bosque
Costa Rican $

(☑6015-4981, 5002-7554; mains US$5-16; ☺5:30am-9pm; 🛜) This restaurant up the hill in Agujitas serves typical Tico cuisine and a range of desserts; it even has free wi-fi.

From left: White-faced capuchin monkeys; Scarlet macaw; Parque Nacional Corcovado (p126)

KRYSSIA CAMPOS/GETTY IMAGES ©

MACIEJ CZEKAJEWSKI/SHUTTERSTOCK ©

From the spacious terrace and a recently added upstairs seating area, it's possible to catch a cool breeze and spot pairs of scarlet macaws coasting over the sea.

Gringo Curt's   International $$

(☏7156-2597; www.gringocurt.com; mains US$10; ⏰noon-9pm) Gringo Curt offers just three things: a fish salad wrap, noodles tossed with vegetables (and sometimes garnished with catch-of-the-day) and super-fresh fish steamed in a banana leaf (serves two). This one-man operation is popular with visitors, and the portions are generous. Curt's a great source of local info, too, and runs nature tours.

Marisquería Roberto's   Seafood $$

(☏6201-2536; mains US$7-12; ⏰noon-9pm) Right near the beach, this open-air restaurant serves up mostly fishy delights, from garlic shrimp spaghetti and *ceviche* to generous helpings of freshly grilled fish, fish tacos and *arroz con mariscos* (seafood fried rice).

Los Coquitos   Seafood

(☏2775-9049; mains US$$; ⏰10am-9pm) Just off the beach on a covered terrace, this delicious restaurant serves up the freshest fish around. The red snapper and marlin get high marks from travelers, as do the the typical Costa Rican *casado* plates, which come with a meat (beef, chicken or fish), beans, rice and a surprisingly tasty salad. Friendly service, too.

❶ GETTING THERE & AWAY

AIR

Departing from San José, NatureAir and Sansa have daily flights to the **Drake airstrip**, which is 2km north of Agujitas. Prices vary according to season and availability, though you can expect to pay around US$80 to US$120 one way.

Alfa Romeo Aero Taxi (☏8632-8150; www.alfaromeoair.com) offers charter flights connecting Drake to Puerto Jiménez (US$430), Carate (US$450) and Sirena (US$420). Flights are best booked at the airport in person; if there are several of you, one-way fares can be less than US$100.

LVALIN/SHUTTERSTOCK ©

MATTEO COLOMBO/GETTY IMAGES ©

Bahía Drake (p136)

Most lodges provide transportation to/from the airport or Sierpe, which involves a jeep or a boat or both, but advance reservation is necessary.

BOAT

An exhilarating boat ride from Sierpe is one of the true thrills of visiting the area. Boats travel along the river through the rainforest and the mangrove estuary. Captains then pilot boats through tidal currents and surf the river mouth into the ocean. All of the hotels offer boat transfers between Sierpe and Bahía Drake with prior arrangements. Most hotels in Drake have beach landings, so wear appropriate footwear.

If you have not made advance arrangements with your lodge for a pick-up, two *colectivo* boats depart daily from Sierpe at 11:30am and 4:30pm, and from Bahía Drake back to Sierpe at 7:15am (US$15) and 2:30pm (US$20).

 GETTING AROUND

Once you reach Bahía Drake, the only way to get around is on foot or by boat.

Sierpe

This sleepy village on the Río Sierpe is the gateway to Bahía Drake, and if you've made a reservation with any of the jungle lodges further down the coast, you will be picked up here by boat. Beyond its function as a transit point, there is little reason to spend any more time here than necessary, though it's well worth taking a peek at one of the celebrated pre-Columbian stone spheres in the main square. If you're visiting the excellent Sitio Arqueológico Finca 6 near Sierpe, you can stop here for lunch. Mangrove cruises can also be arranged in town.

◎ SIGHTS

Sitio Arqueológico Finca 6   Archaeological Site

(☑2100-6000; finca6@museocostarica.go.cr; 4km north of Sierpe; US$6; ☺8am-4pm Tue-Sun) This site offers the best opportunity to view the mysterious pre-Columbian spheres created by the Diquís civilization between 300

BC and 1500 AD. This is their original locale, near culturally significant mounds 30m in diameter. Walking around you can really appreciate their size and perfect sphericity.

 ## INFORMATION

La Perla del Sur (2788-1082; info@perladel
sur.net; ⏰6am-10pm; 📶) is an info center and open-air restaurant located next to the boat dock (the hub of Sierpe). Arrange your long-term parking (US$6 per night), book a tour and take advantage of the free wi-fi before catching your boat to Drake. The food is hit and miss, though.

GETTING THERE & AWAY

Scheduled flights and charters fly into Palmar Sur, 14km north of Sierpe. If you are heading to Bahía Drake, most upmarket lodges will arrange the boat transfer. Should things go awry or if you're traveling independently, there's no shortage of water taxis milling about – be prepared to negotiate a fair price. Regularly scheduled *colectivo* boats depart Sierpe for Drake at 11:30am (US$15) and 4:30pm (US$20).

Buses to Palmar Norte (US$0.70, 40 minutes) depart from in front of Pulpería Fenix at 5:30am, 8:30am, 10:30am, 12:30pm, 3:30pm and 6pm. A shared taxi to Palmar costs about US$10 per person.

Carate

If you make it all the way here, congratulations. A bone-rattling 45km south of Puerto Jiménez, this is where the dirt road rounds the peninsula and comes to an abrupt dead end. There's literally nothing more than an airstrip, a long strip of wild beach and a *pulpería*. Carate is not a destination in itself, but it is the southwestern gateway for anyone hiking into Sirena ranger station in Parque Nacional Corcovado.

A handful of well-designed wilderness lodges in the area make a good night's rest for travelers heading to/from Corcovado or those in search of a quiet retreat surrounded by jungle.

 ## Snorkel & Scuba Drake Bay

Isla del Caño (US$10, diving charge US$4) is one of Costa Rica's top spots for diving, with attractions including intricate rock and coral formations and an amazing array of underwater life. Divers report that the schools of fish swimming overhead are often so dense that they block the sunlight from filtering down.

Bajo del Diablo (Devil's Rock) – one of the best dive sites in the bay – is an astonishing formation of submerged mountains that attracts an incredible variety of fish species, including jacks, snappers, barracudas, puffers, parrotfish, moray eels and sharks.

A two-tank dive runs from US$110 to US$150 depending on the site. Several upscale lodges have on-site dive centers, and there are more dive centers in Agujitas.

Operators include the following.

Osa Divers (📞8994-9309; www.osadivers.com) Competitively priced, recommended diving outfit whisking divers (and snorkelers) off for underwater adventures around Isla del Caño. Snorkeling tours cost US$80; two-/three-tank dives are US$120/160. Equipment could be newer, though, and the dive masters don't have too much patience with novices.

Drake Divers (📞2775-1818; www.drake
diverscr.com; ⏰7am-7pm) This outfit specializes in diving at Isla del Caño, charging US$135/185 for two-/three-tank dives. Snorkelers are welcome to come along (US$80). The equipment is not the newest and the boat is not a purpose-built diving boat, but the divemasters are experienced.

Luna Lodge (📞2206-5859, 888-760-0760 in the USA & Canada; www.lunalodge.com; tent/r/bungalow per person incl all meals US$248/345/433; 🅿📶🏊♿) 🍽A steep road crisscrosses the Río Carate and up the valley to this

Caminos de Osa

Developed in response to the overcrowding of Parque Nacional Corcovado by a cooperation of private, public, academic and nonprofit sectors, the Caminos de Osa (Osa Trails; www.caminosdeosa.com) take visitors along three different routes bisecting the Osa Peninsula. Passing close to the park, they allow visitors to commune with wildlife, while also introducing them to the rural communities that call Osa home.

The **Oro trail** skirts Corcovado and passes through the former gold-mining villages of Rancho Quemado and Dos Brazos, where visitors participate in a host of rural activities, from gold-panning to horseback riding, before finishing in Carate.

Passing through the Sierpe mangroves by boat, the **Agua trail** deposits visitors at San Pedrillo ranger station, also bordering Corcovado, from where they hike into Bahía Drake and cruise out to Caño Island for some underwater exploration.

Finally, the **Selva trail** explores the southeastern part of the peninsula, connecting Dos Brazos to Puerto Jiménez and La Tarde.

Caminos de Osa is actively working together with the communities of Dos Brazos, Rancho Quemado and La Palma, which visitors can easily visit, and their rural tourism infrastructure is developed. The communities are eager to share their way of life with visitors.

enchanting mountain retreat on the border of Parque Nacional Corcovado. Accommodations range from tent cabins to thatched bungalows with open-air garden showers and private terraces, all with stunning views of the pristine jungle rolling down to the ocean. This is the farthest-flung of Carate's accommodations.

La Leona Eco-Lodge (☑2735-5704; www.laleonaecolodge.com; per person tent half-/full board from US$89/99; ▣) ✿On the edge of Parque Nacional Corcovado, this friendly lodge offers all the thrills of camping, without the hassles. The 16 fully screened forest-green tents with beds are nestled between palm trees, with decks facing the beach and allowing frequent wildlife sightings. Solar power provides electricity in the restaurant.

The ride from Puerto Jiménez to Carate is also its own adventure as the narrow, bumpy dirt road winds its way around dense rainforest, through gushing rivers and across windswept beaches. Birds and other wildlife are prolific along this stretch: keep your eyes peeled and hang on tight.

Some places in Carate don't have 24-hour electricity or hot water. Reservations are recommended in the dry season – communication is often through Puerto Jiménez, so messages may not be retrieved every day. For shoestringers, the best option is to camp in the yard in front of the *pulpería;* the expat owner charges US$5 a day to camp in his yard.

Cabo Matapalo

If you didn't know that it was here, you would hardly suspect that the jungle-obscured community of Matapalo existed. There isn't much to the southern tip of the Osa Península save some surfing digs and homes at the entrance to the Golfo Dulce. Matapalo lies just 17km south of Puerto Jiménez, but this heavily forested and beach-fringed cape is a vastly different world. A network of trails traverses the foothills, uninhabited except for migrating

Cabo Matapalo

wildlife from the Reserva Forestal Golfo Dulce. Along the coastline, miles of beaches are virtually empty, except for a few surfers in the know.

Cabo Matapalo is home to wilderness lodges that cater to travelers searching for seclusion and wildlife. Scarlet macaws, pelicans and herons are frequently sighted on the beaches, while all four species of Costa Rican monkeys, several wildcat species, plus sloths, coatis, agoutis and anteaters roam the woods.

Surfers often head to Cabo Matapalo for its righteous breaks at the following beaches.

Playa Matapalo There are three excellent right point breaks off this beach, not far from Encanta La Vida. If there's a south or west swell this is the best time to hit the waves.

Playa Pan Dulce Good for beginners and intermediate surfers, Pan Dulce gets some nice longboard waves most days. You can also go swimming here, but be careful of rip tides.

COSTA BALLENA

Costa Ballena at a Glance...

South of Quepos, the well-trodden central Pacific tourist trail begins to taper off, evoking the Costa Rica of yesteryear – surf shacks and empty beaches, roadside ceviche vendors and a little more space. Intrepid travelers can have their pick of any number of deserted beaches and great surf spots. Known as the Costa Ballena, the stunning length of coastline between Dominical and Ojochal focuses on three things: surfing (Dominical), whale-watching (Uvita) and gourmet cuisine (Ojochal). For the time being, the area largely retains an easygoing, unjaded allure despite the growing numbers discovering its appeal.

One Day on the Costa Ballena

Settle in and head for **Parque Nacional Marino Ballena** (p149), a national marine park with a sandbar shaped like a whale's tail at low tide. Swim, snorkel, frolic about, and then grab a delicious traditional lunch at **Bar y Restaurante Los Laureles** (p152). In the afternoon, get your waterfall on at **Cascada Verde** (p150) or **Cataratas Nauyaca** (p154). Do dinner at **Sabor Español** (p153).

Two Days on the Costa Ballena

Get your dose of Dominical counter-culture. Start by fueling up on *gallo pinto* at **Cafe Mono Congo** (p156) before braving a **surf lesson** (p157) or a **yoga class** (p155). In the afternoon, check out the local rescues at **Alturas Wildlife Sanctuary** (p154) and then feast in foodie beach town Playa Ojochal. Top choices include **Exotica** (p158) and **Ylang-Ylang** (p158).

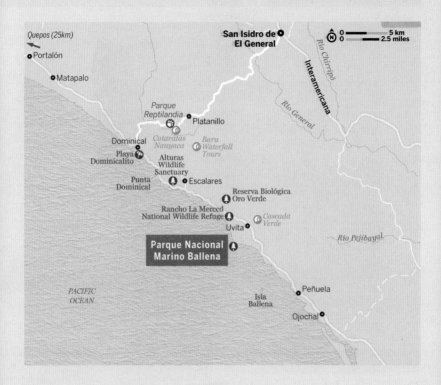

Arriving in the Costa Ballena

This stretch of the coast is well served by frequent buses heading toward the border with Panama and the Osa Peninsula in the south, and Quepos and Jacó in the north. Private and shared shuttles also abound. If you're looking to stay up in the hills, you'll need a 4WD for the rough, steep roads.

Sleeping

Dominical proper is home to the majority of the area's budget accommodations, while midrange and top-end places are popping up on the outskirts of town. There are some terrific, remoter lodges in Uvita and the jungle-clad hills above the coast, and travelers on a budget can camp on the beach.

Humpback whale

CLAUDE HUOT/SHUTTERSTOCK ©

Parque Nacional Marino Ballena

It's appropriate that this stunning national park is shaped like a whale's tail (humpback whales breed here); from the beaches it's possible to spot the migrating giants as they swim near shore.

Created in 1989, this marine park protects coral and rock reefs surrounding several offshore islands. The importance of this area cannot be overstated, especially since it protects migrating humpback and pilot whales, three types of dolphins and nesting sea turtles, not to mention colonies of seabirds and several terrestrial reptiles.

Swimming

The beaches at Parque Nacional Marino Ballena are a stunning combination of golden sand and polished rock. All of them are virtually deserted and perfect for peaceful swimming and sunbathing.

Diving & Snorkeling

The coral reefs around the offshore islands are good places to experience the park's

---

Great For...

☑ **Don't Miss**

In the fall and spring, migrating humpback whales can be viewed here.

Iguana

JOHANN OSWALD - WAS-FUERS-AUGE/GETTY IMAGES ©

lizards.The offshore islands are important nesting sites for frigate birds, brown boobies and brown pelicans, and from May to November, with a peak in September and October, olive ridley and hawksbill turtles bury their eggs in the sand nightly. However, the star attraction are the pods of humpback whales that pass through the national park from July to November and December to April, as well as occasional pilot whales.

Whale- and dolphin-watching trips are run by several tour companies in Uvita, inclduing Bahía Aventuras (p152).

Dangers & Annoyances

The beaches of Parque Nacional Marina Balleno are notorious for bag-snatchings. Do not leave your bag unattended. Local residents are putting pressure on park authorities to improve security in the park and also to provide working toilet facilities.

Information

There are four entrances to the park, the most commonly used being the ranger station in Playa Uvita (take the main road through Uvita), followed by the one along a dirt road that runs past Flutterby House in Uvita. There is now a ranger station (read: wooden shack) there also. All park entrances are open from 7am to 4pm.

underwater world (unlike the coral reefs near the shore that were heavily damaged by sediment run-off from the construction of the coastal highway). Try a trip with Mad About Diving (p150).

Surfing

There is some decent surfing near the river mouth at the southern end of Playa Colonia.

Wildlife-Watching

Heading southeast from Punta Uvita, the park includes mangrove swamps, estuaries and rocky headlands. In the early morning, before other visitors arrive, you'll have the best opportunity for good birdwatching.

The park is home to or frequently visited by a number of wildlife species, including common, bottlenose and pantropical spotted dolphins and a variety of

Uvita

Just 17km south of Dominical, this growing village consists of some dirt roads lined with farms, guesthouses and shops, a cluster of strip malls by the main Costanera Sur entrance, and a scattering of hotels in the jungle-covered hills above. Uvita has retained its gentle pace of life during the low season, but otherwise has become quite a popular and buzzing travel destination thanks to its increasingly sought-after main attraction, Parque Nacional Marino Ballena. The marine reserve has become famous for its migrating pods of humpback whales and its virtually abandoned wilderness beaches, but there are also good waterfalls nearby.

Two of the country's most important tourist events happen yearly in Uvita: an increasingly popular Whale and Dolphin Festival celebrating the arrival of the humpbacks, and the country's biggest hippie-gathering, the Envision Festival (essentially a small-scale Burning Man at the beach).

SIGHTS

Cascada Verde Waterfall

(US$2; 8am-4pm) Around 2.5km inland and uphill (toward the Cascada Verde hostel), this waterfall plunges into an inviting deep pool, perfect for a refreshing dip. The best part? The waterfall also acts as an exhilarating natural waterslide with a 6ft drop at the end; take the path to the top, lie down, cross your arms and let gravity take care of the rest!

Farmers Market Market

(8680-9752; 8am-1pm Sat) Held a short distance from the main entrance to Uvita, along the unpaved road, this sweet little farmers market is a good place to mingle with locals and longtime expats, and purchase psychedelic jewelry, locally grown fruit and vegetables, honey and home-cooked foods.

Rancho La Merced National Wildlife Refuge Nature Reserve

(2743-8032, 8861-5147; www.rancholamerced.com; tours US$35-50, self-guided walk US$6; 7:30am-5:30pm) A few kilometers before Uvita, opposite the turnoff to Oro Verde, is this 506-hectare national wildlife refuge (and former cattle ranch), with primary and secondary forests and mangroves lining the Río Morete. Here you can go on guided nature hikes and birdwatching walks, horseback-ride to Punta Uvita or opt for the 'cowboy experience,' which involves cattle roping, herding cows and riding around with real cowboys.

Reserva Biológica Oro Verde Nature Reserve

(8843-8833) A few kilometers before Uvita you'll see a signed turnoff to the left on a rough dirt road (4WD only) that leads 3.5km up the hill to this private reserve on the farm of the Duarte family, who have lived in the area for more than three decades. Two-thirds of the 150-hectare property is rainforest, and there are guided hikes (US$35), occasional night tours (US$30) and 6am birdwatching walks (US$30). Reserve in advance through Uvita Information Center (p153).

ACTIVITIES

Mad About Diving Diving

(2743-8019; www.madaboutdivingcr.com) Friendly, safe and professional diving operator, offering dives in the Parque Nacional Marino Ballena and full-day scuba excursions to Isla del Caño in Bahía Drake (US$170). Two-tank dives from US$100.

Rancho DiAndrew Outdoors

(8475-1287; http://ranchodiandrew.com; tours from US$65) Super-fun tour operator specializing in surf retreats and nature tours, the most popular of which involves navigating a hidden gorge, plunging off a cliff and feasting on a BBQ by the river. The *rancho* is perched in a patch of jungle near the town of San Josecito, and features open-air

Clockwise from top: Parque Nacional Marino Ballena
(p148); Flowering pineapple plant; Brown booby

cabins and houses (from US$85/96 single/double per night). Sweet views.

Uvita Adventure Tour
Kayaking, Mountain Biking

(2743-8008, 8918-5681; www.uvitadventure tours.com; mountain-biking/kayaking tour from US$45/75) Run by young, enthusiastic owner Victor, this small tour company offers highly recommended tours including exhilarating mountain-biking adventures, kayaking through the mangroves and snorkeling at the marine park. At the time of research, Victor was considering adding electric bike tours.

Bahía Aventuras
Adventure

(2743-8362, 8846-6576; www.bahiaaventuras.com) A well-regarded tour operator in Uvita, Bahía Aventuras has tours running the gamut, including a combo of snorkeling and whale-watching (US$90) in the Marino Ballena National Park, snorkeling around Isla del Caño in Bahía Drake (US$140), and hiking, spanning the Costa Ballena to Corcovado (US$145).

EATING

The more upmarket accommodations have their own restaurants. There are also several *sodas* and a clutch of good restaurants in the main village and along the nearby stretch of Costanera Sur.

Bar y Restaurante Los Laureles
Costa Rican $

(2743-8008; mains US$8-12; ⊙11am-8:30pm Mon-Sat) Adorable family-run restaurant serving mainly Costa Rican and Tex-Mex cuisine, with innovative favorites such as avocado hummus and nacho *patacones*, and staples like chicken wings, chili fries and quesadillas. The margaritas are killer, the service is top-notch and the open-air setting, amid tropical foliage, is super *tranquilo*.

Sibu Cafe
Cafe $

(8308-6604, 2743-8674; coffee US$2-5; ⊙7am-9pm Mon-Sat, from 9am Sun; ❄🅢🖉) Serving the best coffee for miles around, this little cafe hides in the strip-mall part of Uvita. Latte art, chunky brownies and homemade lemon pie are all on the

Playa Uvita

menu. Want something more substantial? The hardworking couple here also make excellent salads, thin-and-crispy pizza pie, veggie juice and fruit smoothies. They recently started selling their own craft beer, Sibu Russian Imperial Stout.

Sabor Español Spanish $$

(☑2743-8312, 8768-9160; mains US$8-22; ☻6-9:30pm Tue-Sun; 🛜) Having had a successful run in Monteverde, charming Spanish couple Heri and Montse realized that they wanted to live by the ocean – to Uvita's good fortune. Thus, their sublime gazpacho, paella, *tortilla española* and other Spanish specialties can now be savored with sangria in a lovely *rancho* setting, at the end of a dirt road in Playa Uvita.

🍷 DRINKING & NIGHTLIFE

Roadshack Deli Bar

(☑8304-6792; ☻11am-7pm Mon-Sat) Around 50m down the main Uvita road from the highway turnoff, this open-air, ramshackle spot is a gathering place for offbeat customers craving wraps, braised pork and other sandwiches (we like the Mother Clucker) and imaginative salads. Wash it all down with homemade craft beer or *kombucha*. This is an informal community center, too, with frequent live music and revelry.

ℹ️ INFORMATION

Uvita Information Center (☑8843-7142, 2743-8072; http://uvita.info; ☻9am-1pm & 2-6pm Mon-Sat) is a fine place to book tours and transport.

ℹ️ GETTING THERE & AWAY

Most buses depart from the sheltered bus stops on the Costanera in the main village; private shuttle companies – Grayline, Easy Ride and Monkey Ride – offer pricier transfers from Uvita to Dominical, San José, Quepos, Jacó, Puerto Jiménez and other popular destinations. It's advantageous to have your own wheels around here.

 Overnight at the Waterfall

Waterfall hikes are a dime a dozen in Costa Rica, and most include a familiar itinerary: hike, swim, eat lunch, maybe rappel, head home. Family-owned Pacific Journeys, based in tiny Las Tumbas, offers something better.

The bilingual, experienced guides lead people up to the top of 600ft Diamante Falls, one of the highest, most beautiful cascades in the country, by scaling hundreds of stairs up through the company's private reserve, amid lush primary forest and past a botanical garden. It takes about three hours and is moderately difficult. Upon arrival at an open-air cavern behind the waterfall, the group unpacks and selects mats to sleep on, with three massive waterfalls visible from the campsite.

Candles and solar-powered lights illuminate the paths and the kind and knowledgeable guides prepare yummy vegetarian meals in an open-air kitchen. The place is decidedly rustic; still, it features flush toilets and picnic benches and is protected from the elements. Rappelling excursions and hikes to nearby swimming holes and cliff-jumping sites get the adrenalin pumping to the point that few will mind the cold, waterfall-fed showers. Those who do mind can warm up with hot tea prepared from spices picked from the botanical garden.

Parque Nacional Marino Ballena (p148)
4FR/GETTY IMAGES ©

From left: Ghost crab; Punta Uvita, Parque Nacional Marino Ballena (p148); Racoon

Dominical

For as long as anybody could remember (which wasn't very long in Dominical), this was a lazy little town that drew a motley crew of surfers, backpackers and affable do-nothings, a place where a traveler could wander the dusty roads, surfboard tucked under an arm, balancing the day's activities between wave riding and hammock hang time.

Those days aren't entirely gone, but in 2015 a bunch of paver stones laid along the beach became the town's first real road. And as an increasing population of expats and gringos began to hunker down, some more sophisticated (though decidedly ecofriendly) businesses began to sprout. Now, the sheer volume of cars, bicycles and pedestrians on the main street, particularly around the time of neighboring Uvita's hippie festival Envision and in the high season, is staggering. Rainier months remain as languidly 'old Costa Rica' as ever.

◎ SIGHTS

Alturas Wildlife Sanctuary
Nature Reserve

(☑2200-5440; www.alturaswildlifesanctuary. org; minimum donation adult/child under 12yr US$25/15; ⊙tours at 9am, 11am, 1pm & 3pm Tue-Sun) Around 1.5km east and uphill from Dominical, this wildlife sanctuary takes in injured and orphaned animals as well as illegal pets. Its mission is to rehabilitate animals and reintroduce them to the wild, and look after those that cannot. During the 60- to 90-minute tour you're introduced to the residents: a macaw missing an eye, monkeys that were caged since infancy, Bubba the famous coatimundi and more. Entertaining, educational and a terrific cause.

Cataratas Nauyaca
Waterfall

(☑2787-0542, 2787-0541; www.cataratasnauy aca.com; horseback tour US$70, pick-up tour US$28, hike admission US$8; ⊙7am-5pm Mon-Sat 8am-4pm Sun) This center, owned and operated by a Costa Rican family, is home to the coast's most impressive waterfalls,

which cascade through a protected reserve of both primary and secondary forest. The family runs horseback-riding tours and tours by pick-up truck to the falls (reservations required; Dominical pickup available), where visitors can swim in the inviting natural pools.

Parque Reptilandia
Zoo

(✆8308-8855, 2787-0343; www.crreptiles.com; adult/child US$12/6; ⊙9am-4:30pm; [P][♿]) Seven kilometers up the Dominical–San Isidro road, this reptile haven is the closest thing humans have to Jurassic Park. It's got everything from crocodiles to turtles and snakes to poison-dart frogs, and our favorite is the viper section, where you can see Costa Rica's deadliest creatures, such as the fer-de-lance, pit viper and the black-headed bushmaster. Friday is feeding day, with live mice introduced into snake enclosures, which your kids may or may not love. Don't miss the the Komodo dragon.

Baru Waterfall Tours
Waterfall

(✆8767-2090; Las Tumbas; US$7; ⊙7am-4pm) A second option for accessing Cataratas

Nauyaca; the hike from this alternative entrance only takes 25 minutes.

ACTIVITIES

Danyasa Yoga Arts School
Yoga

(✆2787-0229; www.danyasa.com; classes incl mat US$16; ⊙shop 9:30am-8pm) This lovely Dominical yoga studio offers a variety of classes for all levels, including unique dance-yoga-flow hybrid styles and even ecstatic moon dance. The studio also serves as a center for retreats of all kinds.

Airborne Arts
Circus

(✆8302-4241; www.airbornearts.com) Ever felt like learning the flying trapeze in the middle of the Costa Rican countryside, with a view of a 100m waterfall? Do it with world-renowned acrobat couple Jonathon Conant and Christine Van Loo, who have constructed a circus-themed paradise south of the remote town of Las Tumbas. It's the perfect escape for those looking to intermittently relax and learn to fly.

Pacific Journeys — Outdoors

(☎2266-1717; www.pacificjourneyscr.com; Las Tumbas; tour per person from US$158) Based in the small town of Las Tumbas north of Dominical, this experienced tour operator runs trips up and around Diamante and Barú Falls, with opportunities for trekking, swimming, cliff jumping, canyoning and even sleeping in a cave behind a 600ft waterfall.

Pineapple Tours — Kayaking

(☎8362-7655, 8873-3283; www.pineapple-kayaktours.com; tours US$20-75) Run by a friendly young couple, Pineapple Tours runs kayaking and stand-up paddleboarding (SUP) trips to local caves, rivers and mangrove forests. Find its office next to the police station in Dominical. It also rents SUP gear, surfboards, kayaks, beach chairs and umbrellas.

✪ EATING

The restaurant scene in Dominical is varied and of a high standard, catering mostly to foreign guests and including many international options. Self-caterers will appreciate the fabulous new health-food store.

Cafe Mono Congo — Cafe $

(www.cafemonocongo.com; mains US$4-9; ☺6:30am-7pm; ☏☑) Perch on a swing at the bar or at a riverside table to enjoy the best espresso in town, hands down. This open-air cafe also dishes up tasty, simple breakfasts like pinto and *huevos rancheros* and (largely veggie) lunches, using organic local produce. Find it at the junction of the road into town and the main drag – couldn't be simpler.

Café de Ensueños — Cafe $

(meals US$5-9; ☺7:30am-8pm) Run by a lovely local family, this cafe is tucked away at the end of the southern spur road. Organic coffee drinks, fresh juices and hearty breakfasts are served al fresco under a covered terrace – an excellent spot for a quiet morning. Extra hungry? Go for the gut-busting Special Breakfast or the Pancake Tropical, which comes with eggs, bacon and fruit.

Meal, Cafe Mono Congo

Del Mar Taco Shop
Tacos $

(☑8428-9050; tacos US$4; ☺11:30am-9pm)
On the approach to the beach, an expat
cooks up some of the Pacific coast's best
tacos in this casual surfer hangout. We
prefer the fish tacos to the shrimp, which
can vary in size. Also delicious are the
daily Hawaiian BBQ specials and chunky
burritos, and the guacamole is superb. On
Taco Tuesday (April to November) tacos
cost just US$2.

El Pescado Loco
Seafood $

(mains US$8-9; ☺11:45am-7:30pm) This little
open-air shack has only a handful of menu
items, but when it comes to fish tacos with
chipotle sauce and chunky guacamole,
well, a taco doesn't get much better than
this. The onion rings and fish and chips
are nothing to sneeze at, either. Our only
quibble: how about real cutlery instead of
disposable?

Soda Nanyoa
Costa Rican $

(☑2787-0013; mains US$2-8; ☺6am-midnight;
☜) In a town that caters to gringo appe-
tites with inflated price tags, Nanyoa is a
gratifying find: an authentic, moderately
priced, better-than-most Costa Rican
soda. The big pinto breakfasts and fresh-
squeezed juice are ideal after a morning
session on the waves. Beer and wine are
available as well.

Phat Noodle
Thai $$

(☑2787-0017; mains US$10-15; ☺11:30am-9pm
Tue-Sun, 5-9pm Mon; ☑) Newish in town,
this expat-owned Thai restaurant and bar
serves up piping hot bowls of rice and
noodles, along with spicy margaritas, all
from the inside of a converted school bus.
Skilfully prepared menu items range from
shrimp and crab rangoon to Thai coconut
ceviche to green curry, and there are a
great many vegan and gluten-free options
as well.

Maracutú
Vegetarian, International $$

(☑2787-0091; www.maracatucostarica.com;
meals US$10-18; ☺noon-9pm, extended bar
hours; ☜☑) This mellow, reggae-spouting
'natural restaurant' hits a lovely high note

 Surfing in Dominical

Dominical owes its fame to its seriously sick point and beach breaks, though
surf conditions here are variable.
There is a great opportunity to learn
surfing in the white-water beach
breaks, but beware of getting in too
deep, as you can really get trashed
out here if you don't know what you're
doing. If you're just getting started,
stay in the white water or make for the
nearby Playa Dominicalito, which is a
bit tamer.

Costa Rica Surf Camp (☑8812-
3625, 2787-0393; www.crsurfschool.
com; Hotel DiuWak; all-inclusive packages
per week US$1145) This locally owned
surf school prides itself on a two-
to-one student-teacher ratio, with
experienced teachers with CPR and
water-safety training. Rainy-season
surf packages start at $1067 per per-
son but get cheaper with more people
involved.

Dominical Surf Adventures (☑2787-
0431; www.dominicalsurfadventures.com;
☺8am-5pm Mon-Sat, 9am-3pm Sun) An
adventurer's one-stop shop on the
main drag, with white-water-rafting
trips (from US$90 for Class II and III
Guabo; or opt for a more challenging
run on the Río Coto Brus Class IV
rapids), kayaking, snorkeling and dive
trips and surf lessons.

Sunset Surf (☑8917-3143; www.sunset
surfdominical.com; MAVI Surf Hotel; all-inclusive packages per week from US$1575;
☺8am-4:30pm) Sunset offers a variety
of packages, including one for women
only. There are day lessons with a
three-to-one student-instructor ratio
and teacher Dylan Parks, who grew up
surfing the waves of Hawaii and Costa
Rica. Organic sunblock is provided; 1%
of proceeds goes toward 'the planet.'

¶○¶ Dining in Ojochal

This laid-back, spread-out village is the Costa Ballena's culinary epicenter, with a multicultural expat population.

Azul (✒2786-5543; El Castillo; lunch mains US$10-26, 2-/3-course dinner US$30/60; ⊙noon-10pm; ⓢ✐) At this chic little restaurant inside El Castillo (✒2786-5543; www.elcastillocr.com; r US$275-395, ste US$525; 𝗣❄ⓢ⋇), with killer views of the Pacific coast, your tastebuds will be singing praises when you treat them to innovative, Tico-style potato skins, goat cheese ravioli and expertly seared steak. There's terrific attention to presentation and taste, and the Mediterranean-style three-course dinners are worth a splurge. Great cocktails and wine list, too.

Ylang-Ylang (✒2786-5054; www.facebook.com/YlangYlangRestaurant; mains US$25; ⊙5-9pm Wed-Sat early Dec-early May; ⓢ✐) The only Indonesian restaurant in Central America, this characterful expat-run place is immensely popular for the authentic, fiery flavors of their dishes (they grow their own Asian herbs). Dishes such as *daging rendang* (beef simmered with spices in coconut milk) and *ikan ketcap* (snapper with galangal and tamarind) are meant to be shared. With only 12 guests per night, advance reservations are essential.

Exotica (✒2786-5050; mains US$10-23; ⊙5-9pm Mon-Sat) This phenomenal gourmet restaurant is worth planning your evening around. In a sultry, jungle ambience with orchids everywhere, the nouveau-French dishes each emphasize a breadth of ingredients brought together in masterful combinations. Some of the highlights include Tahitian fish carpaccio, wild-duck breast with port-pineapple reduction and its signature dessert – the chili-tinged chocolate Devil's Fork. Reservations recommended.

in Dominical. It serves mostly vegetarian and vegan dishes that span the globe, from falafel and burritos to pad Thai and curries, with pescatarian-friendly fish tacos and wasabi tuna thrown in for good measure. The food is made from organic and locally sourced produce where possible.

Maracutú also hosts lots of live music and DJs; Wednesday night is ladies night and the place gets packed.

Dominical Sushi   Sushi $$

(✒8826-7946; www.dominicalsushi.com; mains US$8-13; ⊙1-10pm Sun-Thu, 1-5pm Fri, 5-10pm Sat,) In an open-air setting overlooking the River Barú, this beachfront sushi place takes advantage of the fresh tuna and other fish caught daily in Dominical. We're big fans of its tuna sashimi, unagi, and rainbow rolls. The menu is complemented by a selection of Japanese beers and sake.

Charter   Costa Rican $$

(✒2787-0172; 1.5km north of Dominical; mains US$6-18) This Costa Rican restaurant serves excellent *comida tipica*, but is better known for the old, hollowed-out Allegro airplane parked beside it, which supposedly is being converted into a cocktail bar (or at least that's what staff members have been claiming for years). The steaks are particularly juicy, and the penne pasta with vodka sauce is killer.

🍷 DRINKING & NIGHTLIFE

Fuego Brew Co.   Craft Beer

(✒8992-9559; www.fuegobrew.com; craft beer US$4-6; ⊙11:30am-10:30pm) Glowing electric purple from the center of Dominical, this sleek new establishment is the town's first craft brewery and a place to sip *guanábana*-flavored Hefeweizen all day long. The bartenders are super nice and the bar snacks are tasty, especially the seared tuna. Upstairs is the glistening hardwood bar and restaurant, downstairs are a seven-barrel brewing system and tasting room.

Parque Nacional Marino Ballena (p148)

Tortilla Flats   Bar

(🖉2787-0033; ⏰8am-10pm) The beachfront Tortilla Flats is the de facto place for surfers to enjoy sunset beers after a day in the water (skip the food, though). Its open-air atmosphere and easy vibes reflect the clientele, with surf videos on continuous loop, but continents may drift before you get served.

🛈 DANGERS & ANNOYANCES

○ Waves, currents and riptides in Dominical are very strong, and there have been drownings in the past. Watch for red flags (which mark riptides), follow the instructions of posted signs and swim at beaches that are patrolled by lifeguards. If you're smart, the beach is no problem, but people do die here every year.

○ Dominical attracts a heavy-duty party crowd, which in turn has led to a burgeoning drug problem.

🛈 INFORMATION

On the main strip, near the entrance to Dominical, the **Dominical Information Center** (🖉2787-0454; www.dominicalinformation.com; ⏰9:30am-5pm) has useful maps of town and bus timetables for the entire region. Bus ticket, shuttle and tour booking services available.

🛈 GETTING THERE & AWAY

Gray Line, Easy Ride and Monkey Ride offer private and shared shuttle services to popular destinations such as Jacó, San José, Monteverde, Tamarindo and Sierpe; Easy Ride has direct services to Granada, Nicaragua.

Buses pick up and drop off passengers along the main road in Dominical.

Taxis to Uvita cost US$10 to US$20, while the ride to Quepos costs US$60 and to Manuel Antonio it's US$70. Cars accommodate up to five people, and can be hailed easily in town from the main road.

MANUEL
ANTONIO

Manuel Antonio at a Glance...

For visitors arriving at this small outcrop of land jutting into the Pacific, the air is heavy with humidity, scented with thick vegetation and alive with the calls of birds and monkeys, making it apparent that this is the tropics. The reason to come here is Parque Nacional Manuel Antonio, one of the most picturesque sections of tropical coast in Costa Rica. If you get bored of cooing at the baby monkeys scurrying in the canopy and scanning for birds and sloths, the turquoise waves and perfect sand provide endless entertainment. Despite the area's overdevelopment, the rainforested hills and blissful beaches make the park a stunning destination worthy of the tourist hype.

Two Days in Manuel Antonio

Spend your first day at the **Parque Nacional Manuel Antonio (p164)**, hiking the well-trodden trails and lounging on the picture-perfect beaches. Keep a lookout for monkeys, sloths and other **wildlife**. At the end of the day, head to **Ronny's Place (p179)** for cocktails and splendid sunset views.

Four Days in Manuel Antonio

Spend your second day taking an adventure tour, whether that's a paddleboarding outing with **Paddle 9 (p170)**, a guided coastal hike with **Unique Tours** (p170) or a canopy tour with **Amigos del Río (p176)**. In the evening, head to Quepos for a scrumptious seafood dinner at **Z Gastro Bar (p173)**.

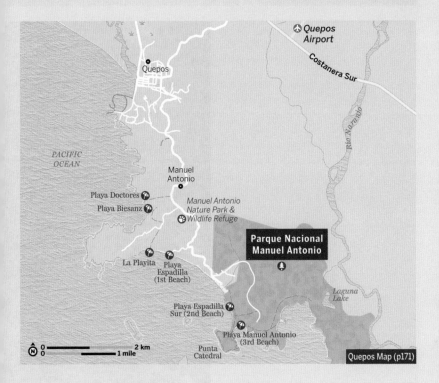

Quepos Map (p171)

Arriving in Manuel Antonio

The area is served by frequent flights and buses, and the roads are good (though the one leading from Quepos to Parque Nacional Manuel Antonio is winding, steep and narrow). Both **NatureAir** (p175) and **Sansa** (p175) service Quepos, with prices varying according to season and availability. The airport is 5km out of town, and taxis make the trip for US$8.

Sleeping

The village of Manuel Antonio is the closest base for exploring the national park, though the selection of sleeping options is more varied in Quepos or on the Quepos–Manuel Antonio stretch of road. The Quepos–Manuel Antonio road is skewed toward ultra-top-end hotels, but plenty of noteworthy midrange and budget options are hidden along the way. Staying in Quepos offers a cheaper alternative to the sky-high prices at many lodges on the road to Manuel Antonio.

Parque Nacional Manuel Antonio

A place of swaying palms and playful monkeys, sparkling blue water and a riot of tropical birds, Parque Nacional Manuel Antonio is the country's smallest (19.83 sq km) and most popular national park.

Great For...

❶ Need to Know

2777-8551; park entrance US$16; ⊘7am-3:30pm Tue-Sun

★ **Top Tip**

Get here early (7am) and head for the park's furthest reaches to avoid the crowds.

Parque Nacional Manuel Antonio is a truly lovely place; the clearly marked trail system winds through rainforest-backed white-sand beaches and rocky headlands, the wildlife (iguanas, sloths, monkeys) is plentiful, and the views across the bay to the pristine outer islands are gorgeous.

The downside? The crowds. Visitors are confined to around 6.8 sq km of the park (the rest is set aside for ranger patrols battling poaching) and the place gets packed when mid-morning tour buses roll in.

Beaches

There are five beautiful beaches – three within the park and two just outside the entrance. The beaches are often numbered – most people call Playa Espadilla (outside the park) '1st beach,' Playa Espadilla Sur '2nd beach,' Playa Manuel Antonio '3rd beach,' Playa Puerto Escondido '4th beach' and Playa Playitas (outside the park) '5th beach.' Some people begin counting at Espadilla Sur, which is the first beach in the park, so it can be a bit confusing trying to figure out which beach people may be talking about. Regardless, they're all equally pristine, and provide sunbathing opportunities; check conditions with the rangers to see which ones are safe for swimming.

Playa Espadilla Sur   Beach
The exposed Playa Espadilla Sur is to the north of Punta Catedral and swimming here can be dangerous. The beach is a half-hour hike from the park entrance.

Punta Catedral   Area
Geographical fun fact: this isthmus, which is the centerpiece of the park, is called a *tombolo* and was formed by the accumu-

lation of sand between the mainland and the peninsula beyond, which was once an island. At its end, the isthmus widens into a rocky peninsula, with thick forest in the middle, encircled by Sendero Punta Catedral. There are good views of the Pacific Ocean and various rocky islets – nesting sites for brown boobies and pelicans.

Playa Manuel Antonio   Beach

With its turquoise waters, this lovely beach fronts a deep bay, sheltered by the Punta Catedral on the west side and a promontory on the east. This is the best beach for swimming, but it also gets the most crowded with picnicking families, so get here early.

☑ Don't Miss

The pre-Columbian turtle trap, built out of rocks, at the western end of Playa Manuel Antonio.

MATTEO COLOMBO/GETTY IMAGES ©

Hiking

Parque Manuel Antonio has an official road, **Sendero El Perezoso**, which is paved and wheelchair-accessible and connects the entrance to the network of short trails. None of them are strenuous, and all are well marked and heavily traversed, though there are some quiet corners near the ends of the trails. Off-trail hiking is not permitted. A new boardwalk stretching from the ranger station to **Playa Espadilla Sur** has opened.

Sendero Principal The longest trail in the park, the 2.2km Sendero Principal fringes Playa Espadilla Sur in the Manuel Antonio village.

Sendero Punta Catedral This 1.4km loop takes in the whole of Punta Catedral, passing through dense vegetation and with glorious views of the Pacific and the offshore islands. The blink-and-you'll-miss-it 200m Sendero La Tampa cuts across part of the loop.

Sendero El Mirador Heading inland and into the forest from the east side of Playa Manuel Antonio, this 1.3km trail climbs to a lookout on a bluff overlooking Puerto Escondido and Punta Serrucho beyond – a stunning vista. Rangers limit the number of hikers on this trail to 45.

Kayaking

Sea kayaking around the park's mangroves is a good way to glimpse the wildlife that this habitat supports. Long-standing operator Iguana Tours (p170) runs responsible kayaking trips.

✗ Take a Break

Discuss animal sightings over fancy coffee drinks on the patio of Café Milagro (p177).

Iguana

FRANCIS WONG/500PX ©

Wildlife-Watching

Capuchin monkeys scurry across idyllic beaches, brown pelicans dive-bomb clear waters and sloths spy on hikers on the trail, in this tiny park that's packed with life.

Great For...

☑ Don't Miss

Howlers crossing the 'monkey bridges' that were erected along the road between Quepos and Manuel Antonio.

Mammals

White-faced capuchins are very used to people, and normally troops of them feed and interact within a short distance of visitors; they can be encountered anywhere along the main access road and around Playa Manuel Antonio. The capuchins are the worst for snatching bags, so watch your stuff.

You'll probably also hear mantled howler monkeys soon after sun rise. Like capuchins, they can be seen anywhere inside the park and even along the road to Quepos – watch for them crossing the monkey bridges that were erected by local conservation groups.

Coatis can be seen darting across various paths and can get aggressive on the beach if you're eating. Three-toed and two-toed sloths are also common in

Coati

CYNTHIA KIDWELL/SHUTTERSTOCK ©

❶ Need to Know

A wildlife guide costs US$15 to US$20 per person for a two-hour tour. Ask to see the guide's ICT license before hiring.

✕ Take a Break

Grab lunch and enjoy the incredible ocean views at Agua Azul (p175).

★ Top Tip

Lenny Montenegro (☎8875-0437) is a recommended wildlife and bird guide.

the park. Guides are extremely helpful in spotting sloths, as they tend not to move around much.

The movements of the park's star and Central America's rarest primate, the Central American squirrel monkey, are far less predictable. These adorable monkeys are more retiring than capuchins, and though they are occasionally seen near the park entrance in the early morning, they usually melt into the forest well before opening time. With luck, however, a troop could be encountered during a morning's walk, and they often reappear in beachside trees and on the fringes of Manuel Antonio village in the early evening.

Marine Animals

Offshore, keep your eyes peeled for pan-tropical spotted and bottlenose dolphins, as well as humpback whales passing by on their regular migration routes. Other possibilities include orcas (killer whales), false killers and rough-toothed dolphins.

Reptiles

Big lizards are also a feature at Manuel Antonio – it's hard to miss the large ctenosaurs and green iguanas that bask along the beach at Playa Manuel Antonio and in vegetation behind Playa Espadilla Sur. To spot the well-camouflaged basilisk, listen for the rustle of leaves along the edges of trails, especially near the lagoon.

Birds

Manuel Antonio is not usually on the serious bird-watchers trail of Costa Rica, though the list of birds here is respectable, and includes the blue-gray and palm tangers, great-tailed grackles, bananaquits, blue dacnises and at least 15 species of hummingbirds. Regional endemics to look out for include the fiery-billed aracaris, black-hooded antshrikes, Baird's trogons, black-bellied whistling ducks, yellow-crowned night herons, brown pelicans, magnificent frigate birds, brown boobies, spotted sandpipers, green herons and ringed kingfishers.

Quepos

Located just 7km from the entrance to Manuel Antonio, the small, busy town of Quepos serves as the gateway to the national park, as well as a convenient port of call for travelers in need of goods and services. Although the Manuel Antonio area was rapidly and irreversibly transformed following the ecotourism boom, Quepos has largely retained an authentic Tico feel.

TOURS

Paddle 9 — Adventure Sports

(☏2777-7436; www.paddle9sup.com; tours US$60-150) These newer kids on the block are a passionate, safety-conscious team who've introduced SUP (stand-up paddleboarding) to Quepos and who delight in showing visitors around the Pacific coast. Apart from its two-hour mangrove or ocean paddleboarding tours, its most popular outing is an eight-hour journey involving paddleboarding, lunch at a tilapia farm and swimming in various waterfalls.

Unique Tours — Adventure Sports

(☏8844-0900, 2777-1119; www.costaricaunique tours.com) This established local operator organizes entertaining rafting tours of the Río Savegre, ocean and mangrove kayaking outings and more. But what makes it unique is that it's the only operator to offer a trip to a hidden, remote hot spring, as well as coastal hikes to Parque Nacional Manuel Antonio. Prices vary depending on group size.

H2O Adventures — Adventure Sports

(Ríos Tropicales; ☏2777-4092; www.h2ocr.com) The venerable Costa Rican rafting company Ríos Tropicales has a hugely popular franchise in Quepos called H2O Adventures, which organizes rafting outings on the Naranjo, El Chorro and Savegre rivers, as well as kayaking and tubing outings. Rates start at US$70 for rapids classes II through IV.

Oceans Unlimited — Diving

(☏2519-9544; www.scubadivingcostarica.com; 2-tank dive US$109) ⚓ This shop takes its diving very seriously, and runs most of its excursions out to Isla Larga and Isla del Caño, which is south in Bahía Drake (connected via a two-hour bus trip). It also has a range of specialized PADI certifications, and regular environmental-awareness projects that make it stand out from the pack.

Manuel Antonio Surf School — Surfing

(MASS; ☏2777-4842, 2777-1955; www.manuel antoniosurfschool.com; group lesson US$65-95) MASS offers friendly, safe and fun small-group lessons daily, lasting for three hours and with a three-to-one student-instructor ratio. Find its stand about 500m up the Manuel Antonio road south of Quepos.

Iguana Tours — Adventure Sports

(☏2777-2052; www.iguanatours.com; ⊗6:30am-9pm) ⚓ With tours that leave for destinations all over the central Pacific coast, this adventure-travel shop offers reputable river rafting, sea kayaking, horseback riding, mangrove tours and dolphin-watching excursions. It's no fly-by-night operation – it's been around since '89 – and has a proven commitment to ecotourism principles.

Tico Loco Adventures — Outdoors

(☏2777-0010; www.ticolocoadventures.com; Selina Hostel; waterfall party tour US$110 minimum 4 people) Based in the Selina Hostel, this tour company offers outdoor adventures that double as parties. The waterfall party tour involves a hike to majestic falls with a cooler of drinks, and is quite popular with the hostel clientele.

Titi Canopy Tours — Adventure Sports

(☏2777-3130; www.titicanopytour.com; Costanera Sur; day/night tours US$80/100; ⊗tours 7:30am, 11am, 2:30pm, 6pm) Offering ziplining, rappelling and Tarzan swinging adventures during the day and night, this outfit has friendly, professional guides

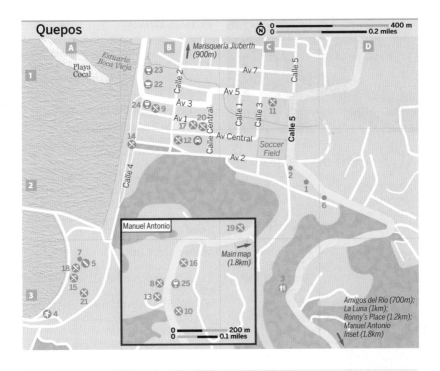

Quepos

and a convenient location just outside of central Quepos (150m south of the hospital). Rates include drinks, snacks and local transportation, and in some cases there's a minimum number of guests required (ask about this in advance).

Planet Dolphin Cruises Wildlife
(2777-1647, in the USA 800-943-9161; www.planetdolphin.com; morning/afternoon trip US$75/85) Planet Dolphin offers dolphin- and whale-watching tours. The cruises include refreshments (such as vodka and *guaro*,

 Sportfishing in Quepos

Sportfishing is big here, and offshore ventures are said to be best from December to April, when sailfish are being hooked. By and large this is a high-dollar activity and you can expect to pay upwards of US$900 to hire a boat for the day. If you want to shop around a bit, visit the office of **Marina Pez Vela** (☏2774-9000; www.marinapezvela.com), 500m south of the town center.

Outfitter **Quepos Sailfishing Charters** (☏2777-2025, 800-388-9957 in USA; www.queposfishing.com) gets good reviews from sportfishers and offers charters on a fleet of variously sized boats, whether you're after sailfish, marlin, dorado or wahoo. Rates vary significantly depending on the season, number of people and size of boat. It also offers packages that include accommodations and transfers.

Striped marlin

a sugarcane liquor), lunch, snorkeling and transfers to your hotel, and depart from Marina Pez Vela. Some customers have complained in the past of misinformation about dolphins and unprofessional behavior by the catamaran crew.

 EATING

One benefit of staying in Quepos proper is the access to a wide range of dining opportunities, and there are also a couple of good markets.

Farmers Market — Market $

(Calle 4; ⊗4pm Fri-noon Sat) Self-caterers should check out the farmers market near the waterfront, where you can buy directly from farmers, fisherfolk, bakers and other food producers.

Brooklyn Bakery — Bakery $

(Av 3; bagels US$1.50, mains US$5-8; ⊗6am-3pm Mon-Sat; 🛜🚲) Real New York–style bagels and lox (a real rarity in Costa Rica)! Rye bread! Iced coffee! This adorable little bakery bakes its fresh wares every morning, as well as serving light bites and amazing salads throughout the day and specials at lunchtime, such as delicious Italian meatball sandwiches.

Marisquería Jiuberth — Seafood $

(☏2777-1292; mains from US$7; ⊗11am-10pm) Run by a hardworking fisherman's family, this institution with brightly tiled floors serves the best seafood in town, yet is practically unknown to visitors because it's tucked away. Whether you have the catch of the day or the satisfying fish soup, the portions are generous and the service attentive. Follow unpaved Calle 2 out of town. Cash only.

L'Angolo — Deli $

(☏8887-9538, 2777-7865; Calle 2; sandwiches US$5-7; ⊗11am-10pm Mon-Sat) This deli makes excellent sandwiches with imported Italian meats and cheeses, served with a side of ill grace from the grumpy waiter, but perfect for toting on excursions to Manuel Antonio.

Soda Come Bien — Cafeteria $

(☏2777-2550; Av 1, Mercado Central; mains US$3.50-8; ⊗6am-5pm Mon-Sat, to 11am Sun) The daily rotation of delicious cafeteria options might include fish in tomato sauce, *olla de carne* (beef soup with rice) or chicken soup, but everything is fresh, the ladies behind the counter are friendly and the burly portions are a dream come true for hungry shoestringers. Or, pick up a fresh *empanada* before or after a long bus ride.

Mercado Central   Market $

(Central Market; Av 1; meals from US$4; ⊘hours vary) The Mercado Central is packed with produce vendors and good *sodas* too numerous to list, so follow your nose and the locals.

Chicken On The Run   Fast Food $

(mains US$4-16; ⊘10am-11am) If it's crispy fried chicken you're craving, this is the best little joint in town. Grab a wing or breast to go, or bring some friends for a sit down meal of an entire roast chicken with all the trimmings. *Casados* are a bargain, too.

Sunrice   Sushi $$

(✆2519-9955; www.sunricerestaurant.com; sushi rolls US$9-12, mains US$9; ⊘noon-9pm Tue-Sun) A newcomer to the Marina Pez Vela, this Latin-influenced sushi and sake bar fills its rolls with fresh tropical produce and local seafood bits. The spicy tuna over crispy rice cakes is a big hit, along with the tuna, avocado and mango poke bowl and the *omusubi* (Japanese rice balls). Dishes tend to be on the smaller side.

Runaway Grill   American $$

(✆2519-9095; Marina Pez Vela; mains US$12-25; ⊘11am-10pm; P❄🕿) An all-round crowd pleaser, Runaway Grill's menu spans steaks, wraps, salads, tacos, burgers, sandwiches and more. Portions are sizable and come with a sea view, the mint lemonades are refreshing and enormous, and the service is friendly (though they struggle sometimes when the place is packed).

Escalofrío   Italian $$

(✆2777-1902; Av Central; mains US$10-22; ⊘2:30-10:30pm Tue-Sun; ❄🕿) Gelato-lovers should make a point of stopping here, to choose from more than 20 flavors of the heavenly stuff. This spacious alfresco restaurant may also be the only game in town on Sunday night during slow season, a godsend especially if you enjoy thin-crust wood-fired pizza.

Z Gastro Bar   Fusion $$

(✆2777-6948; Marina Pez Vela; mains US$15-25; ⊘7am-10pm; P🕿) Bright, open to the breeze from all sides and with colorful cushions strewn on its comfy couches, this

Red-eyed tree frog

is a terrific spot for lingering with a coffee and dessert, or over a meal of dorado *ceviche* in coconut milk, an octopus burger or delicious homemade pasta with mussels. The arty presentation matches the terrific flavors and the service is excellent.

Claro Que Sí
Seafood $$

(☎2777-0777; Hotel Sí Como No; meals US$9-22; ⏲noon-10pm; 🛜🍴) ✿ A casual, family-friendly restaurant that passes on pretension without sacrificing quality, Claro Que Sí proudly serves organic and locally sourced food items that are in line with the philosophy of its parent hotel, **Sí Como No** (☎2777-0777; www.sicomono.com; r US$275-450, child under 6yr free; 🅿❄🛜🏊) ✿. Guilt-free meats and fish are expertly complemented with fresh produce, resulting in flavorful dishes typical of both the Pacific and Caribbean coasts. There's a separate kids' menu.

Gabriella's
Seafood $$$

(☎2519-9300; Marina Pez Vela; mains US$25-35; ⏲4-10pm; 🅿❄🛜) A contender for the region's best restaurant, Gabriella's does many things well. The veranda catches the sunset, the service is attentive, but the food is the real star, with a great emphasis on fresh fish and mouthwatering steak. We're particularly big fans of the seared tuna with chipotle sauce and the spicy sausage and shrimp pasta. In a word: terrific.

🍷 DRINKING & NIGHTLIFE

Café Milagro
Cafe

(☎2777-1707; www.cafemilagro.com; Calle 4; ⏲9am-5pm Mon-Sat) Café Milagro sources its coffee beans from all over Costa Rica and produces a variety of estate, single-origin and blended roasts to suit any coffee fiend's palate. One per cent of its profits gord to environmental causes via international nonprofit, 1% for the Planet. Unlike its other, bigger branch en route to Manuel Antonio, this place has takeout coffee only (US$3.50 to US$7).

Cuban Republik Disco Lounge
Club

(☎8345-9922; cover charge Fri & Sat US$2-4; ⏲10pm-2:30am Thu-Sat) Cuban Republik hosts

Bottlenose dolphins

the most reliable party in central Quepos, and it has various drinks specials. The DJs get loud late into the night and women get in for free before midnight on Friday. It's a nice, mixed Tico and gringo scene.

Dos Locos   Bar
(☑2777-1526; Av Central; ⊙7am-11pm Mon-Sat, 11am-7pm Sun) This popular pseudo-Mexican restaurant is the regular watering hole for the local expat community, and serves as a venue for live music on Wednesday and Saturday. Opening onto the central cross streets of town, it's fun for people-watching (and cheap Imperials). There's an English-language trivia night every Thursday. Added bonus: breakfast is served all day.

El Gran Escape   Bar
(☑2777-7850; Av 3; ⊙11am-10pm Sun-Thu, til late Fri & Sat; 🛜) This long-standing pub is famous for all the fishing hats draped from the ceiling. It offers excellent fresh seafood, sports on the big screen and delicious (though pricey) burgers. Prompt bar staff, too.

❶ GETTING THERE & AWAY

Both **NatureAir** (www.natureair.com) and **Sansa** (www.sansa.com) service Quepos. Prices vary according to season and availability, though you can pay a little less than US$75 for a flight from San José or Liberia. Flights are packed in the high season, so book (and pay) for your ticket well ahead of time and reconfirm often. The airport is 5km out of town, and taxis make the trip for US$8.

All buses arrive at and depart from the busy, chaotic main terminal in the center of town. Scheduled private shuttles, operated by Gray Line, Easy Ride and Monkey Ride, run between Quepos/Manuel Antonio and popular destinations such as Jacó (US$35), Monteverde (US$59), Puerto Jiménez (US$79), San José (US$50) and Uvita (US$35).

❶ GETTING AROUND

A number of international car-rental companies, such as **Budget** (☑2774-0140; www.budget.

 Monkey Business

There are a number of stands on the beach that cater to hungry tourists, though everything is exuberantly over-priced and of dubious quality. Plus, all the food scraps have negatively affected the monkey population. Before you offer a monkey your scraps, consider the following risks to their health.
Monkeys are susceptible to bacteria transmitted from human hands.

Irregular feeding will lead to aggressive behavior as well as create a dangerous dependency (picnickers in Manuel Antonio suffer downright intimidating mobs of them sometimes).

Bananas are not their preferred food, and can cause serious digestive problems.

Increased exposure to humans facilitates illegal poaching as well as attacks from dogs.

It goes without saying: don't feed the monkeys. And, if you do happen to come across someone doing so, take the initiative and ask them politely to stop.

White-faced capuchin monkey
HBRIZARD/GETTY IMAGES ©

co.cr; Quepos Airport; ⊙8am-5pm Mon-Sat, to 4pm Sun), operate in Quepos; reserve ahead and reconfirm to guarantee availability.

Colectivo taxis run between Quepos and Manuel Antonio (US$1 for a short hop). A private taxi will cost a few thousand colones. Catch one at the **taxi stand** (Av Central) south of the market. The trip between Quepos and the park should cost about US$15.

X Marks the Spot

Locals have long believed that a treasure worth billions and billions of dollars lies somewhere in the Quepos and Manuel Antonio area, waiting to be discovered. The legend was popularized by English pirate John Clipperton, who befriended the coastal Quepoa during his years of sailing to and from the South Pacific. Clipperton's belief stemmed from a rumor that in 1670 a number of Spanish ships laden with treasure escaped from Panama City moments before it was burned to the ground by Captain Henry Morgan. Since the ships were probably off-loaded quickly to avoid being raided at sea, a likely destination was the San Bernardino de Quepo Mission, which had strong loyalty to the Spanish crown.

John Clipperton died in 1722 without ever discovering the legendary treasure, and the mission closed permanently in 1746, as most of the Quepoa had succumbed to European diseases. Although the ruins of the mission were discovered in 1974, they were virtually destroyed and had long since been looted. However, if the treasure was indeed as large as it's described in lore, it is possible that a few gold doubloons could still be lying somewhere, waiting to be unearthed.

Playa Manuel Antonio (p165)
HOLGER METTE/GETTY IMAGES ©

Manuel Antonio

◎ SIGHTS

**Manuel Antonio
Nature Park &
Wildlife Refuge**   Wildlife Reserve
(☎2777-0850; adult/child US$15/8; ⊘8am-4pm; 👶) This private rainforest preserve and butterfly garden breeds about three dozen species of butterfly – a delicate population compared to the menagerie of lizards, reptiles and frogs that inspire gleeful squeals from the little ones. A jungle night tour (5:30pm to 7:30pm, US$39/29 per adult/child) showcases the colorful local frogs and their songs, while day tours (US$15/8 per adult/child) introduce you either to the fluttering or the slithering denizens (or both; joint tickets US$25).

La Playita   Beach
At the far western end of Playa Espadilla, beyond a rocky headland (wear sandals), this former nude beach remains one of Costa Rica's most famous gay beaches and a particular draw for young men. The beach is inaccessible around high tide, so time your walk. Also, don't be fooled – you do not need to pay to use the beach, as it's outside the park.

☉ ACTIVITIES

Amigos del Río   Adventure Sports
(☎2777-0082; www.adadventurepark.com; tours US$135) Pack all of your canopy-tour jungle fantasies into one day on Amigos del Río's '10-in-One Adventure,' featuring ziplining, a Tarzan swing, rappelling down a waterfall and more. The seven-hour adventure tour includes a free transfer from the Quepos and Manuel Antonio area as well as breakfast and lunch. Amigos del Río is also a reliable outfit for white-water-rafting trips.

Cala Spa   Spa
(☎2777-0777, ext 220; www.sicomono.com; Hotel Sí Como No; treatments US$70-140; ⊘10am-7pm) If you're sunburned and sore from exploring Manuel Antonio – even better if

Ceviche

you're not – the Cala Spa offers aloe body wraps, citrus salt scrubs and various types of massage to restore body and spirit. Open daily by appointment only.

❽ EATING

The road to Manuel Antonio plays host to some of the best restaurants in the area, and many hotels along this road also have good restaurants open to the public. As with sleeping venues, eating and drinking establishments along this stretch are skewed toward the upmarket. Reservations are recommended on weekends and holidays and during the busy dry season.

Falafel Bar   Mediterranean $
(📞2777-4135; mains US$5-9; ⏰11am-9:30pm Tue-Sun; 🛜🍴) Adding to the diversity of cuisine to be found along the road, this falafel spot dishes up authentic Israeli favorites. You'll also find plenty of vegetarian options, including couscous, fresh salads, stuffed grape leaves, fab fruit smoothies and even french fries for the picky little ones.

Sancho's   Mexican $
(📞2777-0340; tacos from US$3; ⏰11:30am-10pm; 🛜) A great view from the open-air terrace, potent house margaritas, excellent fish tacos and humongous chile verde burritos are just some of the draws at this friendly expat-run joint. A place to knock back a few beers with friends in a convivial, chilled-out atmosphere, rather than woo your date.

Café Milagro   Fusion $$
(📞2777-2272; www.cafemilagro.com; mains from US$7; ⏰7am-9pm) This is a fine stop for fancy coffee drinks, and even better for decadent breakfasts (banana pancakes with macadamia nuts), sandwiches (mango mahimahi wrap) and sophisticated interpretations of Tico fare for dinner (Creole pork tenderloin). The patio itself is a lovely setting surrounded by tropical gardens; you can also order your sandwich packed for a picnic in the park.

Agua Azul   International $$
(📞2777-5280; www.cafeaguaazul.com; meals US$10-25; ⏰11am-10pm Thu-Tue; 🛜) Perched

LGBT Manuel Antonio

For jet-setting gay and lesbian travelers the world over, Manuel Antonio has a reputation as something of a dream destination. Homosexuality has been decriminalized in Costa Rica since the 1970s – a rarity in all-too-often machismo-fueled, conservative Central America – and a well-established gay scene blossomed in Manuel Antonio soon after. It's not hard to understand why.

Not only is the area stunningly beautiful but it has also long attracted liberal-minded individuals, creating a burgeoning artist community and a sophisticated restaurant scene. Check out www.gaymanuelantonio.com for a full list of gay and gay-friendly accommodations, events, restaurants and bars.

The Manuel Antonio area has always been proud to host one of the most sophisticated and cosmopolitan restaurant scenes on the central Pacific coast. A few venues occasionally host gay-oriented events, and **Karma Lounge** is a very friendly spot with an excellent happy hour.

During daylight hours, the epicenter of gay Manuel Antonio is the famous La Playita (p176), a beach with a long history of nude sunbathing for gay men. Alas, the days when you could sun in the buff are gone, but the end of La Playita is still widely regarded as a playful pick-up scene for gay men.

---

on the 2nd floor with uninterrupted ocean views, Agua Azul is a killer lunch spot on this stretch of road – perfect for early-morning park visitors who are heading back to their hotel. The breezy, unpretentious open-air restaurant, renowned for its 'big-ass burger,' also serves up the likes of fajitas, panko-crusted tuna and a tasty fish salad.

Barba Roja   Seafood $$
(☏2777-0331; www.barbarojarestaurant.com; meals US$9-22; ☉11:30am-9pm Tue-Sun) A

Manuel Antonio area institution, the Barba Roja is both a lively bar and a seafood-and-steak spot with a respectable sushi menu and weekly specials (Friday is smoked-rib and blues night). The terrace affords fantastic ocean views, best enjoyed with a local Libertas y La Segua craft brew (pints are US$6) or Mexican-style *michelada* (beer and lime cocktail). Drinks are two-for-one every day, 4pm to 6pm.

La Luna   International $$
(☏2777-9797; www.gaiahr.com; Gaia Hotel; mains US$8-24; ☉6am-11pm; 🛜🏊) Unpretentious and friendly, La Luna makes a lovely spot for a special-occasion dinner, with a spectacular backdrop of jungle and ocean. An international menu offers everything from spicy tuna and mango tacos to mahimahi *ceviche* to lobster tails, with a Tico-style twist – such as grouper baked *en papillote*, with plantain purée and coconut milk. Separate vegetarian and vegan menu available.

Kapi Kapi Restaurant   Fusion $$$
(☏2777-5049; www.restaurantekapikapi.com; meals US$16-40; ☉3-10pm; ❄🛜♿) While there is some stiff competition for the title of best restaurant in the area, this Californian creation certainly raises the bar. The menu at Kapi Kapi (a traditional greeting of the indigenous Maleku) spans the globe from America to Asia. Pan-Asian-style seafood features prominently; macadamia-crusted-mahimahi, lobster ravioli and sugar-cane-skewered prawns are all standouts.

South American wines and Costa Rican coffees complete this globetrotting culinary extravaganza. True to its name, Kapi Kapi welcomes diners with soft lights, earthy tones and soothing natural decor, which perfectly frame the dense forest lying just beyond the perimeter. There's also a separate kids' menu.

🍸 DRINKING & NIGHTLIFE

Bars in several accommodations aside, there's no nightlife in Manuel Antonio village to speak of, though there are several clubs and bars along the road to Quepos.

El Avión   Bar

(☑2777-3378; www.costaverde.com; ⊘noon-
10pm; 🛜) Constructed around a 1954
Fairchild C-123 plane, allegedly purchased
by the US government in the '80s for the
Nicaraguan Contras but never used, this
striking bar-restaurant is a great spot for a
beer and stellar sunset-watching. Skip the
food, though, and double-check the check,
as complaints have been made about
inaccuracies.

In 2000 the enterprising owners of El
Avión purchased the plane for the surprisingly reasonable sum of US$3000 (it
never made it out of its hangar in San José
because of the Iran-Contra scandal that
embroiled Oliver North and his cohorts),
and proceeded to cart it piece by piece to
Manuel Antonio. It now sits on the side of
the main road, where it looks as if it had
crash-landed into the side of the hill.

Ronny's Place   Bar

(☑2777-5120; www.ronnysplace.com; ⊘noon-
10pm) The insane views at Ronny's Place,
of two pristine bays and jungle on all sides,
make it worth a detour for a drink and a
tasty meal. While plenty of places along this
stretch of road boast similar views, the off-
the-beaten-path location makes it feel like
a secret find. Look for the well-marked dirt
road off the main drag.

Karma Lounge   Gay & Lesbian

(☑2777-7230; www.facebook.com/karmalounge
ma; ⊘7pm-2:30am Tue-Sun) Popular mingling
spot for local gay guys and visitors who
want to hang out with them.

ℹ️ GETTING THERE & AWAY

Driving the winding 7km road between Quepos
and Manuel Antonio village on any day but
Monday means spending time in traffic jams and
potentially exorbitant parking fees.

Note that the road to Manuel Antonio is very
narrow and congested, so it's suggested that
you leave your car at your hotel and take an
early-morning bus to the park entrance instead,
then simply walk in.

 Saving the Squirrel Monkey

With its expressive eyes and luxuriant
coat, the *mono tití* (Central American
squirrel monkey) is a favorite among
Costa Rica's four monkey species. It is
also in danger of extinction, as there
are only roughly 1500 of these animals
left in Manuel Antonio, one of its last
remaining native habitats.

Overdevelopment is one of the animal's greatest threats. To remedy this
problem, a conservation project known
as the **Titi Conservation Alliance** (www.
monotiti.org; ☑2777-2306) is taking bold
measures to prevent further decline.
This coalition of organizations is helping
to create a sustainable wildlife corridor
between Parque Nacional Manuel Antonio and the Zona Protectora Cerro Nara
in the northeast.

To achieve this aim, it is reforesting
the Río Naranjo, a key waterway linking
the two locations. More than 65,000
trees have already been planted along
8km of the Naranjo. This not only has
the effect of extending the monkeys'
habitat but also provides a protected
area for other wildlife to enjoy. Scientists
at the Universidad Nacional de Costa
Rica have mapped and selected sites
for reforestation, and business owners
in the area as well as private donations
support the project financially.

SOUTHERN
NICOYA

Southern Nicoya at a Glance...

Word has spread about the hippie-chic outposts of Montezuma and dusty yet developing Santa Teresa. During the dry season, packs of international surfers and wanderers arrive, hungry for the wild beauty and soul-stirring waters on either side of the peninsula. It used to require hours of sweaty bus rides and sluggish ferries from the mainland to access this tropical land's end, but these days there are more roads and regular boat shuttles, making the southern peninsula altogether more accessible.

Two Days in Southern Nicoya

On your first day, relax into your vacay at **Playa Santa Teresa** (p188), one of Costa Rica's most stunning beaches, and throw in a surf or a yoga session if you're keen. Do lunch at **Zwart Cafe** (p190) and a sushi dinner **Koji's** (p191). Spend day two chillin' by the tide pools at **Playa Hermosa** (p188) or exploring the trails at **Reserva Natural Absoluta Cabo Blanco** (p184) and its gorgeous wilderness beach.

Four Days in Southern Nicoya

Base yourself for the next two days in Montezuma, and prioritize the trek to **Montezuma Waterfalls** (p186) for thrilling jumps and cooling dips. Have lunch at **Clandestina** (p196), then head to **Playa Montezuma** (p192) for an afternoon of swimming and sunbathing. Treat yourself to a delectable beachside dinner at **Playa de los Artistas** (p196). On your last day, get an early start on the beach hike to **Playa Cocolito** (p193), where you can luxuriate in some of the most magnificent scenery around.

Montezuma Waterfalls

Reserva Natural Absoluta Cabo Blanco

Montezuma Map (p193)

Arriving in Southern Nicoya

The road from Paquera to Cóbano is paved, but much of the southern peninsula is not, and it's quite a bumpy ride. Ferries carry cars and passengers across the Golfo de Nicoya (from Puntarenas to Paquera), while boats bring passengers from Jacó to Montezuma. A quick flight from San José will deliver you to Tambor.

Sleeping

Montezuma and Santa Teresa are the hubs of the southern peninsula, both with a great range of accommodation options catering to all budgets. But there are *cabinas* and other more interesting accommodations sprinkled all over this region. So if you prefer to nest in a quieter corner of the peninsula, you will surely find somewhere suitable to lay your head.

Reserva Natural Absoluta Cabo Blanco

At the tip of the Península de Nicoya, this unique park is covered by evergreen forests, bisected by a hiking trail and flanked by empty white-sand beaches and offshore islands.

Great For...

☑ Don't Miss

Picnicking and swimming at a deserted beach at the tip of the peninsula.

Just 11km south of Montezuma is Costa Rica's oldest protected wilderness area. Cabo Blanco (p185) comprises 12 sq km of land and 17 sq km of surrounding ocean, and includes the entire southern tip of the Península de Nicoya. The moist micro-climate on the tip of the peninsula fosters the growth of evergreen forests, which are unique when compared with the dry tropical forests typical of Nicoya. The park also encompasses a number of pristine white-sand beaches and offshore islands that are favored nesting areas for various bird species.

Hiking

From the ranger station, the **Sendero Sueco** (Swedish Trail) leads 4.5km down to a wilderness beach at the tip of the peninsula, while the **Sendero Danes** (Danish Trail)

Brown booby

KEVIN SCHAFER/AGE FOTOSTOCK ©

Santa Teresa ●
● Montezuma
Mal País ●
● Cabuya
Reserva Natural Absoluta Cabo Blanco

❶ Need to Know

☑2642-0093; adult/child US$12/2; ⊘8am-4pm Wed-Sun

✕ Take a Break

Pack a picnic with burritos from Zwart Cafe (p190).

★ Top Tip

Cabo Blanco is called an 'absolute' nature reserve because visitors were originally not permitted (prior to the late 1980s).

is a spur that branches from Sendero Sueco and reconnects 1km later. So, you can make this small 2km loop and stay in the woods, or take on the considerably more difficult but much more rewarding hike to the cape, heading down one way and taking the other path back up. Be advised that the trails can get very muddy (especially in the rainy season) and are fairly steep in certain parts – plan for about two hours in each direction.

Monkeys, squirrels, sloths, deer, agoutis and raccoons abound at Cabo Blanco. Armadillos, pizotes (coatis), peccaries and anteaters are also occasionally sighted.

Brown Boobies on the Cabo Blanco

The coastal area is known as an important nesting site for the brown booby, mostly

found 1.6km south of the mainland on **Isla Cabo Blanco** (White Cape Island). In fact, the name 'Cabo Blanco' was coined by Spanish conquistadors when they noticed that the entire island consisted of guano-encrusted rocks.

Beaches

The wide, sandy pebble beach at the end of the trail is magnificent. It's backed by jungle, sheltered by two rugged headlands including one that stretches out into a rock reef with island views just offshore. The water is striped turquoise at low tide, but the cool currents still make for a refreshing dip. Visibility isn't always great for snorkeling but you may want to bring a mask anyway. Driftwood is smooth, weathered and piled haphazardly here and there. There are even picnic tables and a grill, if you care to get ambitious. Simply put, it is a postcard, and should be required for visitors to the southern peninsula. Leave the beach by 2pm to get out before the park closes.

Ziplining

Montezuma Waterfalls

A river hike leads to a waterfall with a delicious swimming hole. Further along the trail, a second set of falls offers a good clean 10m leap into deep water.

Head south past Hotel La Cascada (located at the mouth of the river), where you'll find a parking area. Then take the trail to the right just after the bridge. You'll want proper hiking footwear.

Waterfall Trail

The first waterfall has a lusciously inviting swimming hole, where you'll want to cool off from the hike. Remember that it's shallow and rocky and not suitable for diving.

From here, if you continue on the well-marked trail that leads around and up, you will come to a second set of falls. This is where you'll find a good clean leap into the deep water below. At 10m high, they are also the tallest of the three falls. To reach the jumping point, continue on the trail up the side of the hill until you reach the diving area. Do not attempt to scale the falls. The

Great For...

☑ **Don't Miss**

That agonizing, heart-thumping moment when you have to let go of the rope.

Montezuma
**Montezuma
Waterfalls**
Río Montezuma
**Montezuma
Gardens**
PACIFIC
OCEAN

ⓘ Need to Know

parking US$2

✕ Take a Break

Recover from your adventure with gourmet tacos and craft beer at.Clandestina (p196).

★ Top Tip

Hit the trail early and you may have the falls to yourself.

montezumatraveladventures.com; tours US$45; ⏱9am, 1pm & 3pm) operates a 1½-hour canopy tour. After you've flown down eight ziplines, you'll hike down – rather than up – to the waterfalls. Bring your swimsuit, so you can jump off the rocks and cool off. Park at the canopy entrance (US$4) for quick access to the falls via a suspension bridge. This company has also opened a spotless new lodge, Sun Trails Hotel, on the other side of the swinging bridge, with the latest amenities.

Butterfly Garden

About 1.5km south of town, alongside the waterfall trail, you can tour this lush mariposario (butterfly garden) at **Montezuma Gardens** (Mariposario; ☎2642-1317; www. montezumagardens.com; US$6; ⏱8am-4pm), where the mysterious metamorphoses occur. You'll learn about the life cycles and benefits of a dozen local species, of which you'll see many colorful varieties. Note that it is a long and steep trek from town so you may want to consider a taxi. There's also a modern four-room B&B here that brews its own beer.

rocks are slippery and several travelers have met their death in this way.

From this point, the trail continues up the hill to the third and last set of falls. These are not suitable for jumping, but daring souls can swing out on the rope and drop right into the deeper part of the swimming hole.

Playing It Safe

○ Don't attempt to jump into the lower pool, which is rocky and shallow.

○ Don't attempt to scale the waterfall.

○ Don't jump into the third upper pool without the aid of the swing.

Canopy Tour

Tour company **Sun Trails** (Montezuma Waterfall Canopy Tour; ☎2642-0808; www.

Santa Teresa & Mal País

Santa Teresa didn't even have electricity until the mid-1990s. Then one major land-owner died and his property was subdivided, and the landscape north of the Playa El Carmen intersection changed forever. These days, ATVs are omnipresent, along with gob-smackingly delicious restaurants and transformational ocean-view yoga dens. It's still a wonderful surfing town, though no longer a secret one, and there's a modicum of nightlife. The entire area unfurls along one bumpy coastal road that rambles south from Santa Teresa through Playa El Carmen and terminates in the relaxed, sleepy fishing hamlet of Mal País.

⊙ SIGHTS

Playa Santa Teresa   Beach

Playa Santa Teresa is a long, stunning beach that's famous for its fast and powerful beach break. The surf is pretty consistent and can be surfed at virtually any time of day. At the north end of the beach, Roca Mar – aka Suck Rock – is an awesome point break and a local favorite. The break La Lora is named for the night-club that marks the turnoff from the main road, which is how you find it.

Playa Hermosa   Beach

Somewhere north of town, Playa Santa Teresa ends and Playa Hermosa starts. This gorgeous beach deserves its *hermosa* (beautiful) moniker and then some. It's wide and flat and spectacular at low tide. The beach nearly disappears at high tide. Somewhere between low and high is surf tide, when you can ride the wide beach break left or right from center. You can surf the point break (at the north end of the beach) at any time.

Playa El Carmen   Beach

Playa El Carmen, downhill from the main T intersection coming into town, is a good beach break that can be surfed anytime. The beach is wide and sandy and curls into successive coves, so it makes good beach-combing and swimming terrain too.

Playa Manzanillo   Beach

About 8km north of the Playa El Carmen intersection, past Playa Hermosa, Playa Manzanillo is a combination of sand and rock that's best surfed when the tide is rising and there's an offshore wind.

✪ ACTIVITIES

Freedom Ride SUP   Water Sports

(☎2640-0939, 8737-8781; www.sup-costarica.com; Mal País; rental half-/full day US$25/40, lessons per person US$50; ☺9am-6pm) A stand-up paddle place with sharp management and excellent safety and instruction techniques. Andy offers lessons for first-timers and rentals for old-timers, as well as tours that are entertaining for anyone. Located near the fishing pier in Mal País.

Canopy Mal País   Adventure Sports

(☎2640-0360; www.canopymalpais.com; US$50; ☺9am-3pm) You don't think of ziplining when you come to a surf town? You should. Just south of Mal País, Carlos and crew provide one of the most entertaining experiences around, joking so much you'll forget your fear of heights on the 11 cables, including one that stretches 500m across the jungle below. And the last cable is a surfboard ride!

EATING

If surfing and yoga are the top two activities in Santa Teresa and Mal País, then number three is surely eating. The dining is surprisingly sophisticated for a dusty little surf town. Indulge in gourmet burgers, sublime sushi, multicultural tapas or farm-to-table fusion goodness. Or, keep it real with a *casado* (set meal) from the local *soda*. It's all good.

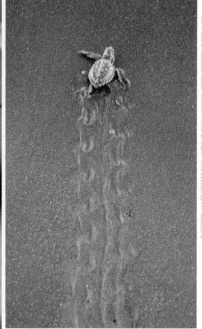

Clockwise from top: Costa Rican breakfast; Olive Ridley turtle; Halloween Crab, Reserva Natural Absoluta Cabo Blanco (p184)

Reserva Natural Absoluta Cabo Blanco (p184)

Zwart Cafe Cafe $

(☏2640-0011; Santa Teresa; mains US$4-8; ◷7am-5pm; 🛜) *Zwart* means 'black' in Dutch, but this shabby-chic, artist-owned gallery and cafe is all white (or mostly, damn dust!). You'll love the surf-inspired Technicolor canvases, the lively outdoor patio and the breakfasts, including chocolate chip pancakes. At lunch it's all about the burritos. About 2km north of the T intersection, on the right if you're heading north. There's a dynamite used bookstore here too.

Mafra's Bakery Bakery $

(mall at entrance to Playa El Carmen; pastries & bread US$2-4; ◷8am-7pm Mon-Sat) Not the biggest bakery in Playa El Carmen, but longtime residents swear by this Italian *panaderia* in the first mall you see as you come into town. Francheska and company whip up a mean *bombolini*, so scrumptious you'll be licking the cream off your fingers afterward. And, a bunch of good focaccia and pizza-like items too. *Buono apettito!*

Burger Rancho Burgers $$

(☏2640-0583; www.facebook.com/Burger Rancho; Santa Teresa; mains US$10-12; ◷11am-10pm; ✐) Get your burger on at this open-air *rancho* across from the soccer field. Check the blackboard for daily changing specials, including veggie choices like a portobello mushroom burger, fish options like a Hawaiian tuna burger, and others such as the interesting chorizo burger. There's other food too, but why would you want to do that? Cash only.

Umi Sushi Sushi $$

(☏2640-0968; Santa Teresa; rolls US$6-14; ◷11:30am-10pm) This new addition to the Santa Teresa smorgasbord serves up the usual sushi roll suspects – California, spicy tuna, and Philadelphia – along with local winners like the mouth-watering Mal País roll (salmon, tuna and avocado). Good food and impeccable presentation make for a win-win. On the main road, about 0.5km north of the T intersection, just before Calle Buenos Aires.

Caracolas
Soda $$

(☎2640-0525; Mal País; mains US$10-16; ⊙11:30am-8:30pm; [P][⊙][♿]) The lone *soda* on this end of the coast. It serves *típica* on timber tables in a garden that rolls on to the rocky beach. The place does all the usual chicken, beef and seafood dishes, as well as sandwiches and salads. But the reason to come here is to feel the ocean breeze and stare at the setting sun.

Restaurante & Pizzeria Playa Carmen
Pizza $$

(☎2640-0110; www.restaurantepizzeriaplaya carmen.com; Playa El Carmen; mains US$10-23; ⊙9am-10pm) The location right on the *playa* is hard to beat, and the list of *ceviche* and cooked fish shows it's more than just a pizzeria. It's a popular spot for sundowners, thanks to the happy-hour specials (two-for-one drinks) and the amazing show that takes place in the sky. Come hobnob with the locals and enjoy.

Bajo El Arbol
Tapas $$$

(Playa El Carmen; mains US$15-18; ⊙6-10pm) If you can't afford a flight to Spain, just sit down 'Beneath the Tree.' Basque chef Julio whips up extraordinary *escalivada* (an eggplant and pepper dish), and the *pulpo a la gallega* (octopus), topped with crunchy sea salt: so damned good it ought to be illegal. Add a half bottle of Spanish wine, and you'll be smiling till the next morning.

Koji's
Japanese $$$

(☎2640-0815; www.santa-teresa.com/kojis; Playa Hermosa; sushi US$5-10; ⊙5:30-9:30pm Tue-Sat) Koji Hyodo's sushi shack is a twinkling beacon of fresh, raw excellence. The atmosphere and service are superior, of course, but his food is a higher truth. The grilled octopus is barely fried and sprinkled with sea salt, and there's a sweet crunch to his lobster sashimi, sliced tracing-paper thin and sprinkled with fresh ginger. Uphill from the main road.

Mary's Restaurant
Fusion $$$

(☎2640-0153; www.maryscostarica.com; Mal País; mains US$10-22; ⊙5:30-10pm Thu-Tue) At

Surfing Southern Nicoya

The long, flat beach stretches for many kilometers along this southwestern coast of the peninsula. The entire area is saturated with surf shops. This is a good place to pick up an inexpensive board, which you can probably sell later. Most of the local shops also do rentals and repairs.

Kina Surf Shop (☎2640-0627; www. kinasurfcr.com; Santa Teresa; lessons per person US$60, board rentals per day US$12-20; ⊙9am-5pm) A terrific, efficient surf shop near the break in Santa Teresa. Kina claims to have the best selection of rental boards in the area, with 60-something quality boards available. The 90-minute lessons for beginner, intermediate and advanced surfers also come highly recommended.

Nalu Surf School (☎2649-0391, 8358-4436; www.nalusurfschool.com; Santa Teresa; board rental per day US$10-20, group/private lessons US$50/65) Located 300m north of the Playa El Carmen intersection (next to Ronny's Supermarket), this surf school is recommended for its fun and professional approach to instruction. Lessons usually take place at Playa El Carmen.

Pura Vida Adventures (☎in USA 1-415-465-2162; www.puravidaadventures.com; Playa El Carmen; weekly rates from US$2795) An excellent women-only retreat in Playa El Carmen that combines surfing and yoga in weeklong experiences that also include all meals. It's on the beach side of the main north–south road, just north of Calle Buenos Aires.

the far end of Mal País village, this unassuming, open-air restaurant has a polished concrete floor, wood oven, pool table and blackboard menu. It offers delicious wood-fired pizzas, homemade bacon and sausages, grilled seafood and fresh produce straight from the farm. It's all fabulous. Its secret? Using only fresh, organic ingredients from local farms and fishers.

Papaya Lounge International $$$

(☑2640-0230; www.moanacostarica.com; Hotel Moana, Mal País; tapas US$6-15; ☉7:30-10am Tue, 7:30-10am & 5-9pm Wed-Mon) The top-shelf restaurant at the **Hotel Moana** (☑2640-0230, toll-free in USA 888-865-8032; r standard/deluxe US$110/145, ste US$245-275, all incl breakfast; P❋☎☀) is on a stunning perch and has jaw-dropping views and Latin-inspired tapas. The emphasis on local ingredients results in delights such as beef braised in chili and coffee, and seafood skewers in habanero-and-passion-fruit glaze. If you're wondering how much to order, two tapas per person should do the trick.

Brisas Del Mar Seafood $$$

(☑2640-0941; Playa El Carmen; mains US$15-22; ☉8-10pm Mon-Sat; P) It's worth the steep climb for sensational views and fancy-looking seafood at the poolside patio restaurant at the Hotel Buenos Aires. Begin with a specialty cocktail as you peruse the day's menu written on the blackboard. Look for fresh *fruits de mer* prepared with international influences; it's almost always fantastic. Cash only.

🍷 DRINKING & NIGHTLIFE

Roca Mar Bar

(☑2640-0250; Santa Teresa; ☉noon-9pm; 🛜) Tucked away at the Blue Surf Sanctuary hotel at the northern end of town, this pretty perfect beach lounge attracts a local expat crowd. Beanbags are stuck in the sand, and hammocks are slung in the trees – all perfectly positioned for sunset. There's an official Sunset Party on Sunday evening – a family-friendly event with live music and fire dancers.

Nativo Sports Bar Sports Bar

(☑2640-0356; www.facebook.com/Nativo SportsBar; Playa El Carmen; ☉11:30am-11pm) Fans above (to cool the place), *fanaticos* below, watching every manner of sport on the four big screens. Baseball, hockey, and of course *fútbol* are all on the offing. For a sports bar, though, there are a variety of food options besides the burger/nacho path: smoothies packed with fruits and vegetables, as well as hummus and salads.

La Lora Amarilla Club

(☑2640-0132; Santa Teresa; ☉noon-2am) There are only four words you need to know: Thursday night reggae party. Come to this enormous concrete hangar – dive bar and dance club in one – to party like you're in the tropics. Santa Teresa's main surf break is named after this bar, as it's just down the dirt road from here.

❶ GETTING THERE & AWAY

The southern Península de Nicoya roads leading to Santa Teresa and Mal País are improving. Nonetheless, whether you catch the bus/ferry, get a lift from a private shuttle or opt to drive yourself, be prepared for a bumpy ride for the last few miles.

❶ GETTING AROUND

Santa Teresa and Mal País are dirt-road types of towns: during the dry season, life gets extremely dusty. The preponderance of ATVs stirs up more grit (and the ire of locals) so consider using a bicycle to get around town, to avoid contributing to the problem. If you must drive, please go slowly. Taxis between Mal País, Playa El Carmen and Santa Teresa range from US$4 to US$8.

Montezuma

◎ SIGHTS

Playa Montezuma Beach

The best beach close to town is just to the north, where the sand is powdery and

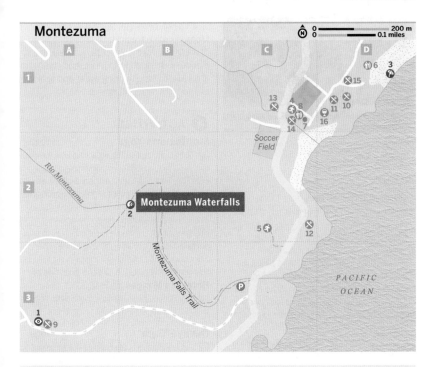

Montezuma

⊙ Sights
1 Montezuma Gardens.................................A3
2 Montezuma Waterfalls............................B2
3 Playa Montezuma.....................................D1

Activities, Courses & Tours
4 Devaya Yoga..C1
5 Montezuma Yoga..C2
6 Peaks & Swells Surf Camp.....................D1
7 Sun Trails..C1
8 Young Vision Surf School........................C1

⊗ Eating
9 Clandestina...A3
10 Cocolores...D1
11 Orgánico...D1
12 Playa de los Artistas................................C2
13 Puggo's..C1
14 Soda El Balcón del Mar...........................C1
15 The Bakery...D1

Drinking & Nightlife
16 Chico's Bar...D1

sheltered from big swells. This is your glorious sun-soaked crash pad. The water's shade of teal is immediately nourishing, the temperature is perfect and fish are abundant. At the north end of the beach, look for the trail that leads to a cove known as Piedra Colorada. A small waterfall forms a freshwater pool, which is a perfect swimming spot.

Playa Grande Beach
About 7km north of town, Playa Grande is the best surf beach in the area. It's a 3km-plus stretch of waves and sand, which never

gets too crowded as it requires a 30-minute hike to get here. But what a hike it is, wandering along between the turquoise waters of the Pacific and the lush greenery of the Montezuma Biological Reserve.

Playa Cocolito Beach
Here's your chance to see a waterfall crashing down a cliff, straight onto the rocks and into the ocean. El Chorro Waterfall is the pièce de résistance of Playa Cocolito, which is itself pretty irresistible.

Yoga

Many surfers know that yoga is the perfect antidote to their sore flippers. Several studios in the area offer drop-in classes.

Casa Zen (⌨2640-0523; www.zencosta rica.com; Santa Teresa; classes per person US$9) Three daily classes take place in a lovely second-story, open-air studio, surrounded by trees. Most of the classes are a hatha-inspired Vinyasa flow, but there's also cardio fit and other styles. Yoga by candlelight is a sublime way to transition from day to night. Multi-class packages are available. Located behind the Plaza Royal.

Yoga Studio at Nautilus (⌨2640-0991; www.hotelnautiluscostarica.com; Santa Teresa; group/private classes US$14/60; ⊙9am & 6pm) What's not to love about rooftop yoga? Twice-daily classes are held on the deck at the Nautilus Boutique Hotel (⌨2640-0991; www.hotelnautiluscostarica. com; Santa Teresa; villa d/q US$165/270; P✱🛜🏊), offering lovely views over the village. It offers Vinyasa flow and kundalini, power and restorative yoga. Look for the Nautilus or Canaima Chill House signs.

Horizon Yoga Hotel (⌨2640-0524; www. horizon-yogahotel.com; Calle Buenos Aires, Santa Teresa; classes per person US$15) Offers two classes daily, in a serene environment overlooking the ocean. As with other schools, weekly and other passes are available.

It's a hot, two-hour, 12km hike from Montezuma: leave at sun rise to spot plenty of wildlife along the way. Alternatively, this is a popular destination for horseback riding. In any case, be sure to bring water and snacks as there are no facilities here.

🎯 ACTIVITIES

Montezuma Yoga   Yoga

(⌨8704-1632, 2642-1311; www.montezumayoga. com; per person US$14; ⊙8:30am Mon-Fri, 6pm Tue, Wed, Sat & Sun) Anusara-inspired instruction, which pairs Iyengar alignment principles with a Vinyasa flow, is available in a gorgeous studio kissed by ocean breezes, sheltered by a peaked tin roof and serenaded by the sounds of nature. The Sunday-night candlelight class is a close-to-heaven experience. On the grounds of **Hotel Los Mangos** (⌨2642-0076; www. hotellosmangos.com; r with/without bathroom US$75/35, bungalows US$90; P✱🛜🏊).

Devaya Yoga   Yoga

(⌨8833-5086; www.devayayoga.com; classes US$12; ⊙classes 8:30am & 4pm Mon-Sat) A studio smack in the middle of town, up-stairs from Pizzeria L'Angolo Allegro. Offers morning and afternoon classes, as well as massage therapy and astrology readings.

**Young Vision
Surf School**   Surfing

(⌨8669-6835; www.youngvisionsurf.com; 2hr lessons US$45) Manny and Alvaro get rave reviews for their knowledge, enthusiasm and patience with new surfers of all ages. Daily lessons take place on Playa Grande, with no more than three people in the class. Surfboard, rash guard and fresh fruit are included. They also offer weeklong camps specifically for families, surfer chicks and yogis. Inquire at **Sano Banano** (⌨2642-0523; www.elsanobanano.com; s/d/ tr/q US$80/86/108/130; P✱🛜) for details.

**Peaks & Swells
Surf Camp**   Surfing

(⌨2642-0067; www.surfcamppeaksnswells.com; 7-day camp per person US$2950; 🛏) Weeklong camps that are geared to women, families and mountain bikers. If one of these is you, here's a chance to learn how to surf, following systematic methods of instruction. Located on the beach, just north of 'downtown' Montezuma.

✖ EATING

Montezuma is experiencing the same food revolution that is taking place on other parts of the peninsula. Local ingredients are meeting international chefs, with magnificent results. Montezuma is also good for traditional Tico fare, often with ocean-side service.

The Bakery Costa Rican $

(Restaurante y Panadería; ⊗6am-10pm) A gentle feeling permeates this no-frills Tico family operation on the beach road, adorned with Hindu tapestries and a mural of the nearby beach. It's cheap, too, and you'll love the refreshing *batidos* (fruit shakes), as well as the filling *casados* and *arrozes* (rice dishes). Early risers go for the homemade pancakes or French toast.

Soda El Balcón del Mar Seafood $

(www.facebook.com/sodaelbalcondelmar; mains US$8-12; ⊗7am-midnight) Hang out below the Tico-themed red-white-and-blue Chinese lanterns on the balcony overlooking the beach, watch flocks of pelicans drift by and kiss the afternoon goodbye. Llip-smacking appetizers include mussels and clams, and you can get a whole-fish catch of the day if that's your thing. Located across from the taxi stand.

Cocolores International $$

(☑2642-0348; mains US$9-22; ⊗5-10pm Tue-Sun) Set on a beachside terrace lit with lanterns, Cocolores is one of Montezuma's top spots for an upscale dinner. The wide-ranging menu includes curries, pasta, fajitas and steaks, all prepared and served with careful attention to delicious details. Prices aren't cheap but it's worth it.

Tierra y Fuego Italian $$

(☑2642-1593; mains US$8-15; ⊗5-10pm; P ✎ ⍟) Take a taxi up to this gem in the hills above Montezuma – fittingly in

Playa Montezuma (p192)

YADID LEVY/GETTY IMAGES ©

Puntarenas-Paquera Ferry

Car and passenger ferries bound for Paquera and Playa Naranjo depart several times a day from the **northwestern dock** (Av 3 btwn Calles 31 & 33) in Puntarenas. If you are driving and will be taking the car ferry, arrive at the dock early to get in line. The vehicle section tends to fill up quickly and you may not make it on. In addition, make sure that you have purchased your ticket from the walk-up ticket window before driving onto the ferry. You will not be admitted onto the boat if you don't already have a ticket.

Schedules change seasonally and can be affected by inclement weather. Check with the ferry office by the dock for any changes. Many of the hotels in town also have up-to-date schedules posted.

Coonatramar (☑2661-1069; www. coonatramar.com; adult/child US$2/1.10, car/bike US$18/4) has daily departures to Playa Naranjo (for transfer to Nicoya and points west) at 6:30am, 10am, 2:30pm and 7pm.

Naviera Tambor (☑2661-2084; www. navieratambor.com; adult/child US$1.60/1, car/bike US$23/4.40) has daily departures to Paquera (for transfer to Montezuma and Mal País) at 5am, 9am, 11am, 2pm, 5pm and 8:30pm.

the Delicias neighborhood. This Italian outpost seems straight out of the Tuscan countryside, with brick ovens, and chickens roasting over the fire. The menu is mostly pizza and pasta, but the flavors are divine – not surprising given the ingredients are all imported or grown onsite.

Puggo's   Middle Eastern $$
(☑8705-1077, 2642-0325; Ruta 624; mains US$10-20; ☺5-11pm) A locally beloved restaurant decorated like a bedouin tent, Puggo's specializes in Middle Eastern cuisine, including falafel, hummus, kebabs and aromatic fish, which are dressed in imported spices and herbs and roasted whole. Cap it off with a strong cup of Turkish coffee.

Puggo's is located just before the soccer field, heading south of town.

Orgánico   Vegetarian $$
(☑2642-1322; www.organicocostarica.com; mains US$8-12; ☺8am-10pm; ☑) When they say 'pure food made with love,' they mean it – this healthy cafe turns out vegetarian and vegan dishes such as spicy Thai burgers, smoothies named for icons like Marley and Hendrix (try the Purple Haze) and more (as well as meaty options, too). Opposite the church square, on the road leading north to the beach.

The avocado ice cream is something everyone should try. There's live music almost nightly, including a wildly popular open mic on Monday nights.

Clandestina   Latin American $$
(Cocina Hispanoamericana; ☑8315-8003; www. facebook.com/clandestinamontezuma; mains US$8-12; ☺noon-9pm Tue-Sat; ☑☑) The secret is out. The hottest restaurant in Montezuma is this awesome, artistic place in the trees at the butterfly gardens. Look for innovative takes on Central American standards, such as daily changing taco specials and delectable chicken mole enchiladas. Vegetarians are joyfully accommodated with yam and lentil cakes or *chilles rellenos* (stuffed peppers). Try the Butterfly Beer, brewed onsite.

Playa de los Artistas   International $$$
(☑2642-0920; www.montezumabeach.com/ playa-de-los-artistas; mains US$9-18; ☺4:30-

Montezuma

8:30pm Tue-Fri, from noon Sat) Most romantic dinner ever. If you're lucky, you'll snag one of the tree-trunk tables under the palms. The international menu with Mediterranean influences changes daily, though you can always count on fresh seafood roasted in the wood oven. The service is flawless, the cooking is innovative and the setting is downright dreamy. Cash only (back to reality), so bring lots.

🍷 DRINKING & NIGHTLIFE

Chico's Bar   Bar
(⊘11am-2am) When it comes to nightlife, Chico's is the main game in town, which means that everybody – old, young, Ticos, tourists, rowdy, dowdy – ends up here

eventually, especially on Thursday night, which is reggae night. Snag a table on the back patio for a lovely view of the beach and beyond. On the main road parallel to the beach.

ℹ️ GETTING THERE & AWAY

The easiest way to reach Montezuma is to abandon your own vehicle and hop on a boat shuttle from Jacó. It's also manageable by bus/ferry or car, and the road into town is now paved. Newer shuttle services offer a more convenient service between Montezuma and other peninsula towns, as far as Liberia airport and beyond in some cases. Interbus (www.interbuscostarica.com) and **Tropical Tours** (📋2640 1900, Whatsapp 8890 9197; www.tropicaltourshuttles.com) are the most notable.

MONTEVERDE

Monteverde at a Glance...

Spread out on the slopes of the Cordillera de Tilarán, this area is a sprawling chain of villages, farms and nature reserves. The Reserva Biológica Bosque Nuboso Monteverde is the most famous one, but there are properties of all shapes and sizes – from tiny family farms to the vast Bosque Eterno de los Niños – that blanket the area in luscious green. As a result, there are trails to hike, birds to spot, waterfalls to swim and adventures to be had at every turn.

Two Days in Monteverde

For your first day, register in advance for a guided tour at the **Bosque Nuboso Monteverde** (p202), taking time afterward to explore independently. Your second day is devoted to getting your adventure on, either flying through the treetops on a **canopy tour** (p208) or climbing trees and canyoning down waterfalls at **Finca Modelo Ecologica** (p215). Don't miss dinner in a fig tree at **Tree House Restaurant** (p219).

Four Days in Monteverde

On your third day, visit a local farm for an enlightening (and energizing) coffee tour. When the sun sets, check out the area nightlife on a night tour at **Bosque Eterno de los Niños** (p213) or **Santuario Ecológico** (p214). Use your final day to learn about bugs at the **Butterfly Garden** (p210) followed by lunch at **Orchid Coffee** (p217).

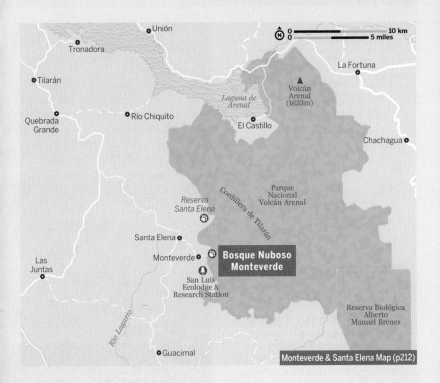

Monteverde & Santa Elena Map (p212)

Arriving in Monteverde

There is no easy way to get to Monteverde and the surrounding environs – by bus or by car, you're in for a bumpy ride. There are three access roads to Santa Elena – to the north via Tilarán, to the west via Las Juntas, and to the south via Guacimal – but all are only partially paved and require at least an hour of winding and bumping up the mountain. That's all supposed to change when the widening and paving of the southern route is completed; work was in progress at the time of research in 2017.

Sleeping

Many lodgings are clustered in the villages of Santa Elena and Monteverde, but many more dot the landscape in the hills above Santa Elena and beyond. Before booking, consider carefully how remote you want to be (and whether or not you'll have your own vehicle). This area has a huge variety of accommodations at all price levels.

Canopy walkway, Bosque Nuboso Monteverde

Bosque Nuboso Monteverde

Here is a virgin forest dripping with mist, dangling with mossy vines, sprouting with ferns and bromeliads, gushing with creeks, blooming with life and nurturing rivulets of evolution.

Great For...

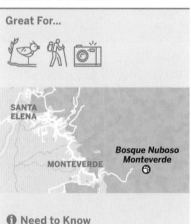

❶ Need to Know

Monteverde Cloud Forest Wildlife Biological Reserve; ☑2645-5122; www.reservamonte verde.com; adult/student/under 6yr US$20/10/free; ☺7am-4pm

★ Top Tip

The reserve's walking trails are almost always muddy, even during the dry season. Bring your boots!

History

This beautiful reserve came into being in 1972 when the Quaker community, spurred on by the threat of encroaching squatters, joined forces with environmental and wildlife organizations to purchase and protect an extra 328 hectares (811 acres) of land. This fragile environment relies almost entirely on public donations to survive. Today, the reserve totals 10,500 hectares (25,946 acres).

Plan Ahead

Due to its fragile environment, the reserve allows a maximum of 160 people at any given time, which is usually reached by 10am in the dry season. Make reservations for a spot on a tour, or arrive before the gates open.

Hiking

There are 13km of marked and maintained trails – a free map is provided with your entrance fee. The three most popular trails, suitable for day hikes, make a rough triangle, El Triángulo, to the east of the reserve entrance. The triangle sides are made up of the popular Sendero Bosque Nuboso, a 1.9km interpretive walk through the cloud forest that begins at the ranger station, paralleled by the more open, 2km El Camino, a favorite of bird-watchers. Sendero Pantanoso forms the far side of El Triángulo, traversing swamps, pine forests and the continental divide. Sendero Río follows the Quebrada Cuecha past a few photogenic waterfalls.

Bisecting the triangle, the gorgeous Chomogo Trail (1.8km) lifts hikers to 1680m, the highest point within the triangle. Other little trails crisscross the region, including the worthwhile Sendero Brillante (300m), with bird's-eye views of a miniature forest. The trail to the Mirador La Ventana (elevation 1550m) is moderately steep and leads

> ✗ **Take a Break**
> Stop at Cafe Colibrí (p220) for a post-hike snack and to snap some hummingbird photos.

further afield to a wooden deck overlooking the continental divide.

Wildlife-Watching

Monteverde is a bird-watching paradise, with the list of recorded species topping out at about 500. The resplendent quetzal is most often spotted during the March and April nesting season, though you may get lucky any time of year. Keep your ears open for the three-wattled bellbird, a kind of cotinga that is famous for its distinctive call. If you're keen on birds, a bird tour is highly recommended.

For those interested in spotting mammals, the cloud forest's limited visibility and abundance of higher primates (human beings) can make wildlife-watching quite difficult. That said, there are some commonly sighted species, including coatis,

Shelf fungus

howler monkeys, capuchins, sloths, agoutis and squirrels (as in 'real' squirrel, not the squirrel monkey). Most animals avoid the main trails, so get off the beaten track.

Tours

Although you can (and should) hike around the reserve on your own, a guide provides an informative overview and enhances your experience. Make reservations at least a day in advance for park-run tours. The English-speaking guides are trained naturalists; proceeds benefit environmental education programs in local schools. The reserve can also recommend guides for private tours.

Bird-watching (☏2645-5112; per person incl entry fee US$64; ⊙tours depart 6am) These early-morning walks usually last four to five hours (for three to six people), checking off as many as 40 species of birds (out of a possible 500).

Natural History (☏2645-5122, reservations 2645-5112; adult/student excl entry fee US$37/27; ⊙tours depart 7:30am, 11am & 1:30pm) Take a 2½- to three-hour guided walk in the woods. You'll learn all about the characteristics of a cloud forest and identify some of its unique flora. Your ticket is valid for the entire day, so you can continue to explore on your own when the tour is over.

Night Tours (☏2645-5122; www.reserva monteverde.com; with/without transportation US$25/20; ⊙tours depart 5:45pm) Observe the 70% of regional wildlife that has nocturnal habits. Tours are by flashlight (bring your own for the best visibility).

☑ Don't Miss

The magical, misty view from the Continental Divide.

NWE PHOTOGRAPHY/SHUTTERSTOCK ©

Coffee beans

Coffee Tours

If you're curious about the magical brew that for many makes life worth living, tour one of the coffee plantations and learn all about how Costa Rica's golden bean goes from plant to cup.

Great For...

☑ **Don't Miss**

Taking a ride in a traditional ox cart.

Tour Operators

Café de Monteverde

Stop by the **shop** (☎2645-7550; www.cafede monteverde.com; Monteverde; tour per person US$18; ☺coffee tasting 7:30am-4.30pm, tours 8am & 1:30pm) ⚑ in Monteverde to take a crash course in coffee and sample the delicious blends. Or, sign on for the three-hour tour on sustainable agriculture, which visits organic fincas implementing techniques like composting and solar energy. Learn how coffee growing has helped to shape this community and how it can improve the local environment. Kind of makes you want to pour yourself another cup!

El Trapiche

Visit this picturesque family **finca** (☎2645-7650; www.eltrapichetour.com; Santa Elena; adult/child US$32/12; ☺tours 10am & 3pm

NICK PEDERSEN/GETTY IMAGES ©

STIG STOCKHOLM PEDERSEN/GETTY IMAGES ©

Don Juan Coffee Tour

Three-in-one tours by **Don Juan** (☎2645-7100; www.donjuancoffeetour.com; Santa Elena; adult/child US$35/15, night tour US$40/20; ⏱7am-4:30pm, tours 8am, 1pm & 6pm) cover all your favorite vices (OK, maybe not all your favorites, but three of the good ones). It's a pretty cursory overview of how sugarcane is harvested and processed; how cacao beans are transformed into dark, decadent chocolate; and how coffee happens, from plant to bean to cup.

Chocolate, Too!

And if you're not a coffee drinker, try the **Caburé Chocolate Tour** (☎2645-5020; www.cabure.net; Monteverde; per person US$15; ⏱tours 1pm & 4pm Mon-Sat). Bob, the owner of the Caburé chocolate shop in Monteverde, shares his secrets about the magical cacao pod and how to transform it into the food of the gods. There are plenty of opportunities for taste testing along the way, and you'll try your hand at making truffles.

Mon-Sat, 3pm Sun) in Santa Elena, where they grow not only coffee but also sugarcane, bananas and plantains. See the coffee process firsthand, take a ride in a traditional ox cart, and try your hand at making sugar. Bonus: lots of samples along the way, including sugarcane liquor, sugarcane toffee and – of course – delicious coffee. Kids love this one.

Coopeldós RL

Coopeldós (☎2693-8441; www.coopeldos. com) 🌿 is a cooperative of 450 small- and medium-sized organic coffee-growers from the area. You can visit this co-op store and buy their coffee in the village of El Dós de Tilarán, about halfway between Tilarán and Monteverde. Or, you might even drink Coopeldós blends back home – this Fairtrade-certified organization sells to Starbucks, among other clients.

Ziplining

DREAMPICTURES/SHANNON FAULK ©

Canopy Tours

The wild-eyed faces and whoop-de-whoop soundtrack are all the proof you need: clipping into a high-speed cable and soaring across the treetops is pure joy.

Santa Elena is the site of Costa Rica's first ziplines, today eclipsed in adrenaline by the many imitators who have followed. If you came to Costa Rica to fly, this is the absolute best place to do it.

Original Canopy Tour

The storied zipline **tour** (☎2645-5243; www.theoriginalcanopy.com; adult/student/child US$45/35/25; ⏰Tours 7:30am, 10:30am & 2:30pm) that started the trend. With 15 cables, a Tarzan swing and a rappel through the center of an old fig tree, it's a lot more fun than most history museums. Your adrenaline rush may not be as big as at some of the other canopy tours, but you'll enjoy smaller groups and more emphasis on the natural surroundings.

Great For...

☑ **Don't Miss**

Howling like Tarzan as you sail through the jungle on the aptly named swing.

SkyTrek

This seriously fast canopy tour consists of 11 platforms attached to steel towers that are spread out along a road and zoom over swatches of primary forest. We're talking serious speeds of up to 64km/h, which is probably why **SkyTrek** (☑2479-4100, toll free USA 1-804-GOTOSKY; www.skyadventures. travel; Santa Elena; adult/student/child SkyWalk US$39/32/27, SkyTrek US$81/67/56; ☺7:30am-5pm) was the first canopy tour with a real brake system. The SkyWalk is a 2km guided tour over five suspended bridges; a night tour is also available.

100% Aventura

Aventura (☑2645-6388; www.aventura canopytour.com; Rte 619, Santa Elena; canopy tour adult/child US$50/40, bridges US$35/30; ☺tours 8am, 11am, 1pm & 3pm) boasts the longest zipline in Latin America (which is nearly 1600m). The 19 platforms are spiced up with a Tarzan swing, a 15m rappel and a Superman zipline that makes you feel as if you really are flying. They also have a network of suspension bridges, laced through secondary forest. Reservations required.

Original Canopy is located way uphill near the Cloud Forest Lodge, 2km off the main Santa Elena–Monteverde Rd.

Selvatura

One of the bigger games in town, **Selvatura** (☑2645-5929; www.selvatura.com; canopy tour US$50, walkways US$30, each exhibit US$5-15; ☺7:30am-4pm) has 3km of cables, 18 platforms and one Tarzan swing over a stretch of incredibly beautiful primary cloud forest. In addition to the cables, it has 3km of 'Treetops Walkways,' as well as a hummingbird garden, a butterfly garden and an amphibian and reptile exhibition.

Selvatura is 6km north of Santa Elena, near the reserve. There's a booking office in town near the church.

Monteverde & Santa Elena

Strung between two lovingly preserved cloud forests, this slim corridor of civilization consists of the Tico village of Santa Elena and the Quaker settlement of Monteverde, each with an eponymous cloud forest reserve. The cloud forests are premier destinations for everyone from budget backpackers to well-heeled retirees.

On a good day, the Monteverde area is a place where you can be inspired about the possibility of a world in which organic farming and alternative energy sources are the norm; on a bad day, it can feel like Disneyland in Birkenstocks. Take heart in the fact that the local community continues to fight the good fight to maintain the fragile balance between nature and commerce.

◎ SIGHTS

The sights in Monteverde and Santa Elena are mostly geared to bringing the wildlife a little closer, whether it's bats, butterflies, frog, snakes or flowers. These stops can be entertaining and educational – especially for children – but it's even more rewarding when you see these creatures in the wild. And you're in the wild now, so go out there and see it.

Butterfly Garden   Zoo
(Jardín de Mariposas; ☏2645-5512; www.monte verdebutterflygarden.com; Cerro Plano; adult/student/child US$15/10/5; ⊗8:30am-4pm) Head here for everything you ever wanted to know about butterflies. There are four gardens representing different habitats; they're home to more than 40 species. Up-close observation cases allow you to witness the butterflies as they emerge from the chrysalis (if your timing is right). Other exhibits feature the industrious leafcutter ant and the ruthless tarantula hawk (actually a wasp that eats tarantulas) and lots of scorpions. Kids love this place, and knowledgeable naturalist guides truly enhance the experience.

Ranario   Zoo
(Monteverde Frog Pond; ☏2645-6320; Santa Elena; per attraction US$14, package ticket US$23, night tour US$30; ⊗9am-4:30pm, frog

Orchids

IMAGES ETC LTD/GETTY IMAGES ©

pond to 8pm) Returning to its former glory as the Ranario, or Frog Pond (it's changed names a few times), this place has added an insect house and a butterfly garden. The frogs are still the highlight – about 25 species reside in transparent enclosures lining the winding indoor jungle paths. Sharp-eyed guides point out frogs, eggs and tadpoles with flashlights. Your ticket entitles you to two visits, so come back in the evening to see the nocturnal species.

San Luis Ecolodge
& Research Station Nature Reserve
(www.ecolodgesanluis.com; San Luis) Formerly a tropical biology research station, this drop-dead gorgeous facility is Monteverde's best-kept secret. Administered by the University of Georgia, it integrates academia with high-quality ecotourism and education. The 62-hectare campus is set on a cinematic jade plateau with cloud forested mountains jackknifing on three sides and keyhole sea views to the west. Travelers can soak up this stunning natural beauty when they stay at the **Ecolodge San Luis** (University of Georgia (UGA) Costa Rica; ☑2645-7363; San Luis; dm/s/d incl meals US$60/90/180; Ⓟ@🛜).

Monteverde
Friends School Cultural Centre
(www.mfschool.org; Monteverde; per person US$15; ⊗tours 8am Tue & Fri; 👬) Spending time at this schoolhouse is a great way for children to learn about and interact with the local culture. With advance reservation, visitors can sit in on morning assembly and tour the grounds. Kids are even invited to attend a class (and recess!) with an English-speaking buddy.

Jardín de Orquídeas Gardens
(Orchid Garden; ☑2645-5308; www.monte verdeorchidgarden.net; Santa Elena; adult/child over 6yr/under 6yr US$12/6/free; ⊗8am-5pm) This sweet-smelling garden in Santa Elena has shady trails winding past more than 400 types of orchids. On your guided tour, you'll see such rarities as *Platystele jungermannioides*, the world's

🍽 Monteverde
Cheese Factory

The **factory** (La Lechería; ☑2645-7090; www.monteverdecheesefactory.com; Monteverde; ⊗7:30am-5pm Mon-Sat, to 4pm Sun) was started in 1953 by Monteverde's original Quaker settlers. The factory produces everything from a creamy Gouda to a very nice sharp white cheddar, as well as other dairy products such as yogurt and, most importantly, ice cream. Don't miss the chance to sample Monte Rico, a Monteverde original. Sadly, it no longer offers tours.

Until the upswing in ecotourism, this was Monteverde's number one employer. The Monteverde Cheese Factory is the second-largest cheese producer in the country. Now owned by the Mexican giant Sigma Alimentos, the factory still uses the original name and recipes.

WESTEND61/GETTY IMAGES ©

smallest orchid. If you have orchids at home, here's your chance to get expert tips on how to keep them beautiful and blooming. If you're expecting massive sprays of colorful blooms, though, think again – most specimens require the magnifying glass given to you at the entrance to be seen.

Bat Jungle Zoo
(☑2645-7701; www.batjungle.com; Monteverde; adult/child US$13/11; ⊗9am-7pm) The Bat Jungle in Monteverde is a small but informative exhibit, with good bilingual educational displays and a habitat housing almost 100 free-flying bats. Make

Monteverde & Santa Elena

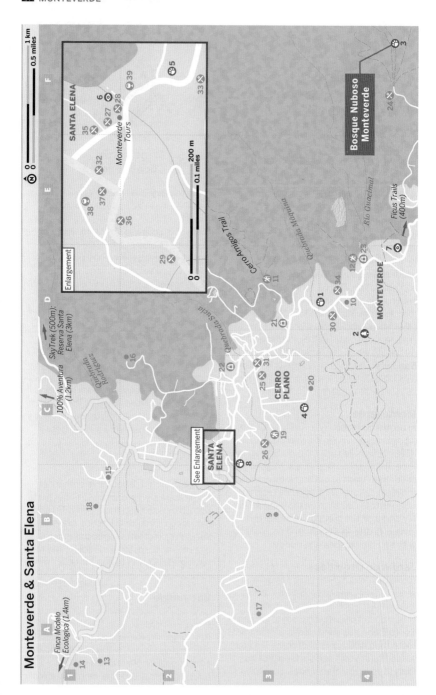

Bosque Nuboso
Monteverde

SANTA ELENA

Monteverde
Tours

CERRO
PLANO

SANTA
ELENA

See Enlargement

MONTEVERDE

Enlargement

Cerro Amigos Trail

Quebrada Sucia

Quebrada Montaña

Quebrada
Rodríguez

Río Guacimal

Finca Modelo
Ecológica (1.4km)

100% Aventura
(1.2km)

SkyTrek (500m);
Reserva Santa
Elena (3km)

Ficus Trails
(400m)

Monteverde & Santa Elena

Sights
1 Bat Jungle D4
2 Bosque Eterno de los Niños D4
3 Bosque Nuboso Monteverde F4
4 Butterfly Garden C3
5 Herpetarium Adventure F2
6 Jardín de Orquídeas F1
7 Monteverde Friends School D4
8 Ranario C3

Activities, Courses & Tours
9 Caballeriza El Rodeo B3
Caburé Chocolate Tour .... (see 1)
10 Café de Monteverde D4
11 Cerro Amigos D3
12 Curi-Cancha Reserve D4
13 Don Juan Coffee Tour A1
14 El Trapiche A1
15 Horse Trek Monteverde B1
16 Original Canopy Tour C2
Reserva Bajo del Tigre .... (see 2)
17 Sabine's Smiling Horses A3
18 Santa Maria Night Walk B1
19 Santuario Ecológico C3
20 Valle Escondido C3

Shopping
Casem .... (see 10)
21 Luna Azul D3
22 Monteverde Art House C3
23 Monteverde Cheese Factory D4

Eating
Café Caburé .... (see 1)
24 Cafe Colibrí F4
25 d'Sofia C3
26 El Jardín C3
27 Morpho's Restaurant F1
28 Orchid Coffee F1
29 Passi Flora D2
30 Pizzería Tramonti D4
31 Quimera's C3
32 Raulito's Pollo Asado E1
33 Sabor Tico F2
34 Stella's Bakery D4
35 Taco Taco F1
36 Toro Tinto E2
37 Tree House Restaurant & Café E1
Whole Foods Market .... (see 10)

Drinking & Nightlife
38 Bar Amigos E1
39 Monteverde Beer House F2

a reservation for your 45-minute tour to learn about echolocation, bat wing aerodynamics and other amazing flying mammal facts.

The bats are on a reversed day/night schedule so they are most active from 9am to 5pm.

ACTIVITIES

In addition to the two biggies anchoring this area at the north and south, Monteverde and Santa Elena are home to dozens of smaller private reserves and the 220 sq km Bosque Eterno de los Niños (Children's Eternal Rainforest). The Monteverde (p202) and Santa Elena (p214) reserves are special – very special – because they are essentially the only cloud forest reserves in the area. But if you want to immerse yourself in nature, get some exercise, spot some monkeys, admire a scenic vista or cool off in a waterfall, there are countless places to do so (most of which will be significantly less crowded than the Monteverde reserve).

Curi-Cancha Reserve — Hiking, Bird-watching

(☎2645-6915, 8356-1431; www.curi-cancha.com; US$15, night tour US$18, natural history tour US$35, bird tour US$75; ⏰7am-3:30pm, guided hike 7:30am & 1:30pm) Bordering Monteverde but without the crowds, this lovely private reserve on the banks of the Río Cuecha is popular among birders. There are about 10km of well-marked trails, a hummingbird garden and a view of the continental divide. Make reservations for the guided hikes, including the early-morning bird walks and specialized three-hour natural history walks.

Bosque Eterno de los Niños — Nature Reserve

(Children's Eternal Rainforest, BEN; ☎2645-5305; www.acmcr.org; adult/child US$12/free, guided night hike US$22/14, transportation per person US$4; ⏰7:30am-5:30pm, night hike

 Santa Elena Reserve

Though Monteverde's cloud forest reserve (p202) gets all the attention, the misty **Reserva Santa Elena** (☑2645-7107, 2645-5390; www.reservasantaelena.org; adult/student US$14/7, guided hike US$15; ⊙7am-4pm) has plenty to recommend it. You can practically hear the epiphyte-draped canopy breathing in as water drops onto the leaf litter and mud underfoot. The odd call of the three-wattled bellbird and the low crescendo of a howler monkey punctuate the higher-pitched bird chatter. While Monteverde entertains almost 200,000 visitors annually, Santa Elena sees fewer than 20,000 tourists each year, meaning its dewy trails are usually far quieter.

This cloud forest is slightly higher in elevation than Monteverde's; as some of the forest is secondary growth, there are sunnier places for spotting birds and other animals. There's a stable population of monkeys and sloths, many of which can be seen on the road to the reserve. Unless you're a trained ecologist, the old-growth forest in Santa Elena will appear fairly similar to that found in Monteverde. At 310 hectares, the community-run **Santa Elena** is much smaller than the **Monteverde forest reserve**. More than 12km of well-marked trails are open for hiking, including four circular trails of varying difficulty and length. Guided hikes (US$15) depart from the reserve four times a day (reservations recommended).

5:30pm; 🐾) ✿ What became of the 1980s efforts of a group of Swedish schoolchildren to save the rainforest? Only this enormous 220 sq km reserve – the largest private reserve in the country. It's mostly inaccessible to tourists, with the exception of the well-marked 3.5km **Sendero Bajo del Tigre** (☑2645-5200; www.acmcr.org/contenido/estaciones-y-senderos/reserva-bajo-del-tigre; adult/student/child US$13/11/8, night hike adult/student/child/transportation US$23/20/14/4; ⊙8am-5pm, night hike 5:30pm; 🐾), which is actually a series of shorter trails. Make reservations in advance for the popular two-hour night hikes.

At the entrance there's an education center for children and a fabulous vista over the reserve.

The Estación Biológica San Gerardo, reachable by a rather gnarly 2½-hour trail from Reserva Santa Elena, is managed by BEN and has dorm beds for researchers and students, but you may be able to stay overnight with prior arrangements.

Santuario Ecológico   Hiking

(Ecological Sanctuary; ☑2645-5869; www.santuarioecologico.com; Cerro Plano; adult/student US$17/14, guided day walk US$30/25, night tour US$27/22; ⊙7am-5:30pm, morning tour 7am, night tour 5:30pm) This smallish sanctuary is set on private property comprising premontane (below mountain) and secondary forest, plus coffee and banana plantations. Descend to an impressive 30m waterfall and cool off with a refreshing dip. These trails are not well trodden – you're more likely to meet a coati or a sloth than another human being. Bird walks and night tours also available.

Cerro Amigos   Hiking

Take a hike up to the highest peak in the area (1842m) for good views of the surrounding rainforest and, on a clear day, Volcán Arenal, 20km away to the northeast. Behind **Hotel Belmar** (☑2645-5201; www.hotelbelmar.net; Cerro Plano; peninsula r US$215-235, deluxe chalets US$249-349, ste US$450-554; 🅿@🛜🏊) ✿ in Cerro Plano, take the dirt road going downhill, then the next left.

View of Volcán Arenal (p226) from Reserva Santa Elena

The trail ascends roughly 300m in 3km. Note that this trail does not connect to the trails in the Monteverde reserve (p202).

Extremo Canopy Adventure

(☑2645-6058; www.monteverdeextremo.com; Santa Elena; canopy tour US$53, bungee US$73, Tarzan swing US$42; ⊙8am-4pm) This place has a canopy ride that allows you to fly Superman-style through the air, the highest and most adrenaline-addled Tarzan swing in the area, and a bungee jump. One way or another, you will scream. While it's located in secondary forest, the views are marvelous but they herd some pretty big groups through here, so it's not exactly a nature experience.

Herpetarium Adventure Zoo

(☑2645-6002; www.skyadventures.travel/herpetarium; Santa Elena; adult/student/child US$15/12/10; ⊙9am-8pm) For those who prefer their reptiles under glass (or at least behind it), a guide will show you around and introduce you to more than 50 species of slithery snakes, frogs, lizards, turtles and other cold-blooded critters. Your ticket entitles you to a return visit after dark, when the nocturnal species come out. Guided tours leave every 90 minutes between noon and 6pm.

TOURS

Finca Modelo Ecologica Adventure

(☑2645-5581; www.familiabrenestours.com; La Cruz; treetop/canyoning/combo US$40/70/100; ⊙treetop 8am-4pm, canyoning 8am, 11am & 2pm) The Brenes family *finca* offers a number of unique and thrilling diversions. Their masterpiece is the two-hour canyoning tour, which descends six glorious waterfalls, the highest of which is 40m. No experience necessary, just an adventurous spirit. The treetop tour involves climbing a 40m ficus tree, using ropes and rappels to go up and down.

The *finca* is located 2km north of Santa Elena in the village of La Cruz; transportation from your hotel is included in the price.

★ **Top Five for Kids**

Selvatura (p209)

Butterfly Garden (p210)

Monteverde Friends School (p211)

El Trapiche (p206)

Ranario (p210)

From left: Butterfly Garden (p210); Two-toed sloth; Hiking through the rainforest

Valle Escondido   Hiking

(Hidden Valley; ☎2645-6601; www.valleescon didopreserve.com; Cerro Plano; day use US$20, night tour adult/child US$25/15; ⏰6am-4:30pm, night tour 5:30pm) Reserve in advance for the popular two-hour guided night tour, then come back the next day to explore the reserve on your own. Located behind Monteverde Inn in Cerro Plano, the well-marked trail winds through a deep canyon into an 11-hectare reserve, passing wonderful vistas and luscious waterfalls.

It's recommended for birding and wildlife-watching during the day, when it's quiet with few tourists.

Santa Maria
Night Walk   Hiking

(☎2645-6548; www.nightwalksantamarias.com; Santa Elena; per person US$25; ⏰tour 5:30pm) Night walks have become so popular because 80 per cent of the cloud forest creatures are nocturnal. This one takes place on a private Santa Elena *finca* with a 10-hectare swath of primary and second-ary forest. Expert guides point out active nocturnal wildlife, ranging from snakes

and spiders to sloths and kinkajous. Flash-lights provided.

Ficus Trails   Hiking

(☎2645-6474; www.ficustrails.com; adult/student/child night hike US$25/20/15, natural history walk US$30/25/20, birding US$45) From the observation deck at this private reserve, you can see from the continental divide down to the San Luis falls, and out to the Golfo de Nicoya. The varied altitude means it's home to a huge diversity of flo-ra and fauna, some of which you can spot on daily bird walks and night hikes.

Tour guides are attentive and patient, guaranteeing a worthwhile experience, but the bird tour seems a bit short for what you're paying.

Take the road to San Luis and follow the signs, or organize a pickup from your hotel.

🛍 SHOPPING

Luna Azul   Jewelry

(☎2645-6638; www.facebook.com/lunaazul monteverde; Cerro Plano; ⏰9am-6pm Mon-Sat,

DREAMPICTURES/SHANNON FAULK/GETTY IMAGES ©

from 10:30am Sun) This super-cute gallery and gift shop is packed to the gills with jewelry, clothing, soaps, sculpture and macramé, among other things. Owner Stephanie's jewelry in particular is stylish and stunning, crafted from silver, shell, crystals and turquoise.

Monteverde
Art House
Arts & Crafts

(Casa de Arte; ☑2645-5275; www.facebook. com/monteverde.arthouse; Cerro Plano; ⊘9am-6pm) You'll find several rooms stuffed with colorful Costa Rican artistry here. The goods include jewelry, ceramic work, Boruca textiles and traditional handicrafts. There's a big variety of offerings, including some paintings and more contemporary work, but it's mostly at the crafts end of the arty-crafty spectrum. Great for souvenirs.

Casem
Arts & Crafts

(Cooperativa de Artesanía Santa Elena Monteverde; ☑2645-5190; www.casemcoop.blogspot. com; Monteverde; ⊘8am-5pm) Begun in 1982 as a women's cooperative representing eight female artists, today Casem has ex-panded to reportedly include almost 150 local artisans (eight of whom are men). It's a nice story, but there's a rather underwhelming selection of stuff, including embroidered clothing, painted handbags, polished wooden tableware and some bookmarks and greeting cards. It's right near the Whole Foods Market (p221) in Monteverde.

EATING

The kitchens of Santa Elena and Monteverde offer high quality but poor value. You'll be delighted by the organic ingredients, local flavors and international zest, but not by the high price tags. Even the local *sodas* (places serving counter lunches) and bakeries are more expensive than they ought to be. Santa Elena has the most budget options.

Santa Elena

Orchid Coffee
Cafe $

(☑2645-6850; www.orchidcoffeecr.com; Santa Elena; mains US$8-12; ⊘7am-7pm; 🛜🖋)
Feeling peckish? Go straight to this lovely

Rufous-tailed hummingbird, Bosque Nuboso Monteverde (p202)

Santa Elena cafe, filled with art and light. Grab a seat on the front porch and take a bite of heaven. It calls itself a coffee shop, but there's a full menu of traditional and nontraditional breakfast items, sweet and savory crepes, interesting and unusual salads and thoroughly satisfying sandwiches.

Taco Taco — Mexican $

(🖉5108-0525; www.facebook.com/tacotaco monteverde; Santa Elena; mains US$5-8; ⊗noon-8pm; 🛜) Quick and convenient, this *taquería* (taco stall) offers tasty Tex-Mex tacos, and burritos and quesadillas filled with shredded chicken. There's also slow-roasted short rib, roasted veggies and battered mahimahi. The only difficulty is deciding what to eat (though you really can't go wrong).

Choose from two locations: this, the original deck location in front of **Pensión Santa Elena** (🖉2645-5051; www.pensionsan taelena.com; incl breakfast, d US$32-38, d without bathroom US$28, ste US$45-60; 🅿@🛜), is perfect for people-watching, but the

new two-toned terrace restaurant next to SuperCompro is a step up in comfort.

Passi Flora — Vegetarian $

(🖉2645-6782; Santa Elena; mains US$7-10; ⊗noon-9pm; 🖋) Good for the body, good for the soul and good for the earth. That's what this joint strives for in its menu of vegetarian and vegan delights. It's a pretty comprehensive offering, with sandwiches, salads, pasta, rice and *rollitos* (empanadas). It's all fresh and deliciously satisfying. Look for the Buddha mosaic and you'll know you're in the right place.

Appropriately next to **Casa Tranquilo** (🖉2645-6782; www.casatranquilohostel. com; Santa Elena; dm/d with bathroom/d without bathroom incl breakfast US$12/35/28; 🅿@🛜).

Raulito's Pollo Asado — Chicken $

(🖉8308-0810; Santa Elena; mains US$4-5; ⊗8am-9:30pm) Scrappy street dogs and chatty *taxistas* vie for attention at this porcelain-countered wonder. Watch as golden, crispy morsels are transferred from the spit to your plate with a heap of rice, fries, salad or *gallo pinto* (blended rice and beans). Wash it down with an icy *horchata* (rice milk and cinnamon drink) and still walk away with some beer money.

Sabor Tico   Soda $

(☑2645-5827; www.restaurantesabortico.com; Centro Comercial, Santa Elena; mains US$5-8; ⏱11am-10pm) Ticos and travelers alike rave about this local joint. Look for tasty twists on the standard fare, such as *olla de carne* (beef soup), *chorreadas Ticas* (fried corn cakes with sour cream) and tamales (holiday fare, typically). The *gallos* (soft tortillas with delicious fillings of your choice) are a perfect alternative to the more filling *casados* (set meals) for lunch.

The original down-home location (7am to 9pm) is opposite the soccer field.

Toro Tinto   Steak $$

(☑2645-6252; www.facebook.com/torotinto. cr; Santa Elena; mains $9-14; ⏱noon-10pm) This Argentinean steakhouse lures in customers with soft lighting and a cozy brick-and-wood interior. It keeps them sated with steaks that are perfectly cut and grilled to order, plus unexpected specials and delicious desserts. The wine selection is good – mostly Chilean and Argentine – but pricey. This place will warm your cloud-soaked soul.

Tree House
Restaurant & Café   Cafe $$$

(☑2645-5751; www.treehouse.cr; Santa Elena; mains US$15-22; ⏱11am-10pm; 🛜) It's a fine line between hokey and happy. But this restaurant, built around a half-century-old *higuerón* (fig) tree, definitely raises a smile. There's a menu of well-prepared if overpriced standards, from *ceviche* to *sopa Azteca* (Mexican tortilla soup) to burgers. The service is spot-on. It's a lively space to have a bite, linger over wine and occasionally catch live music.

Cold? Try the Chocolate Tree House, a devilish dash of coffee and chocolate-flavored liqueurs.

 Horseback Riding

Do like the Ticos do and explore the countryside from the saddle of a horse. You don't have to be an expert rider; most companies (and horses) are used to beginners. There are normally several options for routes and duration, ranging from two hours to full days.

Sabine's Smiling Horses (☑2645-6894, 8385-2424; www.horseback-riding-tour. com; 2hr/3hr/all-day ride per person US$45/65/105; ⏱tours 9am, 1pm & 3pm) Conversant in four languages (in addition to equine), Sabine will make sure you're comfortable on your horse, whether you're a novice rider or an experienced cowboy. Her long-standing operation offers a variety of treks including a popular waterfall tour (three hours) and a magical full moon tour (monthly). And yes, the horses really do smile.

Caballeriza El Rodeo (☑2645-6306, 2645-5764; elrodeo02@gmail.com; Santa Elena; per person US$40-60) Based at a local *finca*, this outfit offers tours on private trails through rainforest, coffee plantations and grasslands, with plenty of pauses to spot wildlife and admire the fantastic landscapes. The specialty is a sunset tour to a spot overlooking the Golfo de Nicoya. *¡Que hermoso!*

Horse Trek Monteverde (☑8379-9827; www.horsetrekmonteverde.com; Rte 606, Santa Elena; per person US$49-85; ⏱7am-7pm Mon-Fri, 10am-6pm Sat-Sun) Owner and guide Marvin Anchia is a Santa Elena native, a professional horse trainer and an amateur naturalist who offers an excellent, intimate horseback-riding experience. Choose between two-hour rides through coffee plantations, scenic half-day rides in the cloud forest and all-day cowboy experiences. The horses are well cared for, well trained and a joy to ride.

El Jardín
International $$$

(☏2645-5057; www.monteverdelodge.com; Monteverde Lodge, Santa Elena; lunch US$8-14, dinner US$16-22; ⊗7am-10pm; 🛜) Arguably the 'finest' dining in the area. The menu is wide ranging, always highlighting the local flavors. But these are not your typical *tipica* (traditional plates) – beef tenderloin served on a sugarcane kebab, and pan-fried trout topped with orange sauce. The setting – with windows to the trees – is lovely and the service is superb. Romantics can opt for a private table in the garden. Worth the drive in off the main road.

Morpho's Restaurant
International $$$

(☏2645-7373; www.morphosrestaurant.com; Santa Elena; mains US$8-20; ⊗11am-9pm; 🖋) Dine among gushing waterfalls and fluttering butterflies at this downtown restaurant. Some call it 'romantic,' others call it 'kitschy' – but nobody can dispute the varied menu, which combines local ingredients with gourmet flair. Veggies, a word of caution: the 'veggie burger' is really just an egg sandwich; there are other vegetarian options such as salads, soups and pastas. Your receipt earns a discount to the adjoining orchid garden (p211).

❎ Cerro Plano & Monteverde

Cafe Colibrí
Cafe $

(☏2645-7768; sandwiches US$5-6; ⊗8am-5pm) Just outside the reserve gates, the 'Hummingbird Cafe' is a top-notch spot to refuel after a hike in the woods. The drinks will warm your body, but the sound of dozens of hummingbirds in the garden will delight your heart. Many say the sandwiches are just OK; come for the coffee (US$2) and *colibris* (humming-birds). Great photo ops. An identification board shows the nine species that you're likely to see.

Stella's Bakery
Bakery $$

(☏2645-5560; Monteverde; mains US$8-15; ⊗6:30am-6pm; 🛜) A bakery for birders. Come in the morning for strong coffee and sweet pastries, or later for rich, warming soup, and sandwiches on home-made bread. Plates such as the *huevos rancheros* satisfy, especially with a heap

of passion-fruit cheesecake for dessert. Whenever you come, keep on eye on the bird feeder, which attracts tanagers, motmots and an emerald-green toucanet.

Whole Foods Market
Supermarket $

(Monteverde; ◷7:30am-5:30pm) This is not the Whole Foods you might think it is, but you'll notice some similarities. It's a good but expensive place to pick up fresh produce, as well as spices and other imported ingredients you might not find in the big supermarket.

Café Caburé
Cafe $$

(✐2645-5020; www.cabure.net; Monteverde; lunch US$6-12, dinner US$16-20; ◷9am-8pm Mon-Sat; ☏) This Argentine cafe above the Bat Jungle specializes in creative and delicious everything, from sandwiches on homemade bread and fresh salads, to more elaborate fare such as sea bass in almond sauce or filet mignon with *chimichurri*. Save room for dessert: the chocolate treats are high art. There's a hot chocolate, an Argentine brownie and (yes!) the cafe's Chocolate Tour (p207).

Quimera's
Tapas $

(✐2645-7037; Cerro Plano; tapas US$7-10; ◷11am-11pm) Come to this casual cafe for unexpected creations, such as sea bass in ginger and rum, shrimp skewers in mango sauce, and roasted eggplant with smoked cheese and sun-dried tomatoes. The place promises 'Latin-infused tapas,' but the menu is actually infused with flavors and ingredients from all over the world. Start yourself off with one of the house caipirinhas.

Pizzería Tramonti
Italian $$

(✐2645-6120; www.tramonticr.com; Monteverde; mains US$10-16; ◷11:30am-9:30pm Mon-Sat) Tramonti offers authentic Italian, specializing in fresh seafood, hearty pastas and wood-fired pizzas. With a greenery-filled dining room twinkling with lights, the ambience is relaxed yet romantic. If you're up in Monteverde and don't feel like venturing into town, this is an acceptable, if somewhat noisy, option. Several pizzas and pastas are suitable for vegetarians. There's a decent selection of wines from Italy and Argentina.

★Top Five for Foodies
El Jardín
d'Sofia (p222)
Quimera's
Morpho's Restaurant
Café Caburé

From left: *Casado*; Orchids; Owl butterfly, Bosque Nuboso Monteverde (p202)

JONATHAN GREGSON/LONELY PLANET ©

FRANCESCO RICCARDO IACOMINO/GETTY IMAGES ©

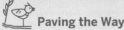

Paving the Way

A 1983 feature article in *National Geographic* billed the Monteverde and Santa Elena area as the place to view one of Central America's most famous birds – the resplendent quetzal. Suddenly, hordes of tourists armed with tripods and telephoto lenses started braving Monteverde's notoriously awful access roads, which came as a huge shock to its Quaker community. In an effort to stem the tourist flow, local communities lobbied to stop developers from paving the roads. It worked for a while, but eventually, the lobby to spur development bested the lobby to limit development. With the paving of the main access road – tentative first steps were being made in 2017 – this precious experiment in sustainable ecotourism will undergo a new set of trials.

Quetzal
CHRISTER FREDRIKSSON/GETTY IMAGES ©

d'Sofia   Fusion $$

(☏2645-7017; Cerro Plano; mains US$12-16; ⏱11:30am-9:30pm; 📶) With its Nuevo Latino cuisine – a modern fusion of traditional Latin American cooking styles – d'Sofia has established itself as one of the best

places in town. Try plantain-crusted sea bass, seafood chimichanga or beef tenderloin with roasted red pepper and cashew sauce. The mood is enhanced by groovy music, picture windows, romantic candle lighting and potent cocktails.

🍷 DRINKING & NIGHTLIFE

Nightlife in these parts generally involves a guided hike and nocturnal critters, but since these misty green mountains draw artists and dreamers, there's a smattering of regular cultural offerings. When there's anything going on, you'll see it heavily advertised around town. You'll see some action at the bars in Santa Elena, especially during the dry season.

Bar Amigos   Bar

(☏2645-5071; www.baramigos.com; Santa Elena; ⏱noon-3am) With picture windows overlooking the mountainside, this Santa Elena mainstay evokes the atmosphere of a ski lodge. But, no, there are DJs, karaoke and billiards plus sports on the screens. This is the one consistent place in the area to let loose, so there's usually a good, rowdy mix of Ticos and tourists.

The food, such as the *chifrijo* (rice and pinto beans with fried pork, capped with fresh tomato salsa and corn chips), is surprisingly good.

Monteverde Beer House   Beer Garden

(☏8659-2054; www.facebook.com/monteverdebeerhouse; Santa Elena; ⏱10am-10pm; 📶) It's not a brewery – contrary to the sign – but it does offer a selection of local craft beers. There's a shady deck out back and smiling servers on hand; it's a perfect atmosphere for kicking back after a day of adventures.

The Middle Eastern food (mains US$6 to US$10) is hit or miss, but if you're hungry, go for the shakshuka.

The Israeli owner was in the process of opening a new bar near the Tree House (p219) at the time of research.

Cocoa fruit

ℹ INFORMATION

Monteverde Tours (Desafío Adventure Company; ☏2645-5874; www.monteverdetours.com; Santa Elena; ⊙7am-7pm Mon-Fri, 10am-6pm Sat & Sun) is a travel agency and vacation planner that can help you find the activity you're looking for. It can make arrangements for guided hikes, horseback riding, canopy tours, coffee tours and more, plus transportation such as the taxi-boat-taxi to Arenal. It's a good resource if you're unsure how you want to spend your time.

ℹ GETTING THERE & AWAY

While most Costa Rican communities regularly request paved roads in their region, preservationists in Monteverde have done the opposite. All roads around here are shockingly rough. Even if you arrive on a newly paved road via Guacimal, you'll still want a 4WD to get to the more remote lodges and reserves.

There are three roads from the Interamericana. Coming from the south, the first

well-signed turnoff is at Rancho Grande (18km north of the Puntarenas exit). The first stretch of this route (from Sardinal to Guacimal) was paved in 2011. The remaining 17km (from Guacimal to Santa Elena) was scheduled to be paved in 2016. That hasn't happened yet; at the time of research, it took about three hours to drive to San José, but that time will be reduced with the road improvements.

A second, shorter road goes via Juntas, but it's not paved except for the first few kilometers.

Finally, if coming from the north, drivers can take the paved road from Cañas via Tilarán and then take the rough road from Tilarán to Santa Elena.

If you're coming from Arenal, consider taking the lakeside route through Tronadora and Río Chiquito, instead of going through Tilarán. The roads are rougher, but the panoramas of the lake, volcano and surrounding countryside are magnificent.

There are two gas stations open for business in the area, one of which is in Cerro Plano.

VOLCÁN ARENAL

Volcán Arenal at a Glance...

You know about the region's main attraction: that volcano, surrounded by old lava fields, bubbling hot springs and a stunning lake. Even though the regular eruptions have ceased, plenty of adventure awaits here. There are trails to hike, waterfalls to rappel down, and sloths to spot. No matter your preferred method of exploring – hiking, biking, horseback riding, ziplining – you can do it here. And when your body's had enough, you can ease into a volcano-heated pool to soak away your aches and pains.

Two Days in Volcán Arenal

On your first day, set out on the well-marked trail system within in **Parque Nacional Volcán Arenal** (p228), venturing to waterfalls, lava flows or crater lakes. Afterwards, head to the **hot springs** (p232) for a well-deserved soak. On your second day, take a detour to El Castillo to visit the **Butterfly Conservatory** (p243) and have lunch at **La Ventanita** (p244).

Four Days in Volcán Arenal

If you have the luxury of a third day, return to the park to hike along old lava flows and spy on sloths. Travel on horseback or by mountain bike if you prefer. Your fourth day is free for a hike and swim at **Catarata Río Fortuna** (p234). Or, take a day trip to **Proyecto Asis** (p237) to support the animal sanctuary.

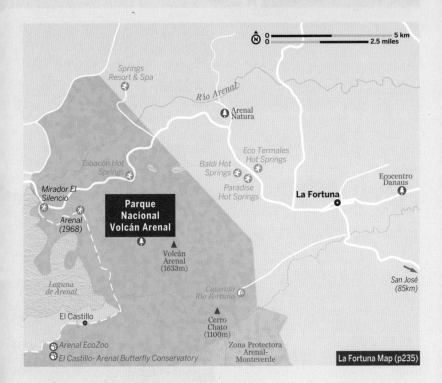

La Fortuna Map (p235)

Arriving in Volcán Arenal

The roads in the region are mostly in fine condition, with good highways branching out from La Fortuna: heading west, past the park entrance and around the lake; heading south through Chachagua and beyond; or heading east toward Muelle and Ciudad Quesada (San Carlos). Buses ply all of these routes. Tour operators and shuttle buses supplement public transportation, making it one of the easiest regions to navigate without your own vehicle.

Sleeping

While there are some decent lodgings in La Fortuna itself (especially budget options), you might want to base yourself uphill – nearer to the hiking, hanging bridges, and hot springs – or a bit south of town where you'll hardly hear a peep at night. Even the lakefront properties around El Castillo and the Laguna de Arenal are close enough to use as a base for exploring the region.

Volcán Arenal

Parque Nacional Volcán Arenal

Volcán Arenal no longer lights up the night sky with molten lava, but it still provides a rugged terrain for hiking and a rich habitat for wildlife.

Great For...

❶ Need to Know

📞2461-8499; adult/child US$15/5; ⊘8am-4pm (last entrance 2:30pm)

★ **Top Tip**
The ranger station has trail maps available.

For most of modern history, Volcán Arenal was just another dormant volcano surrounded by fertile farmland. But for about 42 years – from its destructive explosion in 1968 until its sudden subsiding in 2010 – the volcano was an awe-striking natural wonder, producing menacing ash columns, massive explosions and streams of glowing molten rock almost daily.

The fiery views are gone for now, but Arenal is still a worthy destination, thanks to the dense forest covering her lower slopes and foothills, and her picture-perfect conical shape up top (often shrouded in clouds, but still). The Parque Nacional Volcán Arenal is part of the Area de Conservación Arenal, which protects most of the Cordillera de Tilarán. This area is rugged and varied, rich with wildlife and laced with trails.

Hiking

Although it's no longer erupting (or perhaps because it is not), Volcán Arenal is the big hiking draw here. There is a well-marked trail system within the park, and several private reserves on its outskirts. Waterfalls, lava flows and crater lakes are all worthy destinations, which you can reach without a guide.

From the **ranger station** (📞2461-8499; adult/child US$15/5; ⊗8am-4pm) you can hike the Sendero Los Heliconias, a 1km circular track that passes by the site of the 1968 lava flow. A 1.5km-long path branches off this trail and leads to an overlook. The Sendero Las Coladas also branches off the Heliconias trail and wraps around the volcano for 2km, past the 1993 lava flow. It then connects with the Sendero Los Tucanes, which extends for another

Hiking in Parque Nacional Volcán Arenal

3km through the tropical rainforest at the base of the volcano. To return to the parking area, you'll have to turn back – you'll get good views of the summit on the way.

From the park headquarters (not the ranger station) is the 1.3km Sendero Los Miradores, which leads down to the shores of the volcanic lake and provides a good angle for volcano viewing. Also from park headquarters, the Old Lava Flow Trail is an interesting and strenuous lower-elevation trail following the flow of the massive 1992 eruption. The 4km round trip takes two hours to complete. If you want to keep hiking, combine it with the **Sendero El**

Ceibo, a scenic 1.8km trail through secondary forest.

In 2017 a new 'sector peninsula' set of trails opened, comprising 1.2km of trails, an observation tower, and scenic lake overlook. Although the last entrance to the national park is at 2:30pm, you may be allowed to enter and stay at the new sector later.

There are also trails departing from **Arenal Observatory Lodge** (☑2479-1070, reservations 2290-7011; www.arenalob servatorylodge.com; d/tr/q with bathroom from US$140/155/185, without bathroom US$100/$115/130; P ⊛ @ � 🛰) and on a nearby private reserve, Arenal 1968. This network of trails along the original 1968 lava flow is right next to the park entrance. There's a *mirador* (lookout) that on a clear day offers a picture-perfect volcano view. It's located 1.2km from the highway turnoff to the park, just before the ranger station.

Tours

In addition to hiking, it's also possible to explore the park on horseback, mountain bike or ATV.

Arenal Wilberth Stables (☑2479-7522; www.arenalwilberthstable.com; per person 1/2hr US$40/65; ⊙7:30am, 11am & 2:30pm) Two-hour horseback-riding tours depart from these stables at the foot of Arenal. The ride takes in forest and farmland, as well as lake and volcano views. The stables are opposite the entrance to the national park, but there's an office in La Fortuna, next to Arenal Hostel Resort.

Desafío Adventure Company (p237) A tour agency with the widest range of tours in Fortuna, including horse-riding treks and mountain-bike expeditions to Volcán Arenal.

DENNIS K JOHNSON/GETTY IMAGES ©

☑ **Don't Miss**

When the clouds momentarily clear, you'll have a view of the picture-perfect cone of the volcano.

✕ **Take a Break**

There are no restaurants near the park, so pack a picnic from Rainforest Café (p238).

Tabacón Hot Springs

JOHN COLETTI/GETTY IMAGES ©

Hot Springs

Beneath La Fortuna the lava is still curdling and heating countless bubbling springs.

Great For...

☑ Don't Miss

Sitting in a hot tub with a cool cocktail and a marvelous volcano view.

Eco Termales Hot Springs

Everything from the natural circulation systems in the pools to the soft lighting is understated, luxurious and romantic at this gated, reservations-only **complex** (☎2479-8787; www.ecotermalesfortuna.cr; Via 142; with/without meal US$57/37; ⏰10am, 1pm & 5pm; 🚼) 🍴 about 4.5km northwest of town. Lush greenery surrounds the walking paths that cut through these gorgeous grounds. Only 150 visitors are admitted at a time, to maintain the ambience of serenity and seclusion.

Paradise Hot Springs

This low-key **place** (www.paradisehotsprings cr.com; Via 142; adult/child US$28/16; ⏰11am-9pm) has one lovely, large pool with a waterfall and several smaller, secluded pools, surrounded by lush vegetation and tropical

Tabacón Hot Springs

Some say it's cheesy and some say it's fun. (We say it's both.) At **Tabacón Hot Springs** (☑2519-1999; www.tabacon.com; day pass incl lunch & dinner adult/child US$115/40; ⊙10am-10pm) 🖉, broad-leaf palms, rare orchids and other florid tropical blooms part to reveal a 40°C waterfall pouring over a fake cliff, concealing constructed caves complete with camouflaged cup holders. Lounged across each well-placed stonelike substance are overheated tourists of various shapes and sizes, relaxing.

Baldi Hot Springs

Big enough so that there's something for everyone, **Baldi** (☑2479-9917; www.baldi hotsprings.cr; with/without buffet US$57/35; ⊙9am-10pm; 👪), about 4.5km northwest of town, has 25 thermal pools ranging in temperature from 32°C to a scalding 67°C. There are waterfalls and soaking pools for chill-seekers and 'Xtreme' slides for thrill-seekers, plus a good-size children's play area. At night, the thumping music and swim-up bars attract a young party crowd, but drinks are pricey!

blooms. The pools vary in temperature (up to 40°C), some with hydromassage. Paradise is much simpler than the other larger spring settings, but there are fewer people, and your experience is bound to be more relaxing and romantic.

Springs Resort & Spa

If you're looking for a luxurious hot-spring experience, **Springs** (☑in USA 954-727-8333, 2401-3313; www.thespringscostarica.com; 2-day admission US$65; ⊙8am-10pm; 👪) features 28 free-form pools with varying temperatures, volcano views, landscaped gardens, waterfalls and swim-up bars, including a jungle bar with a waterslide. The whole scene is human-made, yet lovely. The rough 3km road from La Fortuna was being paved during research.

La Fortuna

◎ SIGHTS

Catarata Río Fortuna   Waterfall
(www.cataratariofortuna.com; Diagonal 301; US$15; ☺8am-5pm; P) You can glimpse the sparkling 70m ribbon of clear water that pours through a sheer canyon of dark volcanic rock covered in bromeliads and ferns with minimal sweat equity. But it's worth the climb down and out to see it from the jungle floor. Though it's dangerous to dive beneath the thundering falls, a series of perfect swimming holes with spectacular views tile the canyon in aquamarine. Early arrival means you might beat the crowds: the parking lot fills quickly.

Arenal Natura   Park
(☎2479-1616; www.arenalnatura.com; day/night/bird tour US$35/44/49; ☺8am-5:30pm; 🐾) Located 6km west of La Fortuna, this is a well-manicured nature experience that includes frogs, turtles, snakes and crocs, all in their appointed places. The birdlife is also prolific here. Excellent naturalist guides ensure that you don't miss anything hiding in the trees, and there's a photography tour to help you capture it all. Discounted rates for children and students.

Ecocentro Danaus   Nature Reserve
(☎2479-7019; www.ecocentrodanaus.com; with/without guide US$18/12, guided night tour US$35; ☺7:30am-5pm, night tour 5:30pm; 🐾) 🌿 This center, 4km east of town, has a well-developed trail system that's good for birding, as well as for spotting mammals such as sloths, coatis and howler monkeys. The admission fee also includes a visit to a butterfly garden, a ranarium featuring poison-dart frogs, and a small lake containing caimans and turtles. Reserve in advance for the excellent night tour.

Viento Fresco   Waterfall
(☎2695-3434; www.vientofresco.net; Ruta 145, Campos del Oro; adult/child US$15/10, horseback tour US$55/45; ☺7:30am-5pm; 🐾) Driving between Monteverde and Arenal, there is no good excuse for skipping this stop. Viento Fresco is a series of five cascades, including the spectacular Arco Iris (Rainbow Falls), which drops 75m into a refreshing shallow pool that's perfect for swimming. The 1.3km of trails are well maintained, but there are no crowds or commercialism to mar the natural beauty of this place. You'll probably have the falls to yourself, especially if you go early in the day.

⊙ TOURS

Don Olivo Chocolate Tour   Tours
(☎6110-3556, 2469-1371; www.facebook.com/tourdechocolatedonolivo; Via 142; tour US$25; ☺8am, 10am, 1pm & 3pm; 🐾) Let Don Olivo or his son show you around their family *finca*, showing off their sugarcane, oranges and – of course – cocoa plants. The process of turning this funny fruit into the decadent treat that we all know and love is truly fascinating. Bonus: lots of taste-testing along the way.

Alberto's Horse Tours   Horseback Riding
(☎2479-7711, 2479-9043; www.facebook.com/albertoshorses; Ruta 702; per person US$85; ☺8:30am-1:30pm) Alberto and his son lead popular horseback-riding trips to the Catarata de la Fortuna. It's a three- or four-hour trip, but you'll spend about an hour off your horse, when you hike down to the falls for a swim or a photo op. Beautiful setting, beautiful horses. Cash only. You'll find Alberto on Ruta 702, about 2km south of town.

Arenal Oasis   Bird-Watching, Night Walk
(☎2479-9526; www.arenaloasis.com; night/bird walks US$40/55; ☺bird walk 6am, night tour 5:45pm) The Rojas Bonilla family has created this wild frog sanctuary, home to some 35 species of croaking critters. The frogs are just the beginning of this night

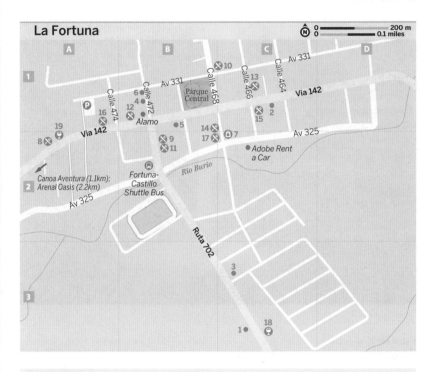

La Fortuna

🌀 Activities, Courses & Tours
1 Alberto's Horse Tours	C3
2 Aventuras Arenal	C1
3 Bike Arenal	C3
4 Desafío Adventure Company	B1
5 Jacamar Naturalist Tours	B1
6 Wave Rafting	B1

🔒 Shopping
7 Hecho A Mano	C2

✖ Eating
8 Anch'io Ristorante & Pizzeria	A2
9 Chifa La Familia Feliz	B2
10 Kappa Sushi	C1
11 La Muerta	B2
12 Lava Lounge	B1
13 Orgánico Fortuna	C1
14 Rainforest Café	B1
15 Restaurant Don Rufino	C1
16 Soda Mima	A1
17 Soda Viquez	B2

🍷 Drinking & Nightlife
18 El Establo	C3
19 La Fortuna Pub	A2

walk, which continues into the rainforest to see what other nocturnal animals await. If you're more of a morning person, it also does a bird-watching tour. Reservations recommended. Located 3km from La Fortuna's center; hotel pick-up costs US$10.

Bike Arenal   Cycling

(☎2479-9020, 2479-7150; www.bikearenal.com; cnr Ruta 702 & Av 319A; rental per day/week US$25/150, half-/full-day tour US$85/135; ☉7am-6pm) This outfit offers a variety of bike tours for all levels of riders, including a popular ride around the lake and a half-day ride to El Castillo. You can also do versions of these rides on your own. Make advance arrangements for rental and an English-speaking bike mechanic will bring the bicycle to you.

La Fortuna waterfall

PureTrek
Canyoning
Canyoning

(📲2479-1313, US toll-free 1-866-569-5723; www.puretrekcanyoning.com; 4hr incl transportation & lunch US$101; ⊙7am-10pm; 👪)
🍃 The reputable PureTrek leads guided rappels down three waterfalls, one of which is 50m high. Also included: rock climbing and 'monkey drop,' which is actually a zipline with a rappel at the end of it. High marks for attention to safety and high-quality gear. It gets some big groups, but it does a good job keeping things moving.

Canoa
Aventura
Canoeing

(📲2479-8200; www.canoa-aventura.com; Via 142; canoe/kayak trip US$57; ⊙6:30am-9:30pm) 🍃 This long-standing family-run company specializes in canoe and float trips (leisurely trips aimed at observation and relaxation) led by bilingual naturalist guides. Most are geared toward wildlife- and bird-watching. Canoa is the sister company of the **Maquenque Lodge**

(📲2479-7785; www.maquenqueecolodge.com; s/d/tr incl breakfast from US$105/130/155; 🅿🛜🏊) 🍃 in Boca Tapada and can arrange an overnight stay there.

Jacamar
Naturalist
Tours
Hiking, Adventure Tour

(📲2479-9767; www.arenaltours.com; Parque Central, Via 142; bird-watching $68; ⊙7am-9pm) Recommended for its variety of naturalist hikes, including Volcán Arenal, waterfall and hanging bridges. Customers rave about the guides' flexibility and attentiveness.

Arenal Paraíso
Canopy Tours
Canopy Tour

(📲2479-1100; www.arenalparaiso.com; Via 142; tours US$50; ⊙8am-5pm; 👪) A dozen cables zip across the canyon of the Río Arenal, giving a unique perspective on two waterfalls, as well as the rainforest canopy. Also includes admission to the resort's swimming pool and 13 thermal pools, which are hidden among the rocks and greenery on the hillside.

Arenal Mundo Aventura
Adventure Sports, Hiking

(📞2479-9762; www.arenalmundoaventura.
com; adult/child canopy tours US$69/52, hiking
US$53/37, Maleku cultural experience $35/19;
⊗8am-1:30pm; 🚼) An all-in-one adventure
park, this place offers various guided
hikes, rappelling and horseback riding, as
well as a canopy tour. It also hosts performances of indigenous Maleku dance and
song. It is 2km south of La Fortuna, on the
road to Chachagua.

Aventuras Arenal
Tours

(📞2479-9133; www.aventurasarenal.com;
Via 142; kayaking US$60, hiking from US$65,
horse riding US$60-75; ⊗7am-8pm) Around
for over 25 years, this outfit organizes a
variety of local day tours on bike, boat and
horseback. It also does trips further afield,
including to Caño Negro and Río Celeste.

Canopy Los Cañones
Canopy Tour

(📞2479-1047; www.hotelloslagos.com; US$55)
🍃 Located at the Hotel Los Lagos, the
Canopy Los Cañones has 12 cables over the
rainforest, ranging from 50m to 500m long.
The price includes admission to a frog farm,
crocodile farm, butterfly farm, hot springs,
natural pools and water-slides, all on the hotel grounds. The hotel is located about 6km
west of La Fortuna, just off Via 142.

Ecoglide
Canopy Tour

(📞2479-7120; www.arenalecoglide.com; adult/
child US$75; ⊗canopy tours at 8am, 10am, 1pm
& 3pm; 🚼) Ecoglide is the biggest canopy
game in town, featuring 13 cables, 15 platforms and a Tarzan swing. The dual-cable
safety system provides extra security and
peace of mind. Located off Via 142, about
5km west (uphill) from La Fortuna.

Wave Rafting
Rafting

(📞2479-7262; www.waveexpeditions.com;
cnr Calle 472 & Av 331; river trips US$70-100;
⊗6am-9pm) Wave Expeditions runs the
wild Ríos Toro and Sarapiquí, as well as
the mellower Balsa, in both rafts and
tubes. There's also hiking, horseback

Community-Based Organization

It's an animal rescue center. It's a
volunteer project. It's Spanish classes.
Proyecto Asis (📞2475-9121; www.
institutoasis.com; adult/child US$31/18,
incl volunteering US$54/31; ⊗tours 8:30am
& 1pm) 🍃 is a community-based organization doing a lot of good, and you can
help. The introductory experience is
a 1½-hour tour of the wildlife rescue
center, but it's worth springing for the
three-hour 'volunteering' experience,
which includes hands-on interaction
with the animals. It's pricey, but the
cause is worthy.

Asis also offers homestays in the local
community. It's located about 20km
west of Quesada, past the village of Flor-
encia. Reserve at least a day in advance.

Mantled howler monkey
KRYSIA CAMPOS/GETTY IMAGES ©

riding, caving, canyoning and tortilla
making on offer, through second-party
tour companies.

Desafío Adventure Company
Adventure Sports

(📞2479-0020; www.desafiocostarica.com;
Calle 2; tours from US$75; ⊗6:30am-9pm) De-
safío is a tour agency that has the widest
range of tours in Fortuna – everything
from paddling trips on the Río Balsa,
horseback-riding treks to Volcán Arenal,
adventure tours rappelling down waterfalls, and mountain-bike expeditions.
It can also arrange your transfer to Monteverde by boat or bike.

SHOPPING

Hecho A Mano   Arts & Crafts

(Handmade Art Shop; ☑8611-0018; www.
facebook.com/handmadeartshop; Calle 468;
⊙9am-9pm Mon-Fri, from 10am Sat & Sun)
There's no shortage of souvenirs for sale
in La Fortuna, but this unique shop is
something special, carrying an excellent
selection of arts and crafts by local and
national artists. You'll find representative
pieces from Costa Rica's many subcul-
tures, including Boruca masks, rasta
handicrafts, lots of macramé and some
lovely handmade jewelry.

Neptune's
House of Hammocks   Homewares

(☑2479-8269; Diagonal 301; hammocks
US$40-50; ⊙8am-6pm) On the road to La
Catarata de la Fortuna, Daniel has been
watching the tourist traffic come and go
for over a decade while he weaves his
magic hammocks. Take a breather and
test one out.

EATING

Unless you're eating exclusively at *sodas,*
you'll find the restaurants in La Fortuna to
be more expensive than in other parts of
the country. But there are some excellent,
innovative kitchens, including a few that
are part of the farm-to-table movement.
The restaurants are mostly clustered in
town, but there are also places to eat on
the road heading west.

Soda Mima   Soda $

(Off Vía 142; ⊙6am-8pm Mon-Sat, to noon Sun)
Nothing fancy from afar, the love radiates
outward from Don Alvaro's kitchen to
warm your belly and your heart. Cheap,
delicious *casados* (set meals) and *gallo
pintos* are standard fare, but add some
marinated peppers from the big jar if you
dare. Customer artwork in various languages adorns the walls, the most fitting
of which reads: 'Don Alvaro Rocks.'

La Muerta   Fast Food $

(Fast Food; ☑2479-1407; Calle 472; mains
US$6-10; ⊙11am-10pm) A slightly healthier
take on fast food, this small stand features a lineup of Latin American favorites
like *tacos al pastor* (shredded pork), *chori-
pan* (sausage sandwich), and *patacones*
(fried green plantains), as well as burritos
and hamburgers, and a bit of bouncy
reggae with your *batido* (fruit shake). If
you dare, go for the El Miedo ('the fear')
hot sauce.

Rainforest Café   Cafe $

(☑2479-7239; Calle 468; mains US$7-10;
⊙7am-10pm; 🐾🍴) We know it's bad form
to start with dessert, but the irresistible
sweets at this popular spot are beautiful
to behold and delicious to devour. The
savory menu features tasty burritos,
casados, sandwiches etc. There's also
a full menu of coffees, including some
tempting specialty drinks (such as Mono
Loco: coffee, banana, milk, chocolate and
cinnamon).

Soda Viquez   Soda $

(☑2479-7133; cnr Calle 468 & Av 325; mains
US$5-10; ⊙8am-10pm; 🍴) Travelers adore
the 'local flavor' that's served up at Soda
Viquez (in all senses of the expression).
It's a super-friendly spot, offering tasty
típico (traditional dishes), especially *casa-
dos*, rice dishes and fresh fruit *batidos.*
Prices are reasonable and portions ample.

Kappa Sushi   Sushi $

(Calle 468, btwn Av 331 & Av 333; sushi & rolls
US$6-12; ⊙noon-10pm; 🍴) When you're
surrounded by mountains and cattle
farms, who's thinking of sushi? Well, you
should. The fish is fresh (you're not *that*
far from the ocean) and the preparations
innovative. The dragon roll (shrimp tem-
pura, avocado and eel sauce) is a favorite.
Enjoy the view of Arenal (or is it Fuji?)
while you feast on raw fish – or go for the
veg options.

Clockwise from top: Volcán Arenal; Parque Nacional
Volcán Arenal; Río Celeste waterfall

Tubing, La Fortuna

Gecko's
Waterfall Grill International $

(☑2479-1569; www.geckoscostarica.com; mains US$6-7; ☺11am-5pm) Good cheap eats (quesadillas, breakfast burritos), rich smoothies and artisanal beers are the payoff at this cafe, located just before the big waterfall. Treat yourself to a breakfast burrito – you walked all the way, didn't you?

Orgánico
Fortuna Vegetarian $$

(☑8572-2115; www.organicofortuna.com; Calle 466; mains US$10-15; ☺11am-9pm) A lovely little family operation that preaches better living through better eating, and the proof is in the pudding (or maybe the falafel). Delicious locally sourced ingredients are prepared with care. Smoothies, coffee with almond milk, and even some gluten-free bread and other options. If you're there long enough, you may even overhear a violin lesson in the back room.

Lava Lounge International $$

(☑2479-7365; www.lavaloungecostarica.com; Via 142; mains US$8-15, specials US$22-24; ☺7am-10:30pm; ℗🛜🖾) This hip, open-air restaurant is a relief when you just can't abide another *casado*. There is pizza and pasta, wraps and salads, and loads of vegetarian options. Service can be variable during peak hours, but the picnic tables and *palapa* (thatched) roof create a cool, rustic vibe. Add colorful cocktails and occasional live music, and the place is pretty irresistible.

Chifa
La Familia Feliz Fusion $$

(☑8469-6327; Calle 472; mains US$8-12; ☺11am-10pm; 🛜🖾🖾) If you're looking for a change of taste – a *real* change from *casados* and pizza – check this out. *Chifa* means 'Chinese food' in Peruvian-Spanish. So what we have here is Peruvian Chinese food, which is something special indeed. The chef goes out of his way to welcome and satisfy all comers.

Brisas Del Lago   Soda $$

(☏2695-3363; San Luis; mains US$6-11; ☺11am-10pm Tue-Sat, from 1pm Sun; P🛜) If you don't mind a little detour, here is your lunch stop between Monteverde and Arenal. Simple Tico fare is done with panache at this dressed-up *soda*. They marinate chicken breasts in their own BBQ sauce, skewer Thai-style shrimp and slather up teriyaki chicken. The garlic fish is sensational. Just past the Catholic church in the community of San Luis.

Anch'io Ristorante
& Pizzeria   Italian $$

(☏2479-7024; Via 142; mains US$10-18; ☺noon-10pm; P🛜🐕) If you have a hankering for pizza, you can't do better than Anch'io, where the crust is crispy thin, the toppings are plentiful and the pie is cooked in a wood-fired oven. Start yourself off with a traditional antipasto. Accompany it with cold beer or a bottle of red. Add super service and pleasant patio seating, and you've got yourself a winner.

Restaurant
Don Rufino   International $$$

(☏2479-9997; www.donrufino.com; cnr Via 142 & Calle 466; mains US$16-40; ☺11am-11pm) The vibe is trendy at this indoor-outdoor grill. The highlight is the perfectly prepared grilled meats: the New York Steak with mushrooms is to die for. If you're cutting back, go for Grandma's BBQ chicken (with chocolate, wrapped in a banana leaf) or the chef's special tuna (seasoned with ginger oil, served with rice noodles, tamarind sauce and cashew nuts).

🍺 DRINKING & NIGHTLIFE

El Establo   Bar

(☏2479-7675; Ruta 702; ☺5pm-2am Wed-Sat) La Fortuna's raucous *sendero* bar with an attached disco fronts the bull ring and attracts an ever-enthusiastic local following. The age demographic here ranges from 18 to 88. That's almost always a good thing. And the beer's cheap, too!

 Represa Arenal

Forget for a moment that there are always ecological issues associated with dams and revel in the fact that this one created a rather magnificent lake (it took a village, or two, in the exchange). In the absence of wind, the glassy surface of Represa Arenal (Arenal Dam) reflects the volcano and the surrounding mountains teeming with cloud forest. Crowds congregate to admire the view and snap photos. Unfortunately, there's no convenient place to stop, so you'll often encounter a minor traffic jam, especially at the dam's western end.

Unlike the fly-by view you'll get on a zipline canopy tour, a walk along **Mistico Hanging Bridges** (Puentes Colgantes de Arenal; ☏2479-8282; www.misticopark.com; adult/child US$24/free, tours US$36-47; ☺7:30am-4:30pm, tours 6am, 9am & 2pm) allows you to explore the rainforest and canopy from six suspended bridges and 10 traditional bridges at a more natural and peaceful pace. All are accessible from a single 3km trail that winds through a tunnel and skirts a waterfall.

Mistico Hanging Bridges
ALEX ROBINSON/GETTY IMAGES ©

La Fortuna Pub   Pub

(www.facebook.com/lafortunapub; Via 142; ☺2pm-midnight Sun-Thu, to 1am Fri-Sat) A new joint just uphill from the town center, these guys are all about Tico artisanal beers, offering a dozen different home-country bottled *cervezas*. They also brew their own beer in small batches that disappear quickly, so watch their

★ **Top Five for Wildlife**

Arenal Oasis (p234)

Aventuras Arenal (p237)

Canoa Aventura (p236)

Jacamar Naturalist Tours (p236)

Ecocentro Danaus (p234)

From left: Spider monkey; Ceiba tree; Sky Adventures

Facebook page for the next arrival. A standard pub-food menu satisfies, while weekend live music and Sunday's open mic add to the buzz.

ⓘ GETTING THERE & AWAY

The fastest route between Monteverde-Santa Elena and La Fortuna is the taxi-boat-taxi combo (formerly known as jeep-boat-jeep, which sounds sexy but it was the same thing). It is actually a minivan with the requisite yellow 'turismo' tattoo, which takes you to Laguna de Arenal, meeting a boat that crosses the lake, where a 4WD van on the other side continues to Monteverde. It's a terrific transportation option that can be arranged through almost any hotel or tour operator in La Fortuna or Monteverde (US$25 to US$35, four hours).

This is now the first transportation choice for many between La Fortuna and Monteverde as it's incredibly scenic and reasonably priced.

ⓘ GETTING AROUND

La Fortuna is easy to access by public transportation, but nearby attractions such as the hot springs, Parque Nacional Volcán Arenal and Laguna de Arenal demand internal combustion (or a tour operator). If you're thinking of doing a day trip to Río Celeste, Caño Negro or Venada Caves, you might also consider renting a car for the day.

Adobe Rent a Car (☎2479-7202; www.adobecar. com; Av 325; ⊙8am-5pm)

Alamo (☎2479-9090; www.alamocostarica.com; cnr Via 142 & Calle 472; ⊙7:30am-5:30pm)

El Castillo

⊙ SIGHTS

Arenal EcoZoo   Zoo

(El Serpentario; ☎2479-1059; www.arenalecoz oo.com; La Fortuna–El Castillo road; adult/child US$15/12, with guide US$23/16; ⊙8am-7pm) This snake house offers a hands-on animal experience: as in, handling and milking a venomous snake. It is also home to

JOHN COLETTI/GETTY IMAGES ©

a red-tailed boa (one of the largest snakes in the world), as well as frogs, amphibious lizards, iguanas, turtles, scorpions, tarantulas and butterflies. Ask about feeding time if you want to see snakes devouring bugs, frogs and even other snakes. Located on the main road uphill from the lake, which connects to La Fortuna.

El Castillo-Arenal Butterfly Conservatory   Wildlife Reserve

(☑2479-1149; www.butterflyconservatory. org; El Castillo–La Fortuna road; adult/student US$15/11; ☺8am-4pm) More than just a butterfly conservatory (although it has one of the largest butterfly exhibitions in Costa Rica). Altogether there are six domed habitats, a ranarium, an insect museum, a medicinal herb garden, and an hour's worth of trails through a botanic garden and along the river. The birding is also excellent here, and there are wonderful volcano views. The conservatory is located on the main road uphill from the lake, which connects to La Fortuna.

⊕ TOURS

La Gavilana   Tours

(☑2479-1747, 8433-7902; www.gavilana.com; El Castillo–La Fortuna road; waterfall tour US$90, base camp day tour $99, Big Forest hike US$159) The adventurous folk at La Gavilana Herbs & Art offer a Big Forest trail hike between El Castillo and San Gerardo (near Santa Elena). Traversing old-growth forests and raging rivers, hikers overnight at the rustic Rancho Maximo. Dinner and breakfast are provided. The office is on the main road uphill from the lake, which connects to La Fortuna.

Sky Adventures   Canopy Tour

(☑2479-4100; www.skyadventures.travel; adult/child Sky Walk US$39/27, Sky Tram US$46/32, Sky River Drift US$72/57, Sky Limit US$81/56, Sky Trek US$81/56; ☺7:30am-4pm) El Castillo's entry in the canopy-tour category has ziplines (Sky Trek), a floating gondola (Sky Tram) and a series of hanging bridges (Sky Walk). It's safe and well run, and visitors tend to leave smiling. A

 Welcome to El Castillo

Just an hour around the bend from La Fortuna, the tiny mountain village of El Castillo is a beautiful, bucolic and bumpy alternative, if you don't mind the somewhat treacherous roads. This picturesque locale, created as a relocation zone after the great eruption of 1968, has easy access to Parque Nacional Volcán Arenal and amazing, up-close views of the looming mountain – with little of the tourist madness of its bigger neighbor.

There is a tight-knit expat community here, some of whom have opened appealing lodges and top-notch restaurants. There are hiking trails and swimming holes. There are even a few worthy attractions – a butterfly house and an eco-zoo. The only thing El Castillo doesn't have is a sidewalk. And maybe that's a good thing.

Mountain lodge, El Castillo
JOHN COLETTI/GETTY IMAGES ©

unique combo, Sky River Drift combines a zipline with tree-climbing and river tubing, while Sky Limit combines ziplining with rappel and other high-altitude challenges.

Rancho Adventure Tours Adventure Sports
(☑8302-7318; www.ranchomargot.com; farm tour US$35, other tours US$55) **Rancho Margot** (cnr El Castillo-La Fortuna road & Rancho Margot road; incl meals dm per person US$80, bungalow s/d US$175/250; P🛜❄) ✈ offers a good selection of guided tours, including

horseback riding on the southern side of Laguna de Arenal, kayaking on the lake, and touring the ranch itself to learn about the workings of a sustainable farm. The activities are free to guests of the Rancho. Located where the El Castillo–La Fortuna road intersects with Rancho Margot Rd.

✖ EATING

La Ventanita Cafe $
(☑2479-1735; El Castillo–La Fortuna road; mains US$3-5; ⏱11am-9pm; ✈) *La Ventanita* is the 'little window' where you place your order. Soon enough, you'll be devouring the best *chifrijo* (rice and pinto beans with fried pork, capped with fresh tomato salsa and corn chips) that you've ever had, along with a nutritious and delicious *batido*. It's typical food with a twist – pulled pork and bacon burritos, for example.

La Gavilana Herbs & Art Bakery $
(☑8533-7902; www.facebook.com/gavilanacr; snacks US$2-6; ⏱8am-5pm Mon-Fri, 9am-2pm Sat) Meet Tomas and Hannah. He's Czech and makes the hot sauce and vinegar; she's American and bakes the cookies and breads. Their place, southwest of El Castillo, is decked with paintings (Hannah), while the grounds contain a food forest (Thomas), filled with medicinal herbs and fruit trees. The whole place is filled with love, beauty and creativity. Reservations requested.

Fusion Grill Fusion $$
(☑2479-1949; www.fusiongrillrestaurant.com; El Castillo–La Fortuna road; mains US$8-15; ⏱7am-10pm) Set in an open-air dining room with an incredible vista of the volcano, Fusion Grill shows off a little swank (at least, more than other restaurants in El Castillo). Chef Adrian Ramirez whips up a mean *parillada mixta* (mixed grill), but your favorite part of the meal might be the specialty desserts like pineapple or banana *flambé*.

DMG337/BUDGET TRAVEL ©

Costa Rican breakfast

🍷 DRINKING & NIGHTLIFE

There's only one place to go out drinking in El Castillo, but it's worth a visit. You have more options in La Fortuna, but it's tricky business getting back here after dark, especially after a few cold ones.

Howlers Bar & Grill   Bar

(📞2479-1785; www.facebook.com/howlers barandgrill; ⏱11:30am-8:30pm Tue-Sun) This lakefront bar is a fun choice for a night out drinking in El Castillo. (Good thing, as it's your only choice.) The American-style pub grub is excellent, as is the cold draught beer. It's a popular place for the expat community to congregate, guaranteeing an upbeat, *pura vida* vibe. Part of the **Majestic Lodge** (📞8703-1561, 2479-1085; www.majesticlodgecostarica.com; El Fósforo–El Castillo road; r US$130; 🅿❄🛜❄) property.

ℹ GETTING THERE & AWAY

El Castillo is located 8km past the entrance to Parque Nacional Volcán Arenal. It's a rough gravel road, and it gets a bit worse once you get to the village.

There is no public transportation, but a private **shuttle bus** (📞8887-9141; Calle 472) runs from the Super Christian in La Fortuna (one hour, US$9) at 7:30am, 12:30pm and 5:30pm. The bus departs Rancho Margot at 6am, 10am and 4pm, returning from La Fortuna at 6am, 10am and 4pm. Contact the father and son drivers Arturo and Luis at 8887-9141, whose van will be either white, grey or green. This bus also will drop you at the entrance to the national park for US$4.

SARAPIQUÍ VALLEY

Sarapiquí Valley at a Glance...

This flat, steaming stretch of finca-dotted lowlands was once part of the United Fruit Company's vast banana holdings. More recently, the river again shot to prominence as one of the premier destinations in the country for kayakers and rafters. With the Parque Nacional Braulio Carrillo as its backyard, this is also one of the best regions for wildlife-watching, especially considering how easy it is to get here.

One Day in Sarapiquí Valley

If you only have one day in the Valle de Sarapiquí, you ought to spend it on the river, **kayaking** or **rafting** (p250) over the thrilling white water. Refuel at the **Rancho Magallanes** (p254) before retiring to your ecolodge to watch the birds.

Two Days in Sarapiquí Valley

Slow things down on day two, with a wildlife-watching **boat tour** (p253) on the Río Sarapiquí or a farm tour (with degustation!) at **Best Chocolate Tour** (p253) or **Organic Paradise** (p253).

Don't leave town without sniffing the tropical flowers over at **Heliconia Island** (p255).

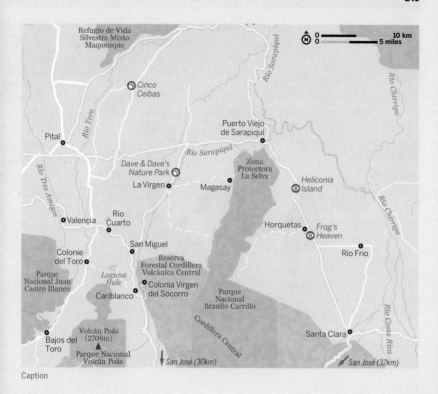

Caption

Arriving in Sarapiquí Valley

Rte 4 connects the region's towns and villages. In the east, the highway hooks up with Rte 32, which continues on to Siquirres. In the west, it joins with Rte 32, continuing south toward San José. The new Vuelta Kooper Chilamate highway opened in 2017, cutting travel time to La Fortuna by half. Buses ply all of these routes.

Sleeping

In addition to raging rapids and prowling animals, there are a slew of stellar lodges in the region, featuring rainforest trails, suspension bridges, pre-Columbian ruins and chocolate tours. Even budget travelers have a few interesting and atmospheric options in and around Chilamate, although the cheapest places to stay are in town (Puerto Viejo or La Virgen).

WOLFGANG KAEHLER/GETTY IMAGES ©

White-Water Rafting

The Río Sarapiquí offers a pretty special package: high-adrenaline kayaking and river-rafting in the midst of wildlife-rich rainforest. Hold on tight as you surf those rapids – but keep your eyes open!

The Río Sarapiquí isn't as wild as the white water on the Río Pacuare near Turrialba, but it will get your heart racing. Even better, the dense jungle that hugs the riverbank is lush and primitive, with chances to glimpse wildlife from your raft. All of the outfitters ride the same rapids, offering roughly the same Class II to IV options at similar prices.

Tour Operators

Aventuras del Sarapiquí (📞2766-6768; www.sarapiqui.com; river trips US$60-95) This highly recommended outfitter offers land, air and water adventures. In addition to white-water rafting (both Class II and III/ IV trips), you can also fly through the air on a 12-cable canopy tour. Or, stay down to earth with horseback riding, mountain

Great For...

☑ Don't Miss

Spotting birds, monkeys and iguanas as you cruise down the river.

Collared aracari

PANORAMIC IMAGES/GETTY IMAGES ©

biking or good old-fashioned hiking. Situated just off the highway.

Sarapiquí Outdoor Center (☏2761-1123; www.costaricaraft.com; 2/4hr rafting trip US$65/90, guided kayak trips from US$90) David Duarte is the local paddling authority. In addition to its own rafting excursions, SOC offers kayak rental, lessons and clinics. Indie paddlers should check in for up-to-date river information. If you need somewhere to sleep before you hit the water, you can crash in the simple rooms or camp in one of the available, all-inclusive tents – no equipment necessary. Located about 18km southwest of Sarapiquí, off Hwy 126.

Green Rivers (☏2766-6265, 2766-5274; www.costaricagreenrive.wixsite.com/sarapiqui rafting; tours US$60-80; 🖼) Operating out of Posada Andrea Cristina B&B, this outfit is run by the ever-amiable Kevín Martínez and his wife Evelyn. They offer a wide variety of rafting and kayaking tours, from family-friendly floats to adrenaline-pumping, rapid-surfing rides. They also know their nature, so they do natural history and bird tours too.

Tropical Duckies (☏8760-3787, 2761-0095; www.tropicalduckies.com; off Hwy 126; adults/children US$56/50; ⊗departs 9am & 1pm) Highly recommended for beginners and families, this outfit does tours and instruction in inflatable kayaks, which allow for a fun paddle even when the river is low. Paddle on flat moving water or Class III rapids (or somewhere in between). Reserve ahead.

Aguas Bravas (☏2761-1645; www.aguas bravascr.com; rafting trips US$75, safari float US$65; ⊗9am-5:30pm) This well-established rafting outfit has set up shop along the Río Sarapiquí (with its own onsite hostel). Aguas Bravas has two tours on offer: take a gentle safari float to spot birds, iguanas, caimans and other wildlife, or sign up to splash through 14km of 'extreme rapids' on the San Miguel section of the river. Both include a spot of lunch.

La Virgen

Tucked into the densely jungled shores of the wild and scenic Río Sarapiquí, La Virgen was one of the small towns that prospered during the heyday of the banana trade. Although United Fruit has long since shipped out, the town remains dependent on its nearby pineapple fields. And it still lives by that river.

For over a decade La Virgen was the premier kayaking and rafting destination in Costa Rica. Dedicated groups of hard-core paddlers spent happy weeks running the Río Sarapiquí. But a tremendous 2009 earthquake and landslide altered the course of the river and flattened La Virgen's tourist economy. Some businesses folded, others relocated to La Fortuna, and a few held on. Now, independent kayakers are starting to come back and there are a couple of river outfitters offering exhilarating trips on the Class II to IV waters of the Río Sarapiquí.

◎ SIGHTS

Cinco Ceibas Wildlife Reserve
(☑2476-0606; www.cincoceibas.com; full-day tour incl lunch US$125) In the huge, 1100-hectare Finca Pangola there is a swath of dense, green primary rainforest, home to some of the oldest and largest trees in all of Costa Rica. This is Cinco Ceibas. And yes, there are five glorious ceiba trees that you see, as you walk 1.2km along the raised wooden boardwalk through the jungle. The stroll is paired with horseback riding, kayaking or an ox-cart ride, plus lunch, for a carefully choreographed adventure.

Frog's Heaven Gardens
(Cielo de Ranas; ☑2764-2724, 8891-8589; www.frogsheaven.org; adult/child US$25/12; ⊙8am-8pm; 👪) 🐾 The frogs hop free in this lovely tropical garden, which provides a perfect habitat for more than 28 species. On guided tours you're likely to see old favorites like the red-eyed tree frog and poison-dart frogs, as well as some lesser-known exotic amphibians, such as the translucent glass

Río Sarapiquí

JOHN COLETTI/GETTY IMAGES ©

frog and the wrinkly Mexican tree frog. Come for the twilight tour to see a whole different frog world.

Dave & Dave's Nature Park
Wildlife Reserve

(☎2761-0801; www.sarapiquieco-observatory. com; US$40; ⊙7am-5pm) Father and son Dave and Dave greet all comers to this 4.5-hectare reserve on the Río Sarapiquí, 200m north of the cemetery. You don't have to be a birder to get great glimpses or photos from the two viewing platforms, with feeders attracting toucans, trogans, tanagers and 10 species of hummingbirds. Follow a self-guided trail system that winds through secondary forest all the way down to the river. A welcome bonus is the free coffee.

TOURS

Hacienda Pozo Azul Adventures
Adventure

(☎2438-2616, in USA & Canada 877-810-6903; www.pozoazul.com; tours US$46-84) Specializes in adventure activities, including horseback-riding tours, a canopy tour over the lush jungle and river, rappelling, mountain biking, and assorted river trips. It's the best-funded tour concession in the area, catering largely to groups and day-trippers from San José. Located about 18km southwest of Sarapiquí, off Hwy 126.

EATING

La Virgen has a few favorite restaurants along the highway serving tried and true Tico favorites. It's nothing extraordinary, but you won't go hungry.

Rusti Tico's
Fusion $

(☎8877-8928; Chilamate; mains US$7-10; ⊙6am-10pm Fri-Wed) Here's a spot for the frugal gourmet. Chef Horacio prepares everything from spaghetti in white sauce, with *patacones* (plantain fritters) on the side, to steamed fish with vegetables, in a savory white mushroom gravy. Carnivores and vegans are given the same attentive

Taking a Farm Tour

While agriculture remains the primary money-maker in the region, many folks recognize that tourism also has a role to play in the local economy. Entrepreneurial local farmers have started supplementing their agricultural activities with farm tours, allowing visitors a view into Tico rural lifestyles, sustainable farming practices, and the ins and outs of producing delicious food.

Costa Rica Best Chocolate (☎8501-7951, 8816-3729; adult/child US$30/20; ⊙tours 8am, 10am, 1pm & 3pm) Where does chocolate come from? This local Chilamate family can answer that question for you, starting with the cacao plants growing on their farm. The two-hour demonstration covers the whole chocolate-making process, with plenty of tasting along the way. Choose from four (chocolate) bars at the end of the tour. About 5km west of downtown Sarapiquí, on the main highway.

Organic Paradise Tour (☎2761-0706; www.organicparadisetour.com; adult/child US$$35/14; ⊙8am, 10am, 1pm & 3pm) Take a bumpy ride on a tractor-drawn carriage and learn everything you ever wanted to know about pineapples (and peppers). The two-hour tour focuses on the production process and what it means to be organic, but it also offers real insight into Costa Rican farm culture, as well as practical tips like how to choose your pineapple at the supermarket.

From left: Achiote fruit seeds; Cocoa pods; Poison dart frog

service at this clean and friendly roadside eatery on the main highway, about 9km west of Sarapiquí.

Restaurante Mar y Tierra
Costa Rican $

(☏8434-2832; mains US$8-10; ⏰8am-10pm) You can't miss this roadside seafood and steak restaurant, set in an A-frame in the middle of town. It's popular with both locals and travelers. Try the *arroz Mar y Tierra*, a Tico take on surf and turf.

Rancho Magallanes
Costa Rican $

(☏2766-5606; chicken US$5-12; ⏰10am-10pm) Rancho Magallanes is a sweet roadside restaurant with a wood-burning brick oven where they roast whole chickens and serve them quite simply with tortillas and banana salsa. You can dine with the truckers by the roadside or in the more upscale riverside dining area, painted with colorful jungle scenes.

🍷 DRINKING & NIGHTLIFE

Bar & Cabinas El Río
Bar

(☏2761-0138; ⏰noon-10pm) At the southern end of town, turn off the main road and make your way down to this atmospheric riverside hangout, set on rough-hewn stilts high above the river. Locals congregate on the upper deck to sip cold beers and nosh on filling Tico fare.

ℹ️ GETTING THERE & AWAY

La Virgen lies on Hwy 126, about 8km north of San Miguel and 17km west of Puerto Viejo de Sarapiquí. It's a paved but curvy route (especially heading south, where the road starts to climb into the mountains). Buses ply this route from San José via San Miguel to Puerto Viejo, stopping in La Virgen along the way. Local buses run hourly between La Virgen and Puerto Viejo de Sarapiquí (US$1, 30 minutes) from 6am to 8pm.

NIKPAL/GETTY IMAGES ©

Puerto Viejo de Sarapiquí

The scenic confluence of the Ríos Puerto Viejo and Sarapiquí was once the most important port in Costa Rica. Boats laden with fruit, coffee and other commercial exports plied the Sarapiquí as far as the Nicaraguan border, then turned east on the Río San Juan to the sea.

Today it is simply a gritty but pleasant palm-shaded market town. The town has made concessions to the new economy, with the local polytechnic high school offering students advanced tourism, ecology and agriculture degrees. The school even has its own reserve, laced with trails. Visitors, meanwhile, can choose from any number of activities in the surrounding area, such as bird-watching, rafting, kayaking, boating and hiking.

◉ SIGHTS

Heliconia Island   Gardens
(☏2764-5220; www.heliconiaisland.com; self-guided/guided tours US$10/18, d/q from

US$82/104; ⊗8am-5pm; P 🐾) 🌿 Drive down a rugged road, walk across the bridge and enter a masterpiece of landscape architecture that is home to more than 80 varieties of heliconias, tropical flowers, plants and trees. The 2-hectare island overlooking the Río Puerto Viejo is also a refuge for 228 species of birds, including a spectacled owl who returns every year to raise her family. There are resident howler monkeys, river otters, sloths and a few friendly dogs that will greet you upon arrival.

⊕ TOURS

The boat traffic at the dock in Puerto Viejo is no longer transporting commuters who have somewhere to go. Nowadays it's used primarily for tourist boats, which cruise the Ríos Sarapiquí and Puerto Viejo, looking for birds and monkeys. On a good day, passengers might spot an incredible variety of water birds, not to mention crocodiles, sloths, two kinds of monkeys and countless iguanas sunning

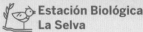
Estación Biológica La Selva

Estación Biológica La Selva is a working biological research station equipped with laboratories, experimental plots, a herbarium and an extensive library. The station is usually teeming with scientists and students researching the nearby private reserve.

The area protected by La Selva is 16 sq km of premontane wet tropical rainforest, much of which is undisturbed. It's bordered to the south by the 476-sq-km Parque Nacional Braulio Carrillo, creating a protected area large enough to support a great diversity of life. More than 886 bird species have been recorded here, as well as 120 mammal species (including 70 species of bats and five species of big cats), 1850 species of vascular plants (especially from the orchid, philodendron and legume families) and thousands of insect species – with 500 types of ants alone.

Reservations are required for three-hour **guided hikes** (☑2766-6565, www.threepaths.co.cr; guided hike US$35, bird-watching hike US$50; ☺guided hike 8am & 1:30pm, bird-watching hike 5:45am) with a bilingual naturalist guide. You'll head across the hanging bridge and into 57km of well-developed jungle trails, some of which are wheelchair accessible. Unguided hiking is forbidden, although you'll be allowed to wander a bit after your guided tour. You should also make reservations for the popular guided bird-watching hikes.

Shining honeycreeper
MAREK STEFUNKO/ALAMY STOCK PHOTO ©

themselves on the muddy riverbanks or gathering in the trees.

Oasis Nature Tours
Boating
(☑2766-6108, 2766-6260, 8816-6462; www.oasisnaturetours.com; full-day tour incl transportation from San José per person US$85-100, safari boat tour per person US$35) This is just one of several guides that runs boat tours on the local rivers. Also offers ziplining, rafting and other guided adventures. Right next to the bus terminal, down the alley in a blue house.

Anhinga Tours
Boating
(☑8346-1220, 2766-5858; www.anhinga.jimdo.com; Av 7; tours per person US$25) This local guide takes travelers out to explore the Río Sarapiquí and its tributaries. Located on the east–west road at the end of town leading to the river.

😋 EATING

Most of the lodgings in and around Puerto Viejo have onsite restaurants or provide meals. Otherwise, there are several *sodas* in Puerto Viejo de Sarapiquí and a supermarket at the western end of town. A couple of interesting restaurants are along the highway between Puerto Viejo and La Virgen (not your typical *sodas*), and the Hotel El Bambú restaurant has some nice choices.

Restaurante y Pizzeria La Casona
Pizza $$
(☑2766-7101; www.hotelaraambigua.com; meals US$8-16; ☺8am-10pm; 🛜👪) The restaurant at **Hotel Ara Ambigua** (☑2766-7101; s/d/tr/q incl breakfast from US$95/95/112/128; 🅿✳🛜🏊) is particularly recommended for its pizza and traditional, homemade cuisine served in an open-air *rancho*. If you're looking for something beyond the pizza/*casado* routine, try the tangy Frida Kahlo chicken. The deck offers a sweet view of the gardens, where birds flutter by as you enjoy your meal.

Clay-colored thrush, the national bird of Costa Rica

Congo Jack's BBQ American $

(📞8447-6684; Calle 1, near Av 3; mains US$6-10; ⏱11am-9pm) Here's a clean, tiny box of a restaurant that seems to have borrowed its gleaming white tiles from the clinic next door. It's borrowed its menu, certainly, from North America, with BBQ pulled-pork sandwiches and other 'fast food,' all claiming to be not fried. Except the french fries, of course.

🛈 GETTING THERE & AWAY

Puerto Viejo de Sarapiquí has been a transportation center longer than Costa Rica has been a country, and it's easily accessed via paved major roads from San José, the Caribbean coast and other population centers. There's a taxi stop across from the bus terminal, and drivers will take you to the nearby lodges for US$5 to US$10.

Volcán Arenal (p226)

In Focus

Painted oxcart wheel

Costa Rica Today

Costa Rica remains one of the more prosperous and stable countries in Central America. It's also one of the only nations in the region without an army. Sound environmental management is a prominent issue, and green proposals were recurring themes in political campaigns during the lead-up to the 2018 general election. Agriculture is one of Costa Rica's main industries, but tourism is its economic backbone.

Carbon Neutrality

Costa Rica has long had a reputation for being green but, to paraphrase Kermit: it ain't easy. In 2009 then-president Óscar Arias set a big goal: that Costa Rica would achieve carbon neutrality by the year 2021. Achieving this would have made Costa Rica the world's first carbon-neutral country and would coincide auspiciously with its bicentennial.

Some measures have not yet been implemented as scheduled, and the numbers suggest that the 2021 target may have been overly ambitious. In 2016 Costa Rica produced 98% of its electricity from renewables. That same year, the nation ran without fossil fuel–generated electricity for 271 days, including a 110-day run between June 17 and October 6. This feat was achieved using hydro, wind and geothermal power to

belief systems
(% of population)

73	15	1	3	8
Catholic	Protestant/ Evangelical	Jehovah's Witnesses	Other	None

if Costa Rica were 100 people

84 would be White & mestizo
7 would be Mulatto
3 would be Indigenous
3 would be Unspecified
2 would be African
1 would be Asian

population per sq km

👤 ≈ 15 people

Costa Rica   Nicaragua   USA

deliver electricity to homes. However, despite Costa Rica's best efforts, it has an oil-reliant transport infrastructure, so in big-picture terms non-renewables make up most of the country's energy use.

Costa Rica's Elections

On April 1 2018 Costa Rica elected a new president, Carlos Alvarado Quesada, of the center-left Citizen Action Party (PAC). Although the polls predicted that the run-off would be a close one, it wasn't. Alvarado – a 38-year-old novelist, musician and former cabinet minister – won more than 60% of the vote, handily defeating Fabricio Alvarado Munoz (a right-wing former TV anchor and evangelical preacher from the National Restoration Party). The decisive victory was particularly good news for progressives and proponents of gay rights. Key challenges the new president faces include an escalating murder rate and a widening national deficit.

Alvarado will take the reigns from former President Luis Guillermo Solís, also a member of PAC. Solís was Costa Rica's first president in half a century not to come from the two-party system, under which the social-democratic National Liberation Party and the center-right Social Christian Unity Party took turns holding power.

Relations with Nicaragua

The Río San Juan forms the eastern stretch of the border between Nicaragua and Costa Rica. This quiet waterway has been the source of much discord between the two countries, and the International Court of Justice (ICJ) has had to preside over several legal disputes.

The latest flap started with Nicaragua dredging Isla Calero's river delta in late 2010. This involved trees being felled and earth being dumped into the river. With Nicaraguan soldiers present during the process, the Costa Rican government decided that this was reason enough to claim invasion, and the situation deteriorated from there. In March 2011, when the ICJ considered the case and reiterated the validity of the Cañas-Jerez Treaty, both sides interpreted the language as a win.

Subsequently, then-president of Costa Rica Laura Chinchilla called for emergency funds to begin construction of a road along the Costa Rican bank of the river, without proper environmental or engineering reviews. This caused consternation not only in Nicaragua but also in Costa Rica about the road's environmental and political impact. Nicaraguan president Daniel Ortega, for his part, has proposed the construction of a trans-oceanic canal in the Río San Juan.

At the beginning of 2017 the Costa Rican government filed a new case with the ICJ concerning continued Nicaraguan military presence on its territory. It also asked for a new deadline and a compensation amount for the 2015 settlement to be issued.

Manzanillo (p94)

INGA LOCMELE/SHUTTERSTOCK ©

History

Costa Rica's history remains a loose sketch during the reign of its pre-Columbian tribes, and European 'discovery' of the New World was followed by the subjugation and evangelization of its indigenous peoples. But in the mid-20th century, it radically departed from the script by abolishing its army, diversifying its economy and brokering peace in the region, paving the way for today's stable, environmentally friendly nation.

11,000 BC
The first humans occupy Costa Rica and populations quickly flourish due to the rich land and marine resources.

1000 BC
The Huetar power base in the Central Valley is solidified following the construction and habitation of the ancient city of Guayabo.

1502
Christopher Columbus docks off the coast and, due to all the gold he sees, dubs it *costa rica* ('rich coast').

Coffee fruit

KRYSSIA CAMPOS/GETTY IMAGES ©

Lost Worlds of Ancient Rica

The coastlines and rainforests of Central America have been inhabited by humans for at least 10,000 years, but ancient civilizations in Costa Rica are largely the subject of speculation. It is thought that the area was something of a backwater straddling the two great civilizations of the Andes and Mesoamerica, with the exception of the Diquís Valley along the Pacific coast. Archaeological finds here suggest that a great deal of trading took place between early inhabitants of Costa Rica and their more powerful neighbors. On the eve of European discovery some 500 years ago, an estimated 400,000 people were living in today's Costa Rica.

Unlike the massive pyramid complexes found throughout other parts of Latin America, the ancient towns and cities of Costa Rica (with the exception of Guayabo) were loosely organized and had no centralized government or ceremonial centers. The settlements fought among each other, but for the purpose of getting slaves rather than to extend their territory. Not known for building edifices that would stand the test of

1563	1737	1808
The first permanent Spanish colonial settlement in Costa Rica is established in Cartago by Juan Vásquez de Coronado.	The future capital of San José is established, sparking a rivalry with neighboring Cartago that culminates in a civil war.	Coffee, set to become the nation's main agricultural crop, arrives from Cuba.

★ **Pre-Columbian Sites**

Monumento Nacional Arqueológico Guayabo (Turrialba)

Hacienda Barú (Dominical)

Sitio Arqueológico Finca 6 (Sierpe)

Finca Cántaros (San Vito)

time, Costa Rica's early inhabitants did, however, leave behind mysterious relics: enormous stone spheres, liberally scattered around the Diquís Valley.

Heirs of Columbus

On his fourth and final voyage to the New World in 1502, Christopher Columbus was forced to drop anchor near present-day Puerto Limón after a hurricane damaged his ship. While waiting for repairs, Columbus ventured into the verdant terrain and exchanged gifts with hospitable and welcoming chieftains. He returned from this encounter claiming to have seen 'more gold in two days than in four years in Española.' Columbus dubbed the stretch of shoreline from Honduras to Panama 'Veraguas,' but it was his excited descriptions of *costa rica* (the 'rich coast') that gave the region its lasting name. At least that's how the popular story goes.

Anxious to claim the country's bounty, Columbus petitioned the Spanish Crown to have himself appointed governor. But by the time he returned to Seville, his royal patron Queen Isabella was on her deathbed, which prompted King Ferdinand to award the prize to Columbus' rival, Diego de Nicuesa. Although Columbus became a very wealthy man, he never returned to the New World. He died in 1506 after being worn down by ill health and court politics.

To the disappointment of his conquistador heirs, Columbus' tales of gold were mostly lies and the locals were considerably less than affable. Nicuesa's first colony in present-day Panama was abruptly abandoned when tropical disease and warring tribes decimated its ranks. Successive expeditions launched from the Caribbean coast also failed as pestilent swamps, oppressive jungles and volcanoes made Columbus' paradise seem more like a tropical hell.

A bright moment in Spanish exploration came in 1513 when Vasco Núñez de Balboa heard rumors about a large sea and a wealthy, gold-producing civilization across the mountains of the isthmus – these almost certainly referred to the Inca empire of present-day Peru. Driven by equal parts ambition and greed, Balboa scaled the continental divide, and on September 26 1513 he became the first European to set eyes upon the Pacific Ocean. Keeping up with the European fashion of the day, Balboa immediately proceeded to claim the ocean and all the lands it touched for the king of Spain.

The thrill of discovery aside, the conquistadors now controlled a strategic western beachhead from which to launch their conquest of Costa Rica. In the name of God and king, aristocratic adventurers plundered indigenous villages, executed resisters and enslaved survivors throughout the Península de Nicoya. However, none of these bloodstained campaigns led to a permanent presence, as intercontinental germ warfare caused

1821	**1838**	**1856**
Following a declaration by Mexico on behalf of Central America, Costa Rica gains its independence from Spain.	Costa Rica becomes entirely independent.	Costa Rica quashes the expansionist aims of hawks in the US by defeating William Walker and his invading army.

outbreaks of feverish death on both sides. The indigenous people mounted a fierce resistance to the invaders, which included guerrilla warfare, destroying their own villages and killing their own children rather than letting them fall into Spanish hands.

New World Order

It was not until the 1560s that a Spanish colony was firmly established in Costa Rica. Hoping to cultivate the rich volcanic soil of the Central Valley, the Spanish founded the village of Cartago on the banks of the Río Reventazón. Although the fledgling colony was extremely isolated, it miraculously survived under the leadership of its first governor, Juan Vásquez de Coronado. Some of Costa Rica's demilitarized present was presaged in its early colonial government: preferring diplomacy over firearms to counter the indigenous threat, Coronado used Cartago as a base to survey the lands south to Panama and west to the Pacific, and secured deed and title over the colony.

Though Coronado was later lost in a shipwreck, his legacy endured. Costa Rica was an officially recognized province of the Virreinato de Nueva España (Viceroyalty of New Spain), which was the name given to the viceroy-ruled territories of the Spanish empire in North America, Central America, the Caribbean and Asia.

For roughly three centuries, the Captaincy General of Guatemala (also known as the Kingdom of Guatemala), which included Costa Rica, Nicaragua, Honduras, El Salvador, Guatemala and the Mexican state of Chiapas, was a loosely administered colony in the vast Spanish empire. Since the political and military headquarters of the kingdom were in Guatemala, Costa Rica became a minor provincial outpost that had little if any strategic significance or exploitable riches.

As a result of its status as a swampy, largely useless backwater, Costa Rica's colonial path diverged from the typical pattern in that a powerful landholding elite and slave-based economy never gained prominence. Instead of large estates, mining operations and coastal cities, modest-sized villages of small-holders developed in the interior Central Valley. According to national lore, the stoic, self-sufficient farmer provided the backbone for 'rural democracy' as Costa Rica emerged as one of the only egalitarian corners of the Spanish empire.

Equal rights and opportunities were not extended to the indigenous groups, and as Spanish settlement expanded, the local population decreased dramatically. From 400,000 at the time Columbus first sailed, the population was reduced to 20,000 a century later, and to 8000 a century after that. While disease was the main cause of death, the Spanish were relentless in their effort to exploit the natives as an economic resource by establishing the *encomienda* system. It applied to indigenous males and gave the Spaniards the right to demand free labor, with many worked to death. Central Valley groups were the first to fall, though outside the valley several tribes managed to survive a bit longer under forest cover, staging occasional raids. However, as in the rest of Latin America, repeated military campaigns eventually forced them into submission and slavery, though throughout that

1889	**1919**	**1948**
Costa Rica's first democratic elections are held.	Federico Tinoco Granados is ousted as the dictator of Costa Rica in one of the few violent episodes in an otherwise peaceful history.	Conservative and liberal forces clash, resulting in a six-week civil war that leaves 2000 Costa Ricans dead and many more wounded.

Bahía Drake's Plundered Treasure

British explorer, government-sponsored pirate and slaver Sir Francis Drake is believed to have anchored in Bahía Drake in 1579. Rumor has it that he buried some of his plundered treasure here, but the only solid memorial to the man is a monument that looks out to his namesake bay.

period many clergymen protested the brutal treatment of indigenous subjects and implored the Spanish Crown to protect them.

Fall of an Empire

Spain's costly Peninsular War with France from 1808 to 1814 – and the political turmoil, unrest and power vacuums that it caused – led Spain to lose all its colonial possessions in the first third of the 19th century.

In 1821 the Americas wriggled free of Spain's imperial grip following Mexico's declaration of independence for itself as well as the whole of Central America. Of course, the Central American provinces weren't too keen on having another foreign power reign over them and subsequently declared independence from Mexico. However, all of these events hardly disturbed Costa Rica, which learned of its liberation a month after the fact.

The newly liberated colonies pondered their fate: stay together in a United States of Central America or go their separate national ways. At first they came up with something in between, namely the Central American Federation (CAF), though it could neither field an army nor collect taxes. Accustomed to being at the center of things, Guatemala also attempted to dominate the CAF, alienating smaller colonies and hastening the CAF's demise. Future attempts to unite the region would likewise fail.

Meanwhile, an independent Costa Rica was taking shape under Juan Mora Fernández, the first head of state (1824–33). He tended toward nation building, and organized new towns, built roads, published a newspaper and coined a currency. His wife even partook in the effort by designing the country's flag.

Life returned to normal, unlike in the rest of the region, where post-independence civil wars raged on. In 1824 the Nicoya-Guanacaste region seceded from Nicaragua and joined its more easygoing southern neighbor, defining the territorial borders. In 1852 Costa Rica received its first diplomatic emissaries from the US and Great Britain.

Coffee Rica

In the 19th century the riches that Costa Rica had long promised were uncovered when it was realized that the soil and climate of the Central Valley highlands were ideal for coffee cultivation. Costa Rica led Central America in introducing the caffeinated bean, which transformed the impoverished country into the wealthiest in the region.

1949

Hoping to heal old wounds and look forward, the temporary government enacts a new constitution that abolishes the army.

1963

Reserva Natural Absoluta Cabo Blanco becomes Costa Rica's first federally protected conservation area.

1977

The Indigenous Law of 1977 is passed, protecting the rights of indigenous communities to ownership of their territories.

When an export market was discovered, the government actively promoted coffee to farmers by providing free saplings. At first Costa Rican producers exported their crop to nearby South Americans, who processed the beans and re-exported the product to Europe. By the 1840s, however, local merchants had already built up domestic capacity and learned to scope out their own overseas markets. Their big break came when they persuaded the captain of HMS *Monarch* to transport several hundred sacks of Costa Rican coffee to London, percolating the beginning of a beautiful friendship.

The Costa Rican coffee boom was on. The drink's quick fix made it popular among working-class consumers in the industrializing north. The aroma of riches lured a wave of enterprising German immigrants, enhancing technical and financial skills in the business sector. By century's end, more than one-third of the Central Valley was dedicated to coffee cultivation, and coffee accounted for more than 90% of all exports and 80% of foreign-currency earnings.

The coffee industry in Costa Rica developed differently from those in the rest of Central America. As elsewhere, there arose a group of coffee barons – elites who reaped the rewards of the export bonanza. But Costa Rican coffee barons lacked the land and labor to cultivate the crop. Coffee production is labor intensive, with a long and painstaking harvest season. Costa Rica's small farmers became the principal planters, and the coffee barons monopolized processing, marketing and financing. The coffee economy in Costa Rica created a wide network of high-end traders and small-scale growers, whereas in the rest of Central America a narrow elite controlled large estates worked by tenant laborers.

Coffee wealth became a power resource in politics. Costa Rica's traditional aristocratic families were at the forefront of the enterprise. At mid-century, three-quarters of the coffee barons were descended from just two colonial families. The country's leading coffee exporter at this time was President Juan Rafael Mora Porras (1849–59), whose lineage went back to the colony's founder, Juan Vásquez de Coronado. Mora was overthrown by his brother-in-law after the president proposed to form a national bank independent of the coffee barons. The economic interests of the coffee elite would thereafter become a priority in Costa Rican politics.

Banana Empire

The coffee trade unintentionally gave rise to Costa Rica's next export boom: bananas. Getting coffee out to world markets necessitated a rail link from the central highlands to the coast, and Limón's deep harbor made an ideal port. Inland was dense jungle and insect-infested swamps, which prompted the government to contract the task to Minor Keith, the nephew of an American railroad tycoon.

The project was a disaster. Malaria and accidents churned through workers as Tico recruits gave way to US convicts and Chinese indentured servants, who were in turn replaced by freed Jamaican slaves. To entice Keith to continue, the government turned

1987
President Óscar Arias Sánchez wins the Nobel Peace Prize for his work on the Central American peace accords.

1994
The indigenous people of Costa Rica are finally granted the right to vote.

2000
The population of Costa Rica tops four million.

Banana plantation

JOHN COLETTI/GETTY IMAGES ©

over 3200 sq km of land along the route and provided a 99-year lease to run the railroad. In 1890 the line was finally completed and running at a loss.

Keith had begun to grow banana plants along the tracks as a cheap food source for the workers. Desperate to recoup his investment, he shipped some bananas to New Orleans in the hope of starting a side venture. He struck gold, or rather yellow. Consumers went crazy for the elongated finger fruit. By the early 20th century, bananas surpassed coffee as Costa Rica's most lucrative export and the country became the world's leading banana exporter. Unlike in the coffee industry, the profits were exported along with the bananas.

Costa Rica was transformed by the rise of Keith's banana empire. He joined another American importer to found the infamous United Fruit Company, known locally as Yunai, which was soon the largest employer in Central America. To locals it was known as *el pulpo* (the octopus) – its tentacles stretched across the region, becoming entangled with the local economy and politics. United Fruit owned huge swaths of lush lowlands,

2006	2010	2010
Óscar Arias Sánchez is elected president for the second time on a pro-Cafta (Central American Free Trade Agreement) platform.	Costa Rica elects its first female president, National Liberation Party candidate Laura Chinchilla.	Volcán Arenal, the country's most active volcano for over four decades, stops spitting lava and enters a resting phase.

much of the transportation and communication infrastructure, and bunches of bureaucrats. The company drew a wave of migrant laborers from Jamaica, changing the country's ethnic complexion and provoking racial tensions. In its various incarnations as the United Brands Company and, later, Chiquita, Yunai was virulently anti-union and maintained control over its workforces by paying them in redeemable scrip rather than cash for many years.

Bitter Fruit

For details on the role of Minor Keith and the United Fruit Company in lobbying for a CIA-led coup in Guatemala, pick up a copy of the highly readable *Bitter Fruit* (1982) by Stephen Schlesinger and Stephen Kinzer.

Amazingly, the marks that *el pulpo* left on Costa Rica are still present, including the rusting train tracks and a locomotive engine in Palmares.

Birth of a Nation

The inequality of the early 20th century led to the rise of José Figueres Ferrer, a self-described farmer-philosopher. The son of Catalan immigrant coffee planters, Figueres excelled in school and went to Boston's MIT to study engineering. Upon returning to Costa Rica to set up his own coffee plantation, he organized the hundreds of laborers on his farm into a utopian socialist community and appropriately named the property La Luz Sin Fin (The Struggle Without End).

In the 1940s Figueres became involved in national politics as an outspoken critic of President Calderón. In the midst of a radio interview in which he bad-mouthed the president, police broke into the studio and arrested Figueres. He was accused of having fascist sympathies and was banished to Mexico. While in exile he formed the Caribbean League, a collection of students and democratic agitators from all over Central America who pledged to bring down the region's military dictators. When he returned to Costa Rica, the Caribbean League, now 700 men strong, went with him and helped protest against those in power.

When government troops descended on the farm with the intention of arresting Figueres and disarming the Caribbean League, it sparked a civil war. The moment had arrived: the diminutive farmer-philosopher now played the man on horseback. Figueres emerged victorious from the brief conflict and seized the opportunity to put into place his vision of Costa Rican social democracy. After dissolving the country's military, Figueres quoted HG Wells: 'The future of mankind cannot include the armed forces.'

As head of a temporary junta government, Figueres enacted nearly a thousand decrees. He taxed the wealthy, nationalized the banks and built a modern welfare state. His 1949 constitution granted full citizenship and voting rights to women, AfricanAmericans, indigenous groups and Chinese minorities. Today Figueres' revolutionary regime is regarded as the foundation of Costa Rica's unarmed democracy.

2013
The murder of 26-year-old environmentalist Jairo Mora Sandoval brings international attention.

2014
Costa Rica advances to the quarterfinals of the 2014 FIFA (Fédération Internationale de Football Association) World Cup in Brazil.

2014
Volcán Poás, one of the most visited attractions in Costa Rica, erupts, prompting park closures until further notice.

The Little Drummer Boy

During your travels through the countryside, you may notice statues of Juan Santamaría, a drummer boy from Alajuela. He is one of Costa Rica's most beloved national heroes.

In April 1856 the North American mercenary William Walker and his ragtag army attempted to invade Costa Rica during an ultimately unsuccessful campaign to conquer all of Central America. Walker had already managed to seize control of Nicaragua, taking advantage of the civil war that was raging there. It didn't take him long after that to decide to march on Costa Rica, though Costa Rican president Juan Rafael Mora Porras guessed Walker's intentions and recruited a volunteer army of 9000 civilians. They surrounded Walker's army in an old hacienda (estate) in present-day Parque Nacional Santa Rosa. The Costa Ricans won the battle and Walker was forever expelled from Costa Rican soil, but Santamaría was ostensibly killed while daringly setting fire to Walker's defenses.

The American Empire

Throughout the 1970s and '80s, the sovereignty of the small nations of Central America was limited by their northern neighbor, the US. Big sticks, gunboats and dollar diplomacy were instruments of a Yankee policy to curtail socialist politics, especially the military oligarchies of Guatemala, El Salvador and Nicaragua.

In 1979 the rebellious Sandinistas toppled the American-backed Somoza dictatorship in Nicaragua. Alarmed by the Sandinistas' Soviet and Cuban ties, fervently anticommunist president Ronald Reagan decided it was time to intervene. Just like that, the Cold War arrived in the hot tropics.

The organizational details of the counterrevolution were delegated to Oliver North, an eager-to-please junior officer working out of the White House basement. North's can-do creativity helped to prop up the famed Contra rebels to incite civil war in Nicaragua. While both sides invoked the rhetoric of freedom and democracy, the war was really a turf battle between left-wing and right-wing forces.

Under intense US pressure, Costa Rica was dragged in. The Contras set up camp in northern Costa Rica, from where they staged guerrilla raids. Not-so-clandestine CIA operatives and US military advisors were dispatched to assist the effort. A secret jungle airstrip was built near the border to fly in weapons and supplies. To raise cash for the rebels, North allegedly used this covert supply network to traffic illegal narcotics through the region.

The war polarized Costa Rica. From conservative quarters came a loud call to reestablish the military and join the anticommunist crusade, which was largely underwritten by the US Pentagon. In May 1984 more than 20,000 demonstrators marched through San José to give peace a chance, though the debate didn't climax until the 1986 presidential election. The victor was 44-year-old Óscar Arias Sánchez, who, despite being born into coffee wealth, was an intellectual reformer in the mold of José Figueres Ferrer, his political patron.

Once in office, Arias affirmed his commitment to a negotiated resolution and reasserted Costa Rican national independence. He vowed to uphold his country's pledge of neutrality and to vanquish the Contras from the territory. The sudden resignation of the US ambassador around this time was a suspected result of Arias' strong stance. In a public ceremony, Costa Rican schoolchildren planted trees on top of the CIA's secret airfield. Most notably, Arias became the driving force in uniting Central America around a peace plan, which ended the Nicaraguan war and earned him the Nobel Peace Prize in 1987.

In 2006 Arias once again returned to the presidential office, winning the popular election by a 1.2% margin and subsequently ratifying the controversial Central American Free Trade Agreement (Cafta), which Costa Rica entered in 2009.

When Laura Chinchilla became the first female president of Costa Rica in 2010, she promised to continue with Arias' free-market policies, in spite of the divisive Cafta agreement (the referendum in 2007 barely resulted in a 'yes' vote at 51%). She also pledged to tackle the rise of violent crime and drug trafficking, on the increase due to Costa Rica's being used as a halfway house by Colombian and Mexican cartels. Ironically, a month after discussing the drug-cartel problem with then-US-president Barack Obama during his visit to Costa Rica, Chinchilla herself became embroiled in a drug-related scandal over the use of a private jet belonging to a man under investigation by Costa Rican intelligence for possible links to international drug cartels.

2016	**2017**	**2018**
Volcán Turrialba erupts, engulfing the country's major cities in a toxic ash cloud.	The government files a new case with the ICJ concerning Nicaraguan military presence on its territory.	Carlos Alvarado Quesada, a 38-year-old novelist and musician from the center-left PAC party, is elected president.

La Fortuna (p234)

Costa Rica Outdoors

Whether you're hiking through the jungle, riding powerful waves on the coast or zipping through the dripping rainforest canopy, Costa Rica is one adrenaline-pumping destination. Families will appreciate the easy-going rafting expeditions and short hikes in the country's national parks, while experienced adventurers will get their kicks in depths of Costa Rica's varied and untamed wildernesses.

Hiking & Trekking

Hiking opportunities around Costa Rica are seemingly endless. With extensive mountains, canyons, dense jungles, cloud forests and two coastlines, this is one of Central America's best and most varied hiking destinations.

Hikes come in an enormous spectrum of difficulty. At tourist-packed destinations such as Monteverde, trails are clearly marked and sometimes paved. This is fantastic if you're traveling with kids or aren't confident about route-finding. For long-distance trekking, there are many more options in the remote corners of the country.

Opportunities for moderate hiking are typically plentiful in most parks and reserves. For the most part, you can rely on signs and maps for orientation, though it helps to have some navigational experience (your phone compass might come in handy). Good hiking

Diving at Isla del Coco (p277)

shoes, plenty of water and confidence in your abilities may enable you to combine several shorter day hikes into a lengthier expedition. Tourist-information centers at park entrances are great resources for planning your intended route.

If you're properly equipped with camping essentials, the country's longer and more arduous multiday treks are at your disposal. Costa Rica's top challenges are scaling Cerro Chirripó, traversing Corcovado and penetrating deep into the heart of La Amistad. While Chirripó can be undertaken independently, local guides are required for much of La Amistad and for all of Corcovado.

Make it Happen

If you're planning your trip around long-distance trekking, it's best to visit during the dry season (December to April). Outside this window, rivers become impassable and trails (and roads!) are prone to flooding. In the highlands, journeys become more taxing in the rain, and the bare landscape offers little protection.

Costa Rica is hot and humid: hiking in these tropical conditions, harassed by mosquitoes, can really take it out of you. Wear light clothing that will dry quickly. Overheating and dehydration are the main sources of misery on the trails, so be sure to bring plenty of water and take rest stops. Make sure you have sturdy, comfortable footwear and a lightweight rain jacket.

Unfortunately, people have reported robberies while on some of the more remote trails. Although this rarely happens, it is always advisable to hike in a group for added safety. Hiring a local guide is another excellent way to enhance your experience, avoid getting lost and learn an enormous amount about the flora and fauna around you.

Baby sloth

Some of the local park offices have maps, but this is the exception rather than the rule. If you are planning to undertake independent hiking on long-distance trails, be sure to purchase your maps in San José in advance.

A number of companies offer trekking tours in Costa Rica.

Osa Wild (p129) Offers a huge variety of hikes in the Osa, in partnership with a sustainability organization.

Costa Rica Trekking Adventures (p120) Offers multiday treks in Chirripó, Corcovado and Tapantí.

Osa Aventura (p129) Specializes in treks through Corcovado.

Surfing

Point and beach breaks, lefts and rights, reefs and river mouths, warm water and year-round waves make Costa Rica a favorite surfing destination. For the most part, the Pacific coast has bigger swells and better waves during the latter part of the rainy season, but the Caribbean cooks from November to May. Basically, there's a wave waiting to be surfed at any time of year.

For the uninitiated, lessons are available at almost all of the major surfing destinations – especially popular towns include Jacó, Dominical, Sámara and Tamarindo on the Pacific coast. Surfing definitely has a steep learning curve, and it can be dangerous if the currents are strong. With that said, the sport is accessible to children and novices, though it's advisable to start with a lesson and always inquire locally about conditions before you paddle out.

Throughout Costa Rica, waves are big (though not massive), and many offer hollow and fast rides that are perfect for intermediates. As a bonus, Costa Rica is one of the few places on the planet where you can surf two different oceans in the same day. Advanced surfers with plenty of experience can contend with some of the world's most famous waves. The top ones include Ollie's Point and Witch's Rock, off the coast of the Santa Rosa sector of the Área de Conservación Guanacaste (featured in *Endless Summer II*); Mal País and Santa Teresa, with a groovy scene to match the powerful waves; Playa Hermosa, whose bigger, faster curls attract a more determined (and experienced) crew of wave-chasers; Pavones, a legendary long left across the sweet waters of the Golfo Dulce; and the infamous Salsa Brava in Puerto Viejo de Talamanca, for experts only.

Make it Happen

Most international airlines accept surfboards (they must be properly packed in a padded board bag) as one of the two pieces of checked luggage, though this is getting harder and pricier in the age of higher fuel tariffs. Domestic airlines offer more of a challenge: they will accept surfboards for an extra charge, but the board must be under 2.1m in length. On full flights, there's a chance your board won't make it on because of weight restrictions.

An alternative is to buy a new or used board in Costa Rica and then sell it before you leave. Great places to start your search include Jacó, Mal País and Santa Teresa, and Tamarindo. It's usually possible to buy a cheap longboard for about US$250 to US$300, and a cheap shortboard for about US$150 to US$200. Many surf shops will buy back your board for about 50% of the price you paid.

Outfitters in many of the popular surf towns rent all kinds of boards, fix dings, give classes and organize excursions. Jacó, Tamarindo, Pavones and Puerto Viejo de Talamanca are good for these types of activities.

Costa Rica Surf Camp (p157) Excellent teachers with safety certification and low teacher-student ratios.

Dominical Surf Adventures (p157) An excellent source of surf lessons in Dominical.

Caribbean Surf School (p83) Based in Puerto Viejo de Talamanca, Hershel is widely considered to be one of the best teachers on the Caribbean side.

Pura Vida Adventures (p191) An excellent women-only surf-and-yoga camp at Playa El Carmen.

Wildlife-Watching & Birding

Costa Rica's biodiversity is legendary, and the country delivers unparalleled opportunities for bird- and wildlife-watching. Most people are already familiar with the most famous, yet commonly spotted, animals. You'll instantly recognize monkeys bounding through the treetops, sloths clinging to branches and toucans gliding beneath the canopy. Young children, even if they have been to the zoo dozens of times, typically love the thrill of spotting creatures in the wild.

For slightly older visitors, keeping checklists is a fun way to add an educational element to your travels. If you really want to know what you're looking at, pick up wildlife and bird guides before your trip – look for ones with color plates for easy positive IDs (Rainforest Publications produces easy-to-store laminated foldouts of birds, flowers and fauna).

A quality pair of binoculars (starting at US$200 to US$300) is highly recommended and can really make the difference between far-off movement and a veritable face-to-face encounter (some guides and lodges can lend you a pair). For expert birders, a spotting scope is essential, and multipark itineraries will allow you to quickly add dozens of new species to your all-time list. Optics are heavy and expensive, though, so consider that when packing.

Make it Happen

Costa Rica is brimming with avian life at every turn, but sometimes it takes an experienced guide to help you notice it.

Aratinga Tours (p117) Some of the best bird tours in the country are led by Belgian ornithologist Pieter Westra.

Tropical Feathers (☑2771-9686; www.costaricabirdingtours.com) Local owner and guide Noel Ureña has over 16 years' experience leading birding tours.

Birding Eco Tours (☑in USA 614-932-1430; www.birdingecotours.com) An international birding-tour company with highly entertaining and qualified guides in Costa Rica.

Pink spatula and ducks

White-water Rafting & Kayaking

White-water rafting has remained one of Costa Rica's top outdoor pursuits since the '80s. Ranging from family-friendly Class I riffles to nearly non-navigable Class V rapids, the country's rivers offer highly varied experiences.

First-time runners are catered for year-round, while seasoned enthusiasts arrive en masse during the wildest months from June to October. There is also much regional variation, with gentler rivers located near Manuel Antonio along the central Pacific coast, and world-class runs along the Río Pacuare in the Central Valley. Since all white-water rafting in Costa Rica requires the presence of a certified guide, you will need to book trips through a reputable tour agency. No matter the run, you'll get totally soaked and tossed about, so pack a sense of humor, but no fancy clothes or jewelry.

River kayaking has its fair share of loyal fans. The tiny village of La Virgen in the northern lowlands is the unofficial kayaking capital of Costa Rica and the best spot to hook up with other paddlers. The neighboring Río Sarapiquí has an impressive variety of runs that cater to all ages and skill levels.

With 1228km of coastline, two gulfs and plentiful mangrove estuaries, Costa Rica is also an ideal destination for sea kayaking. This is a great way for paddlers to access remote areas and catch glimpses of rare birds and wildlife. Access varies considerably, and is largely dependent on tides and currents.

June to October is considered peak season for river rafting and kayaking, though some rivers offer good runs all year. Government regulation of outfitters is shoddy, so ask lots of questions about your guide's water-safety, emergency and medical training. If you suspect they're bluffing, move along – there are plenty of legit outfits.

River kayaking can be organized in conjunction with white-water-rafting trips if you are experienced; sea kayaking is popular year-round.

Aguas Bravas (☏2479-7645; www.aguasbravascr.com; rafting US$80-100; ☺7am-7pm) In La Fortuna, this is the best outfitter on Costa Rica's best white water.

Exploradores Outdoors (p77) This outfit offers one- and two-day trips on the Ríos Pacuare, Reventazón and Sarapiquí.

Green Rivers (p251) A young and fun Sarapiquí-based outfit working out of the Posada Andrea Cristina.

Pineapple Tours (p156) Exciting half-day kayak trips go through caves and mangrove channels.

H2O Adventures (p170) Arranges two- and five-day adventures on the Río Savegre.

Hiking near Quepos (p170)

KATHRIN ZIEGLER/GETTY IMAGES ©

Ríos Tropicales (p101) Multiday adventures on the Río Pacuare and two days of kayaking in Tortuguero.

Costa Rica Expeditions (☑2521-6099; www.costaricaexpeditions.com) This outfitter handles small groups and offers rafting trips that cater to foodies.

Diving & Snorkeling

The good news is that Costa Rica offers body-temperature water with few humans and abundant marine life. The bad news is that visibility is low because of silt and plankton, and soft corals and sponges are dominant.

However, if you're looking for fine opportunities to see massive schools of fish, as well as larger marine animals such as turtles, sharks, dolphins and whales, then jump right in. It's also worth pointing out that there are few places in the world where you could feasibly dive in the Caribbean and the Pacific on the same day – though why not take your time?

The Caribbean Sea is better for novice divers and snorkelers, with the beach towns of Manzanillo and Cahuita particularly well suited to youngsters. Puerto Viejo de Talamanca lays claim to a few decent sites that can be explored on a discovery dive. Along the Pacific, Isla del Caño ups the ante for those with solid diving experience.

Isla del Coco is the exception to the rule – this remote island floating in the deep Pacific is regarded by veteran divers as one of the best spots on the planet. To dive the wonderland of Coco, you'll need to visit on a liveaboard and have logged some serious time underwater.

Make it Happen

Generally, visibility isn't great during the rainy months, when rivers swell and their outflow clouds the ocean. At this time, boats to offshore locations offer better viewing opportunities.

The water is warm – around 24°C (75°F) to 29°C (84°F) at the surface, with a thermocline at around 20m below the surface where it drops to 23°C (73°F). If you're keeping it shallow, you can skin-dive.

Surfing, Guanacaste

PANORAMIC IMAGES/GETTY IMAGES ©

If you're interested in diving but aren't certified, you can usually complete a one-day introductory course that will allow you to do one or two accompanied dives. If you love it – and most people do – certification courses take three to four days and cost around US$350 to US$500.

Mountain Biking & Cycling

Although the winding, potholed roads and aggressive drivers can be a challenge, cycling is on the rise in Costa Rica. Numerous less-trafficked roads offer plenty of adventure – from scenic mountain paths with sweeping views to rugged trails that take riders through streams and past volcanoes.

The best long-distance rides are along the Pacific coast's Interamericana, which has a decent shoulder and is relatively flat, and on the road from Montezuma to the Reserva Natural Absoluta Cabo Blanco on the southern Península de Nicoya. The hills around Bahía Salinas in the northwest are good fun, too.

Mountain biking has taken off in recent years and there are good networks of trails around Corcovado and Arenal, as well as more rides in the central mountains.

Make it Happen

Most international airlines will fly your bike as a piece of checked baggage for an extra fee. Pad it well, because the box is liable to be handled roughly.

Alternatively, you can rent mountain bikes in almost any tourist town, but the condition of the equipment varies greatly. For a monthly fee, Trail Source (www.trailsource.com) can provide you with information on trails all over Costa Rica and the world.

Outfitters in Costa Rica and the US can organize multiday mountain-biking trips. If you want to tour Costa Rica by bicycle, be forewarned that the country's cycling shops are decidedly more geared toward utilitarian concerns. Bring any specialized equipment (including a serious lock) from home.

Envision Festival (p22)

LINDSAY FENDT/ALAMY STOCK PHOTO ©

The Tico Way of Life

*Blessed with natural beauty and a peaceful,
army-less society, it's no wonder Costa Rica has long
been known as the Switzerland of Central America.
While nowadays the country is certainly challenged
by its lofty eco-conscious goals and modern intercontinental maladies (such as drug trafficking), the
Tico attitude remains sunny and family-centered,
with a good balance between work and play.*

The Pura Vida

Pura vida – pure life – is more than just a slogan that rolls off the tongues of Ticos (Costa Ricans) and emblazons souvenirs. In the laid-back tone in which it is constantly uttered, the phrase is a bona fide mantra for the Costa Rican way of life. Perhaps the essence of the pure life is something better lived than explained. But hearing *'pura vida'* again and again while traveling across this beautiful country – as a greeting, a stand-in for goodbye, 'cool,' and an acknowledgement of thanks – makes it evident that the concept lives deep within the DNA of this country.

The living seems particularly pure when Costa Rica is compared with its Central American neighbors such as Nicaragua and Honduras; there's little poverty, illiteracy or political tumult, the country is crowded with ecological jewels, and the standard of living is high. What's more, Costa Rica has flourished without an army for the past 60 years. The sum of the parts is a country that's an oasis of calm in a corner of the world continuously degraded by warfare. And though the Costa Rican people are justifiably proud hosts, a compliment to the country is likely to be met simply with a warm smile and an enigmatic two-word reply: *pura vida*.

Daily Life

With its lack of war, long life expectancy and relatively sturdy economy, Costa Rica enjoys the highest standard of living in Central America. For the most part, Costa Ricans live fairly affluent and comfortable lives, even by North American standards.

As in many places in Latin America, the family unit in Costa Rica remains the nucleus of life. Families socialize together and extended families often live near each other. When it's time to party it's also largely a family affair; celebrations, vacations and weddings are a social outlet for rich and poor alike, and those with relatives in positions of power – nominal or otherwise – don't hesitate to turn to them for support.

Given this mutually cooperative environment, it's no surprise that life expectancy in Costa Rica is slightly higher than in the US. In fact, most Costa Ricans are more likely to die of heart disease or cancer as opposed to the childhood diseases that plague many developing nations. A comprehensive socialized health-care system and excellent sanitation systems account for these positive statistics, as do a generally stress-free lifestyle, tropical weather and a healthy and varied diet – the *pura vida*.

Still, the divide between rich and poor is evident. The middle and upper classes largely reside in San José, as well as in the major cities of the Central Valley highlands (Heredia, Alajuela and Cartago), and enjoy a level of comfort similar to their economic brethren in Europe and the US. City dwellers are likely to have a maid and a car or two, and the lucky few have a second home on the beach or in the mountains.

The home of an average Tico is a one-story construction built from concrete blocks, wood or a combination of both. In the poorer lowland areas, people often live in windowless houses made of *caña brava* (a local cane). For the vast majority of *campesinos* (farmers) and *indígenas* (people of indigenous origin), life is harder than in the cities, poverty levels are higher and standards of living are lower than in the rest of the country. This is especially true along the Caribbean coast, where the descendants of Jamaican immigrants have long suffered from lack of attention by the federal government, and also in indigenous reservations. However, although poor families have few possessions and little financial security, every member assists with working the land or contributing to the household, which creates a strong safety net.

As in the rest of the world, globalization is having a dramatic effect on Costa Ricans, who are increasingly mobile, international and intertwined in the global economy – for better or for worse. These days, society is increasingly geographically mobile – the Tico who was born in Puntarenas might end up managing a lodge on the Península de Osa. And, with the advent of better-paved roads, cell coverage, and the increasing presence of North American and European expats (and the accompanying malls and big box stores), the Tico family unit is subject to the changing tides of a global society.

Women in Costa Rica

By the letter of the law, Costa Rica's progressive stance on women's issues makes the country stand out among its Central American neighbors. A 1974 family code stipulated equal duties and rights for men and women. Additionally, women can draw up contracts, assume loans and inherit property. Sexual harassment and sex discrimination are also against the law, and in 1996 Costa Rica passed a landmark law against domestic violence that was one of the most progressive in Latin America. With women holding more and more roles in political, legal, scientific and medical fields, Costa Rica has been home to some historic firsts: in 1998 both vice presidents (Costa Rica has two) were women, and in February 2010 Arias Sánchez's former vice president, Laura Chinchilla, became the first female president.

Still, the picture of sexual equality is much more complicated than the country's bragging rights might suggest. Byproducts of the legal prostitution trade include illicit underground activities such as child prostitution and the trafficking of women. Despite the cultural reverence for the matriarch (Mother's Day is a national holiday), traditional Latin American machismo is hardly a thing of the past and anti-discrimination laws are rarely enforced. Particularly in the countryside, many women maintain traditional societal roles: raising children, cooking and running the home.

Sport

From the scrappy little matches that take over the village pitch to the breathless exclamations of 'Goal!' that erupt from San José bars on the day of a big game, no other Costa Rican sporting venture can compare with *fútbol* (soccer). Every town has a soccer field (which usually serves as the most conspicuous landmark) where neighborhood aficionados play in heated matches.

The *selección nacional* (national selection) team is known affectionately as La Sele. Legions of Tico fans still recall La Sele's most memorable moments, including an unlikely showing in the quarterfinals at the 1990 World Cup in Italy and a solid (if not long-lasting) performance in the 2002 World Cup. More recently, La Sele's failure to qualify for the 2010 World Cup led to a top-down change in leadership and the reinstatement of one-time coach Jorge Luis Pinto, a Colombian coach who has had mixed results on the international stage. In general, Pinto seemed to be a good fit for the team's ferocious young leaders such as record-setting scorer Álvaro Saborío, goalkeeper Keylor Navas and forward Bryan Ruiz. And in fact, Pinto led the team to qualify for the 2014 World Cup in Brazil, where the team reached the quarterfinals, making them national heroes. At the time of research Costa Rica's national team was set to battle it out in the 2018 World Cup qualifiers.

With such perfect waves, surfing has steadily grown in popularity among Ticos, especially those growing up in surf towns. Costa Rica hosts numerous national and international competitions annually that are widely covered by local media, as well as holding regular local competitions such as the weekly contest at Playa Hermosa (south of Jacó).

For a nation that values its wildlife, it may be surprising that the controversial sport of bullfighting is still popular, particularly in the Guanacaste region, though the bull isn't killed in the

Marriage Equality

Since 1998 there have been laws on the books to protect 'sexual option,' and discrimination is generally prohibited in most facets of society. The country is becoming increasingly gay-friendly, but traditional culture has been slower to respond.

In January 2012 Costa Rica's primary newspaper, *La Nación,* conducted a poll in which 55% of the respondents believed that same-sex couples should have the same rights as heterosexual couples. Then in July 2013 the Costa Rican legislature 'accidentally' passed a law legalizing gay marriage, due to a small change in the bill's wording. In 2015 a Costa Rican judge granted a same-sex common-law marriage, making Costa Rica the first country in Central America to recognize gay relationships.

Legal recognition of same-sex partnerships was a major point of contention in the 2010 and 2018 presidential races, and President Carlos Alvarado has expressed support for gay rights.

Costa Rica by the Book

Costa Rica's history and culture have been detailed in a number of books. **Tycoon's War**, by Stephen Dando-Collins, is a well-told tale of US business tycoon Cornelius Vanderbilt's epic struggle to maintain his economic stranglehold over the Central American isthmus.

Bananas: How United Fruit Company Shaped the World, by Peter Chapman, tells the story of the meteoric rise and inevitable collapse of the megalith known to locals as 'el pulpo' (the octopus).

Nation Thief, by Robert Houston, is a novelistic telling of William Walker's excursions into Central America.

Green Phoenix, by William Allen, details the ultimate victory of a cohort of Costa Rican and US scientists and volunteers in halting deforestation.

Walking with Wolf, by Kay Chornook and Wolf Guindon, recounts the life of one of Monteverde's pioneering Quakers and his decades-long dedication to preserving his cloud-forest home.

Cocorí, by Joaquín Guitiérrez, is an illustrated tapestry of life lessons gleaned by a young boy in the rainforest.

Guanacaste: Rutas de Viaje (Travel Routes), by Luciano Capelli and Yazmin Ross, is a stunning coffee-table book of the province's festivals, farmers, and frogs, among other things.

Costa Rican version of the sport. More aptly described, bullfighting is really a ceremonial opportunity to watch an often tipsy cowboy run around with a bull. Travelers should consider the ethics of the spectacle when deciding to attend.

Arts

Literature

Costa Rica has a relatively young literary history and few works of Costa Rican writers or novelists are available in translation. Carlos Luis Fallas (1909–66) is widely known for *Mamita Yunai* (1940), an influential 'proletarian' novel that took the banana companies to task for their labor practices, and he remains very popular among the Latin American left.

Carmen Naranjo (1928–2012) is one of the few contemporary Costa Rican writers to have risen to international acclaim. She was a novelist, poet and short-story writer who also served as ambassador to India in the 1970s, and a few years later as minister of culture. In 1996 she was awarded the prestigious Gabriela Mistral medal by the Chilean government. Her collection of short stories, *There Never Was a Once Upon a Time,* is widely available in English. Two of her stories can also be found in *Costa Rica: A Traveler's Literary Companion.*

José León Sánchez (b 1929) is an internationally renowned memoirist of Huetar descent, hailing from the border of Costa Rica and Nicaragua. After being convicted for stealing from the famous Basílica de Nuestra Señora de Los Ángeles in Cartago, he was sentenced to serve his term at Isla San Lucas, one of Latin America's most notorious jails. Illiterate when he was incarcerated, Sánchez taught himself how to read and write, and clandestinely authored one of the continent's most poignant books: *La isla de los hombres solos* (called *God Was Looking the Other Way* in the translated version).

Music & Dance

Although there are other Latin American musical hotbeds of more renown, Costa Rica's central geographical location and colonial history have resulted in a varied musical culture that incorporates elements from North and South America and the Caribbean islands.

San José features a regular lineup of domestic and international rock, folk and hip-hop artists, but you'll find that the regional sounds also survive, each with their own special rhythms, instruments and styles. For instance, the Península de Nicoya has a rich musical history, most of its sound made with guitars, maracas and marimbas. The common sounds on the Caribbean coast are reggae, reggaetón (a newer version of reggae mixed with hip-hop beats) and calypso, which has roots in Afro-Caribbean slave culture.

Popular dance music includes Latin dances, such as salsa, merengue, bolero and *cumbia*. Guanacaste is also the birthplace of many traditional dances, most of which depict court-ship rituals between country folk. The most famous dance – sometimes considered the national dance – is the *punto guanacasteco*. What keeps it lively is the *bomba,* a funny (and usually racy) rhymed verse shouted by the male dancers during the musical interlude.

Visual Arts

The visual arts in Costa Rica first took on a national character in the 1920s, when Te-odórico Quirós, Fausto Pacheco and their contemporaries began painting landscapes that differed from traditional European styles, depicting the rolling hills and lush forest of the Costa Rican countryside, often sprinkled with characteristic adobe houses.

The contemporary scene is more varied and it's difficult to define a unique Tico style. The work of several artists has garnered acclaim, including the magical realism of Isidro Con Wong, the surreal paintings and primitive engravings of Francisco Amighetti and the mystical female figures painted by Rafa Fernández. The Museo de Arte y Diseño Contem-poráneo in San José is the top place to see this type of work, and its permanent collection is a great primer.

Many galleries are geared toward tourists and specialize in 'tropical art' (for lack of an official description): brightly colored, whimsical folk paintings depicting flora and fauna that evoke the work of French artist Henri Rousseau.

Folk art and handicrafts are not as widely produced or readily available here as in other Central American countries. However, the dedicated souvenir hunter will have no problem finding the colorful Sarchí oxcarts that have become a symbol of Costa Rica. Indigenous crafts include intricately carved and painted masks made by the Boruca indigenous peo-ple, as well as handwoven bags and linens, and colorful Chorotega pottery. These can also be found in San José and more readily along Costa Rica's Pacific coast.

Film

While film is not a new medium in Costa Rica, young filmmakers have been upping the country's ante in this arena. Over the last decade or so, a handful of Costa Rican filmmakers have submitted their work for Oscar consideration, and many others have received critical acclaim for their pictures nationally and internationally. Such films include an adaptation of Gabriel García Márquez's magical-realism novel *Del amor y otro demonios* (Of Love and Other Demons, 2009), directed by Hilda Hidalgo, and a comedic coming-of-age story of young Ticos on the cusp of adulthood in contemporary Costa Rica in *El cielo rojo* (The Red Sky, 2008), written and directed by Miguel Alejandro Gomez. There's also the light-hearted story of a Costa Rican farmer who embarks on the journey to Europe to raise money and save his farm in *Maikol Yordan de viaje perdido* (Maikol Yordan Traveling Lost, 2014), again directed by Gomez.

A film-festival calendar has also been blossoming in Costa Rica, though dates vary year on year. Sponsored by the Ministerio de Cultura y Juventud, the Costa Rica Festival Inter-nacional de Cine (www.facebook.com/CostaRicaCineFest) takes place in San José (check the website for current dates) and features international films fitting the year's theme. The longer-running Costa Rica International Film Festival (CRIFF; www.filmfestivallife.com) takes place in early June, with an associated documentary film festival the week afterwards.

Catarata Río Fortuna (p234)

Landscapes & Ecology

*Despite its diminutive size, Costa Rica's land is an
astounding collection of habitats. On one coast
are the breezy skies and big waves of the Pacific,
while only 119km away lie the languid shores of the
Caribbean. In between, there are active volcanoes,
alpine peaks and crisp high-elevation forest. Few
places can compare with Costa Rica's spectacular
interaction of natural, geological and climatic forces.*

The Land

The Pacific Coast

Two major peninsulas hook out into the ocean along the 1016km-long Pacific coast: Nicoya in the north and Osa in the south. Although they look relatively similar from space, on the ground they could hardly be more different. Nicoya is one of the driest places in the country and holds some of Costa Rica's most developed tourist infrastructure; Osa is wet and rugged, run through by wild, seasonal rivers and rough dirt roads that are always under threat from the creeping jungle.

Just inland from the coast, the Pacific lowlands are a narrow strip of land backed by mountains. This area is equally dynamic, ranging from dry deciduous forests and open cattle country in the north to misty, mysterious tropical rainforests in the south.

Central Costa Rica

Move a bit inland from the Pacific coast and you immediately ascend the jagged spine of the country: the majestic Cordillera Central in the north and the rugged, largely unexplored Cordillera de Talamanca in the south. Continually being revised by tectonic activity, these mountains are part of the majestic Sierra Madre chain that runs north through Mexico.

Home to active volcanoes, clear trout-filled streams and ethereal cloud forest, these mountain ranges generally follow a northwest to southeast line, with the highest and most dramatic peaks in the south near the Panamanian border. The highest peak in the country is windswept Cerro Chirripó (3820m).

In the midst of this powerful landscape, surrounded on all sides by mountains, are the highlands of the Meseta Central – the Central Valley. This fertile central plain, some 1000m above sea level, is the agricultural heart of the nation and enjoys abundant rainfall and mild temperatures. It includes San José and cradles three more of Costa Rica's five largest cities, accounting for more than half of the country's population.

The Caribbean Coast

Cross the mountains and drop down the eastern slope and you'll reach the elegant line of the Caribbean coastline – a long, straight 212km along low plains, brackish lagoons and waterlogged forests. A lack of strong tides allows plants to grow right over the water's edge along coastal sloughs. Eventually, these create the walls of vegetation along the narrow, murky waters that characterize much of the region. As if taking cues from the slow-paced, Caribbean-influenced culture, the rivers that rush out of the central mountains take on a languid pace here, curving through broad plains toward the sea.

While there are smoothly paved main roads along the southern Caribbean coast, the northern Caribbean is still largely inaccessible except by boat or plane.

Geology

If all this wildly diverse beauty makes Costa Rica feel like the crossroads between vastly different worlds, that's because it is. As it's part of the thin strip of land that separates two continents with hugely divergent wildlife and topographical character, and right in the middle of the world's two largest oceans, it's little wonder that Costa Rica boasts such a colorful collision of climates, landscapes and wildlife.

The country's geological history began when the Cocos Plate, a tectonic plate that lies below the Pacific, crashed headlong into the Caribbean Plate, which is off the isthmus' east coast. Since the plates travel about 10cm every year, the collision might seem slow by human measure, but it was a violent wreck by geological standards, creating the area's subduction zone. The plates continue to collide, with the Cocos Plate pushing the Caribbean Plate toward the heavens and making the area prone to earthquakes and ongoing volcanic activity.

Despite all the violence underfoot, these forces have blessed the country with some of the world's most beautiful and varied tropical landscapes.

Out on the Reef

Compared with the rest of the Caribbean, the coral reefs of Costa Rica are not a banner attraction. Heavy surf and shifting sands along most of the Caribbean coast produce conditions that are unbearable to corals. The exceptions are two beautiful patches of reef in the south that are protected on the rocky headlands of Parque Nacional Cahuita and Refugio Nacional de Vida Silvestre Gandoca-Manzanillo. These diminutive but vibrant reefs are home to more than 100 species of fish and many types of coral, and make for decent snorkeling and diving.

Unfortunately, the reefs themselves are in danger due to global warming and increased water temperatures, tourism (divers and snorkelers damaging the reefs), and pollutants, like sediments washing downriver from logging operations and toxic chemicals that wash out of nearby agricultural fields. Although curbed by the government, these factors persist. Along with these threats, a major earthquake in 1991 lifted the reefs as much as 1.5m, stranding and killing large portions of this fragile ecosystem.

Wildlife

Nowhere else are so many types of habitats squeezed into such a tiny area, and species from different continents have been commingling here for millennia. Costa Rica has the world's largest number of species per 10,000 sq km – a whopping 615. This simple fact alone makes Costa Rica the premier destination for nature-lovers.

The large number of species here is also due to the country's relatively recent appearance. Roughly three million years ago, Costa Rica rose from the ocean and formed a land bridge between North and South America. As species from these two vast biological provinces started to mingle, the number of species essentially doubled in the area where Costa Rica now sits.

Flora

Simply put, Costa Rica's floral biodiversity is mind-blowing – there are more than 500,000 species in total, including close to 12,000 species of vascular plant, and the list gets more and more crowded each year. Orchids alone account for about 1400 species. The diversity of habitats created when this many species mix is a wonder to behold.

Rainforest

The humid, vibrant mystery of the tropical rainforest connects acutely with a traveler's sense of adventure. These forests, far more dense with plant life than any other environment on the planet, are leftover scraps of the prehistoric jungles that once covered the continents. Standing in the midst of it and trying to take it all in can be overwhelming: tropical rainforests contain more than half of the earth's known living organisms. Naturally, this riotous pile-on of life requires lots of water – the forest typically gets between 5m and 6m of rainfall annually (yes, that's *meters*!).

Classic rainforest habitats are well represented in the parks of southwestern Costa Rica or in the mid-elevation portions of the central mountains. Here you will find towering trees that block out the sky, long, looping vines and many overlapping layers of vegetation. Large trees often show buttresses – wing-like ribs that extend from their trunks for added structural support. And plants climb atop other plants, fighting for a bit of sunlight. The most impressive areas of primary forest – a term designating completely untouched land that has never been disturbed by humans – exist on the Península de Osa.

Cloud Forest

Visiting the unearthly terrain of a cloud forest is a highlight for many visitors; there are amazing swaths of it in Monteverde, along the Cerro de la Muerte and below the peaks of Chirripó. In these regions, fog-drenched trees are so thickly coated in mosses, ferns, bromeliads and orchids that you can hardly discern their true shapes. These forests are created when humid trade winds off the Caribbean blow up into the highlands, then cool and condense to form thick, low-hanging clouds. With constant exposure to wind, rain and sun, the trees here are crooked and stunted.

Cloud forests are widespread at high elevations throughout Costa Rica and any of them warrant a visit. Be forewarned, however, that in these habitats the term 'rainy season' has little meaning because it's always dripping wet from the fog – humidity in a cloud forest often hovers around 100%.

Tropical Dry Forest

Along Costa Rica's northwestern coast lies the country's largest concentration of tropical dry forest – a stunningly different

Don't Disturb the Dolphins

Swimming with dolphins has been illegal since 2006, although shady tour operators out for a quick buck may encourage it. Research indicates that in some heavily touristed areas, dolphins are leaving their natural habitat in search of calmer seas. When your boat comes across these amazing creatures of the sea, avoid the temptation to jump in with them – you can still have an awe-inspiring experience peacefully observing them without disturbing them.

scene to the country's wet rainforests and cloud forests. During the dry season many trees drop their foliage, creating carpets of crackling, sun-drenched leaves and a sense of openness that is largely absent in other Costa Rican habitats. The large trees here, such as Costa Rica's national tree, the guanacaste, have broad, umbrella-like canopies, while spiny shrubs and vines or cacti dominate the understory. At times, large numbers of trees erupt into spectacular displays of flowers, and at the beginning of the rainy season everything is transformed with a wonderful flush of new, green foliage.

This type of forest was native to Guanacaste and the Península de Nicoya, though it suffered generations of destruction for its commercially valuable lumber. Most was clear-cut or burned to make space for ranching. Guanacaste and Santa Rosa national parks are good examples of the dry forest and host some of the country's most accessible nature hiking.

Mangroves

Along brackish stretches of both coasts, mangrove swamps are a world unto themselves. Growing on stilts out of muddy tidal flats, five species of tree crowd together so densely that no boats and few animals can penetrate. Striking in their adaptations for dealing with salt, mangroves thrive where no other land plant dares tread and are among the world's most relentless colonizers. Mangrove seeds are heavy and fleshy, blooming into flowers in the spring before falling off to give way to fruit. By the time the fruit falls, the mud is covered with spiky seedlings that anchor in the soft mud of low tides. In only 10 years, a seedling has the potential to mature into an entire new colony.

Mangrove swamps play extremely important roles in the ecosystem. Not only do they buffer coastlines from the erosive power of waves but also they have high levels of productivity because they trap nutrient-rich sediment and serve as spawning and nursery areas for innumerable species of fish and invertebrates. The brown waters of mangrove channels – rich with nutrients and filled with algae, shrimp, crustaceans and caimans – form tight links in the marine food chain and are best explored in a kayak, early in the morning.

There are miles of mangrove channels along the Caribbean coast, and a vast mangrove swamp on the Pacific, near Bahía Drake.

Fauna

Though tropical in nature – with a substantial number of tropical animals such as poison-dart frogs and spider monkeys – Costa Rica is also the winter home for more than

200 species of migrating birds that arrive from as far away as Alaska and Australia. Don't be surprised to see one of your familiar backyard birds feeding alongside trogons and toucans. Birds are one of the primary attractions for naturalists, who scan endlessly for birds of every color, from strawberry-red scarlet macaws to the iridescent jewels called violet sabrewings (a type of hummingbird). Because many birds in Costa Rica have restricted ranges, you are guaranteed to find different species everywhere you travel.

Visitors will almost certainly see one of Costa Rica's four types of monkeys or two types of sloths, but there are an additional 230 types of mammals awaiting the patient observer. More exotic sightings might include the amazing four-eyed opossum or the silky anteater, while a lucky few might spot the elusive tapir or have a jaguarundi cross their path. The extensive network of national parks, wildlife refuges and other protected areas are prime places to spot wildlife.

If you are serious about observing birds and animals, the value of a knowledgeable guide cannot be underestimated. Their keen eyes are trained to notice the slightest movement in the forest, and they recognize the many exotic sounds. Most professional bird guides are proficient in the dialects of local birds, greatly improving your chances of hearing or seeing these species.

No season is a bad one for exploring Costa Rica's natural environment, though most visitors arrive during the peak dry season, when trails are less muddy and more accessible. A bonus of visiting between December and February is that many of the wintering migrant birds are still hanging around. A trip after the peak season means fewer birds, but this is a stupendous time to see dry forests transform into vibrant greens and it's also when resident birds begin nesting.

Endangered Species

As expected in a country with unique habitats and widespread logging, there are numerous species whose populations are declining or in danger of extinction. Currently, the number-one threat to most of Costa Rica's endangered species is habitat destruction, followed closely by hunting and trapping.

Costa Rica's four species of sea turtles – olive ridley, leatherback, green and hawksbill – deservedly get a lot of attention. All four species are classified as endangered or critically endangered, meaning they face an imminent threat of extinction. While populations of some species are increasing, thanks to various protection programs along both coasts, the risk for these *tortugas* (turtles) is still very real.

Destruction of habitat is a huge problem. With the exception of the leatherbacks, all of these species return to their natal beach to nest, which means that the ecological state of the beach directly affects that turtle's ability to reproduce. All of the species prefer dark, undisturbed beaches, and any sort of development or artificial lighting (including flashlights) will inhibit nesting.

Hunting and harvesting eggs are two major causes of declining populations. Green turtles are hunted for their meat. Leatherbacks and olive ridleys are not killed for meat, but their eggs are considered a delicacy – an aphrodisiac, no less. Hawksbill turtles are hunted for their unusual shells, which are sometimes used to make jewelry and hair ornaments. Of course, any trade in tortoiseshell products and turtle eggs and meat is illegal, but a significant black market exists.

The ultra-rare harpy eagle and the legendary quetzal – the birds at the top of every naturalist's must-see list – teeter precariously as their home forests are felled at an alarming rate. Seeing a noisy scarlet macaw could be a birdwatching highlight in Costa Rica, but trapping for the pet trade has extirpated these magnificent birds from much of their former range. Although populations are thriving on the Península de Osa, the scarlet macaw is now extinct over most of Central America, including the entire Caribbean coast.

A number of Costa Rica's mammals are highly endangered, including the elusive jaguar and the squirrel monkey, both due to destruction of habitat. The two survive in the depths of Parque Nacional Corcovado, with the latter also found in some numbers in Parque Nacional Manuel Antonio.

Harassment and intimidation of conservationists in Costa Rica is nothing new, and although the brutal murder of 26-year-old environmentalist Jairo Mora Sandoval in Limón Province in 2013 brought the issue to international attention, those accused of his murder were initially acquitted. In 2015 seven men were accused of Sandoval's murder. Four of the men were not convicted of murder but of assault, kidnapping and aggravated robbery for a crime that took place after Mora's murder. Then in 2016, after an appeal, the not-guilty verdict was overturned. Each of the men is serving 50 years in prison, the maximum sentence in Costa Rica.

National Parks & Protected Areas

The national-park system began in the 1960s, and has since been expanded into the Sistema Nacional de Areas de Conservación (National System of Conservation Areas; Sinac), with an astounding 186 protected areas, including 27 national parks, eight biological reserves, 32 protected zones, 13 forest reserves and 58 wildlife refuges. At least 10% of the land is strictly protected and another 17% is included in various multiple-use preserves. Costa Rican authorities take pride in the statistic that more than 27% of the country has been set aside for conservation, but multiple-use zones still allow farming, logging and other exploitation, so the environment within them is not totally protected. The smallest number might be the most amazing of all: Costa Rica's parks are a safe haven to approximately 5% of the world's wildlife species.

In addition to the system of national preserves, there are hundreds of small, privately owned lodges, reserves and haciendas (estates) that have been set up to protect the land. Many belong to longtime Costa Rican expats who decided that this country was the last stop in their journey along the 'gringo trail' in the 1970s and '80s. The abundance of foreign-owned protected areas is a bit of a contentious issue with Ticos. Although these are largely nonprofit organizations with keen interests in conservation, they are private and often cost money to enter. There's also a number of animal rescue and rehabilitation centers (also largely set up by expats), where injured and orphaned animals and illegal pets are rehabilitated and released into the wild, or looked after for life if they cannot be released.

Although the national-park system appears glamorous on paper, the Sinac authority still sees much work to be done. A report from several years ago amplified the fact that much of the protected area is, in fact, at risk. The government doesn't own all of this land – almost half of the areas are in private hands – and there isn't the budget to buy it. Technically, the private lands are protected from development, but there have been reports that many landowners are finding loopholes in the restrictions and selling or developing their properties, or taking bribes from poachers and illegal loggers in exchange for access.

On the plus side is a project by Sinac that links national parks and reserves, private reserves and national forests into 13 conservation areas. This strategy has two major effects. First, these 'megaparks' allow greater numbers of individual plants and animals to exist. Second, the administration of the national parks is delegated to regional offices, allowing a more individualized management approach. Each conservation area has regional and subregional offices charged with providing effective education, enforcement, research

Volunteer Opportunities

Cloudbridge Nature Reserve (www. cloudbridge.org) Trail building, construction, tree planting and projects monitoring the recovery of the cloud forest are offered to volunteers, who pay for their own housing with a local family. Preference is given to biology students, but all enthusiastic volunteers can apply.

Tropical Science Center (www.cct. or.cr) This long-standing NGO offers volunteer placement at Reserva Biológica Bosque Nuboso Monteverde. Projects can include trail maintenance and conservation work.

Fundación Corcovado (www.corcovado foundation.org) An impressive network of people and organizations committed to preserving Parque Nacional Corcovado.

Monteverde Institute (www.monte verde-institute.org) A nonprofit educational institute offering training in tropical biology, conservation and sustainable development.

and management, although some regional offices play what appear to be only obscure bureaucratic roles.

In general, support for land preservation remains high in Costa Rica because it provides income and jobs to so many people, plus important opportunities for scientific investigation.

Environmental Issues

No other tropical country has made such a concerted effort to protect its environment, and a study published by Yale and Columbia Universities in 2012 ranked Costa Rica in the top five nations for its overall environmental performance. At the same time, as the global leader in the burgeoning ecotourism economy, Costa Rica is proving to be a case study in the pitfalls and benefits of this kind of tourism. The pressures of overpopulation, global climate change and dwindling natural resources have also made it a key illustration of the urgency of environmental protection.

Deforestation

Sometimes, when the traffic jams up around the endless San José sprawl, it is hard to keep in mind that this place was once covered in a lush, unending tropical forest. Tragically, after more than a century of clearing for plantations, agriculture and logging, Costa Rica lost about 80% of its forest cover before the government stepped in with a plan to protect what was left. Through its many programs of forest protection and reforestation, 54% of the country is forested once again – a stunning accomplishment.

Despite protection for two-thirds of the remaining forests, cutting trees is still a major problem for Costa Rica, especially on private lands that are being cleared by wealthy landowners and multinational corporations. Even within national parks, some of the more remote areas are being logged illegally because there is not enough money for law enforcement.

Apart from the loss of tropical forests and the plants and animals that depend on them, deforestation leads directly or indirectly to a number of other severe environmental problems. Forests protect the soil beneath them from the ravages of tropical rainstorms. After deforestation, much of the topsoil is washed away, lowering the productivity of the land and silting up watersheds and downstream coral reefs.

Cleared lands are frequently planted with a variety of crops, including acres of bananas, the production of which entails the use of pesticides as well as blue plastic bags to protect the fruit. Both the pesticides and the plastic end up polluting the environment. Cattle ranching has been another historical motivator for clear-cutting. It intensified during the 1970s, when Costa Rican coffee exports were waning in the global market.

Because deforestation plays a role in global warming, there is much interest in rewarding countries such as Costa Rica for taking the lead in protecting their forests. The US has forgiven millions of dollars of Costa Rica's debt in exchange for increased efforts to preserve rainforests. The Costa Rican government itself sponsors a program that pays landowners for each hectare of forest they set aside, and has petitioned the UN for a global program that would pay tropical countries for their conservation efforts. Travelers interested in taking part in projects that can help protect Costa Rica's trees should look to volunteer opportunities in conservation and forestry.

Tourism

The other great environmental issue facing Costa Rica comes from the country being loved to death, directly through the passage of around two million foreign tourists a year, and less directly through the development of extensive infrastructure to support this influx. For years, resort hotels and lodges continued to pop up, most notably on formerly pristine beaches or in the middle of intact rainforest. Too many of these projects were poorly planned, and they necessitate additional support systems, including roads and countless vehicle trips, with much of this activity unregulated and largely unmonitored.

As tourism continues to become a larger piece of the Costa Rican economy, the bonanza invites more and more development. Taking advantage of Costa Rica's reputation as a green destination, developers promote mass tourism by building large hotels and package tours that, in turn, drive away wildlife, hasten erosion and strain local sewer and water systems. The irony is painful: these businesses threaten to ruin the very environment that they're selling.

It's worth noting that many private lodges and reserves are also doing some of the best conservation work in the country, and it's heartening to run across the ever-increasing homespun efforts to protect Costa Rica's environment, spearheaded by hardworking families or small organizations tucked away in some quiet corner of the country. These include projects to boost rural economies by raising native medicinal plants, efforts by villagers to document their local biodiversity, and resourceful fundraising campaigns to purchase endangered lands.

Sustainable Travel

Costa Rica's visitors presently account for the largest sector of the national economy and thus have unprecedented power to protect this country. How? By spending wisely, asking probing questions about sustainability claims and simply avoiding businesses that threaten Costa Rica's future.

In its purest form, sustainable tourism simply means striking the ideal balance between the traveler and their surrounding environment. This often includes being conscientious about energy and water consumption, and treading lightly on local environments and communities. Sustainable tourism initiatives support their communities by hiring local people for decent wages, furthering women's and civil rights, and supporting local schools, artists and food producers.

On the road, engage with the local economy as much as possible; for example, if a local artisan's handiwork catches your eye, make the purchase – every dollar infuses the micro-economy in the most direct (and rewarding) way.

Gallo pinto (blended rice and beans)

JEF_M/GETTY IMAGES ©

Food & Drink

Bordered by two oceans and heavily populated with expats, Costa Rica is a foodie's delight – the sort of place where you can dig into an oh-so-satisfying casado, the Tico's staple rice-beans-and-meat platter, or feast on five-star sushi. French and Italian pastry chefs sate morning munchies; taquerias and American bar-food tempt nocturnal noshers. And the regional Nicoya diet has proven one of the healthiest in the world. Dig in!

What to Eat

Meals

Breakfast for Ticos is taken in the early morning, usually from 6am to 8am, and consists of *gallo pinto*. Many hotels offer a tropical-style continental breakfast, usually consisting of toast with butter and jam, accompanied by fresh fruit. American-style breakfasts are also available in many eateries and are, needless to say, heavy on the fried foods and fatty meats.

A midday lunch (served between 11:30am and 2:30pm) at most *sodas* (lunch counters) usually involves a *casado* (set meal; literally, 'married'), a cheap, well-balanced plate of rice, beans, meat, salad and sometimes *plátanos maduros* (fried sweet plantains) or *patacones* (twice-fried plantains), which taste something like french fries.

Seabass *ceviche* with plantain chips

BARRY VINCENT/ALAMY STOCK PHOTO ©

For dinner (6pm to 9pm), a *casado* is on offer at most restaurants. Upscale Tico establishments may serve *lomito* (a lean cut of steak) and dishes like *pescado en salsa palmito* (fish in heart-of-palm sauce). Some of the more forward-thinking restaurants in San José may drop an experimental vegetable plate in front of you.

Local Specialties

Considering the extent of the coastline, it's no surprise that seafood is plentiful, and fish dishes are usually fresh and delicious. While it's not traditional Tico fare, *ceviche* is on most menus, usually made from *pargo* (red snapper), *dorado* (mahi-mahi), octopus or tilapia. The fish is marinated in lime juice with some combination of chilis, onions, tomatoes and herbs. Served chilled, it is a delectable way to enjoy fresh seafood. Emphasis is on 'fresh' here – it's raw fish, so if you have reason to believe it's not fresh, don't risk eating it. Sushi is also finding a place in many towns.

Food is not heavily spiced, unless you're having traditional Caribbean-style cuisine. Most local restaurants will lay out a bottle of Tabasco-style sauce, homemade salsa or Salsa Lizano, the Tico version of Worcestershire sauce and the 'secret' ingredient of *gallo pinto*. Some lay out a tempting jar of pickled hot peppers as well.

Most bars also offer the country's most popular *boca* (snack), *chifrijo,* which derives its name from two main ingredients: *chicharrón* (fried pork) and frijoles (beans). Diced tomatoes, spices, rice, tortilla chips and avocado are also thrown in for good measure. Fun fact about *chifrijo:* in 2014 a restaurant owner named Miguel Cordero claimed he officially invented it. He brought lawsuits against 49 businesses and demanded a cool US$15 million in damages. So far he has not been able to collect.

Habits & Customs

When you sit down to eat in a restaurant, it is polite to say *buenos días* (good morning), *buenas tardes* (good afternoon) or *buenas noches* (good evening) to the waitstaff and any people you might be sharing a table with – and it's generally good form to acknowledge everyone in the room this way. It is also polite to say *buen provecho,* which is the equivalent of *bon appetit,* at the start of the meal.

Caribbean cuisine is the most distinctive in Costa Rica, having been steeped in indigenous, *criollo* (Creole) and Afro-Caribbean flavors. It's a welcome cultural change of pace after seemingly endless *casados*. Regional specialties include *rondón* (whose moniker comes from 'rundown,' meaning whatever the chef can run down), a spicy seafood gumbo; Caribbean-style rice and beans, made with red beans, coconut milk and curry spices; and *patí,* the Caribbean version of an *empanada* (savory turnover), the best street food, bus-ride snack and picnic treat.

Vegetarians & Vegans

Costa Rica is a relatively comfortable place for vegetarians to travel. Rice and beans, as well as fresh fruit juices, are ubiquitous, but there's a lot more than that. The Happy Cow has a handy list of veggie restaurants nationwide (www.happycow.net/north_america/costa_rica). Visit farmers markets to sample what's in season: Costa Rica is a growers' paradise.

Most restaurants will make veggie *casados* on request and many places are now including them on the menu. These set meals usually include rice and beans, cabbage salad and one or two selections of variously prepared vegetables or legumes.

With the high influx of tourism, there are also many specialty vegetarian restaurants or restaurants with a veggie menu in San José and tourist towns. Lodges in remote areas that offer all-inclusive meal plans can accommodate vegetarians with advance notice.

Vegans, macrobiotic and raw-food-only travelers will have a tougher time, as there are fewer outlets accommodating those diets, although this is slowly changing. If you intend to keep to your diet, it's best to choose a lodging where you can prepare food yourself. Many towns have *macrobióticas* (health-food stores), but the selection varies. Fresh vegetables can be hard to come by in isolated areas and will often be quite expensive, although farmers markets are cropping up throughout the country.

What to Drink

Coffee

Coffee is probably the most popular beverage in the country, and wherever you go, someone is likely to offer you a cafecito. Traditionally, it is served strong and mixed with hot milk to taste, also known as café con leche. Purists can get café negro (black coffee); if you want a little milk, ask for leche al lado (milk on the side). Many trendier places serve espresso drinks.

Fruit Drinks

For a refresher, nothing beats *batidos* – fresh fruit shakes made either *al agua* (with water) or *con leche* (with milk). The array of available tropical fruit can be intoxicating and includes mango, papaya, *piña* (pineapple), *sandía* (watermelon), *melón* (cantaloupe), *mora* (blackberry), *carambola* (starfruit), *cas* (a type of tart guava), *guanabana* (soursop or cherimoya) and *tamarindo* (fruit of the tamarind tree). If you are wary about the condition of the drinking water, ask that your *batido* be made with *agua enbotellada* (bottled water) and *sin hielo* (without ice), though water is generally safe to drink throughout the country.

Pipas are green coconuts that have had their tops hacked off with a machete and then been spiked with a straw for drinking the coconut water inside – super refreshing when you're wilting in the tropical heat. If you're lucky enough to find it, *agua dulce* is sugarcane water, a slightly grassy, sweet juice that's been pressed through a heavy-duty, hand-cranked mill.

On the Caribbean coast, look for *agua de sapo* (literally 'toad water'), a beautiful lemonade laced with fresh ginger juice and *tapa de dulce* (brown sugar). *Resbaladera*, found mostly in the Guanacaste countryside, is a sweet milk – much like *horchata*

Green Treats

Feria Verde de Aranjuez (p49) San José's 'green market,' and an all-around winner for breakfast, produce, smoothies, everything.

Punta Mona (www.puntamona.org; cabinas per person incl 3 organic meals US$90; @) The sprawling garden at this secluded eco-retreat near Manzanillo has one of the world's largest collections of edible tropical plants.

Costa Rica Cooking (2479-1569; www. costaricacooking.com; per person US$125) Help to whip up your own meal in La Fortuna, based on local and almost entirely organic produce.

(the Mexican rice drink) – made from rice, barley, milk and cinnamon. Other local drinks you may encounter include *linaza* (a flaxseed drink said to aid digestion) and *chan* (a drink made from chia seed and lemon) – which can be an acquired taste due to its slimy (yum!) texture.

Beer

The most popular alcoholic drink is *cerveza* (beer; aka *birra* locally), and there are several national brands. Imperial is the most popular – either for its smooth flavor or for the ubiquitous merchandise emblazoned with the eagle-crest logo. Pilsen, which has a higher alcohol content, is known for its saucy calendars featuring las chicas Pilsen (the Pilsen girls). Both are tasty pilsners. Bavaria produces a lager and Bavaria Negro, a delicious, full-bodied dark beer; this brand is harder to find. A most welcome burgeoning craft-beer scene is increasing the variety of Costa Rican beers and broadening local palates.

Guaro

After beer, the poison of choice is *guaro*, which is a colorless alcohol (most similar to *aguardiente*) distilled from sugarcane and usually consumed as a sour or by the shot, oftentimes with hot sauce and lime juice. This spicy concoction is called a *chili guaro,* and in the last few years it has become a staple in San José and certain beach towns. *Guaro* goes down mighty easily but leaves one hell of a hangover.

Rum

As in most of Central America, the local rums are inexpensive and worthwhile, especially the Ron Centenario, which recently shot to international fame. And at the risk of alienating the most patriotic of Ticos, it would be remiss not to mention the arguably tastier Flor de Caña from Nicaragua (pause for rotten tomatoes). The most popular rum-based tipple is a *cuba libre* (rum and cola), which hits the spot on a hot, sticky day, especially when served with a fresh splash of lime. Premixed cans of *cuba libre* are also available in stores, but it'd be a lie to say the contents don't taste weirdly like aluminum.

Keel-billed toucan

ONDREJ PROSICKY/SHUTTERSTOCK ©

Survival Guide

Directory A–Z

Accommodations

Accommodations come at every price and comfort level: from luxurious ecolodges and sparkling all-inclusive resorts and backpacker palaces to spartan rooms with little more than a bed and four cinderblock walls. The variety and number of rooms on offer, coupled with online booking, means that advance booking is not usually required.

Note that the term *cabina* (cabin) is a catch-all that can define a wide range of prices and amenities, from very rustic to very expensive.

Pricing

Many lodgings lower their prices during the low (rainy, aka 'green' season) season, from May to November. Prices change quickly and many hotels charge per person rather than per room – read rates carefully and always check ahead.

US dollars are the preferred currency for listing rates in Costa Rica. However, colones are accepted everywhere and are usually exchanged at current rates without an additional fee.

Paying with a credit card sometimes incurs a surcharge and cash discounts are sometimes on offer.

Hotels

○ It's always advisable to ask to see a room – including the bathroom – before committing to a stay, especially in budget lodgings. Rooms within a single hotel can vary greatly.

○ Some pricier hotels will require confirmation of a reservation with a credit card. Before doing so, note that some top-end hotels require a 50% to 100% deposit up front when you reserve. This rule is not always clearly communicated.

○ In most cases reservations can be canceled and refunded with enough notice. Ask the hotel about its cancellation policy before booking. It is often easier to make the reservation than to unmake it.

○ Many hotels charge a hefty service fee for credit-card use.

Climate

San José

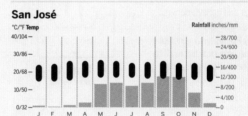

Puerto Limón

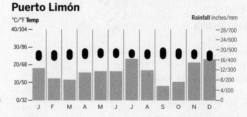

Puntarenas

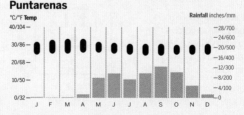

○ Have the hotel fax or email you a confirmation. Hotels often get overbooked, and if you don't have a confirmation, you could be out of a room.

○ To compete with online booking services, some hotels offer a discount if you book direct, or if you pay in cash.

Booking Services

Costa Rica Innkeepers Association (www.costarica innkeepers.com) A nonprofit association of B&Bs, small hotels, lodges and inns.

Escape Villas (www.villascosta rica.com) High-end accommodations across Costa Rica, most near Parque Nacional Manuel Antonio, which are suitable for families and honeymooners looking for luxury.

Lonely Planet (www.lonelyplan et.com/costa-rica/hotels) Recommendations and bookings.

Customs Regulations

○ All travelers over the age of 18 are allowed to enter the country with 5L of wine or spirits and 500g of processed tobacco (roughly 400 cigarettes or 50 cigars).

○ Camera gear, binoculars, and camping, snorkeling and other sporting equipment are readily allowed into the country.

○ Dogs and cats are permitted entry providing they

have obtained both general health and rabies-vaccination certificates.

○ Pornography and illicit drugs are prohibited.

Electricity

Type A
120V/60Hz

Type B
120V/60Hz

Gay & Lesbian Travelers

In Costa Rica the situation facing gay and lesbian travelers is better than in most Central American countries, and some areas of the country – particularly Quepos and Parque Nacional Manuel Antonio – have been gay vacation destinations for two decades. Homosexual acts are legal, and in 2015 Costa Rica became the first country in Central America to recognize gay relationships. Still, most Costa Ricans are tolerant of homosexuality only at a 'don't ask, don't tell' level. Same-sex couples are unlikely to be the subject of harassment, though public displays of affection might attract unwanted attention.

The undisputed gay and lesbian capital of Costa Rica is Manuel Antonio; while there, you can pick up an issue of *Playita* (www. gaymanuelantonio.com/ playita-magazine.html). The Spanish-language magazine *Gente 10* (www.gente10. com) is available at gay bars in San José.

Agua Buena Human Rights Association (☎2280-3548; www.aguabuena.org) This noteworthy nonprofit organization has campaigned steadily for fairness in medical treatment for people living with HIV/AIDS in Costa Rica.

Center of Investigation & Promotion of Human Rights in Central America (CIPAC; ☎2280-7821; www.cipacdh.org) The leading gay activist organization in Costa Rica.

Toto Tours (☎800-565-1241, in USA 773-274-8686; www.toto tours.com) Gay-travel specialist that organizes regular trips to Costa Rica, among other destinations.

Health

Travelers to Central America need to be vigilant about food- and mosquito-borne infections. Most of the illnesses frequently caught while on holiday here are not life threatening, but they can certainly ruin your trip. Besides getting the proper vaccinations, it's important to use a good insect repellent and exercise care in what you eat and drink.

Before You Go

Health Insurance

High-risk adventure activities or water sports such as diving are not on all travel policies: make sure you pay for the appropriate level of insurance coverage. Yours may cover basic activities, such as walking, but not ziplining or surfing; if diving, some companies may only cover you up to a certain number of dives or a certain depth. If unsure, check with your insurer before leaving your home country.

A list of medical-evacuation and travel-insurance companies can be found on the US State Department (www.travel.state.gov) website under the 'Before You Go' tab.

Recommended Vaccinations

● Get necessary vaccinations four to eight weeks before departure.

● Ask your doctor for an International Certificate of Vaccination (otherwise known as the 'yellow booklet'), which will list all the vaccinations you've received. This is mandatory for countries that require proof of yellow-fever vaccination upon entry (Costa Rica only requires such proof if you are entering from a country that carries a risk of yellow fever).

In Costa Rica

Availability & Cost of Health Care

● Good medical care is available in most major cities but may be limited in rural areas.

● For an extensive list of physicians, dentists and hospitals, visit https://cr.usembassy.gov and look under 'U.S. Citizen Services/Medical Assistance/Medical Practitioners List'.

● Most pharmacies are well supplied and a handful are open 24 hours. Pharmacists are licensed to prescribe medication. If you're

taking any medication on a regular basis, make sure you know its generic (scientific) name, since many pharmaceuticals go under different names in Costa Rica.

Infectious Diseases

Dengue fever (breakbone fever) Dengue is transmitted by *Aedes aegypti* mosquitoes, which often bite during the daytime and are usually found close to human habitations, often indoors. Dengue is especially common in densely populated urban environments. It usually causes flu-like symptoms including fever, muscle aches, joint pains, headaches, nausea and vomiting, often followed by a rash. Most cases resolve uneventfully in a few days. There is no treatment for dengue fever except taking analgesics such as acetaminophen/paracetamol (Tylenol) and drinking plenty of fluids. Severe cases may require hospitalization for intravenous fluids and supportive care. There is no vaccine. The key to prevention is taking insect-protection measures.

Hepatitis A The second-most common travel-related infection (after traveler's diarrhea). It's a viral infection of the liver that is usually acquired by ingestion of contaminated water, food or ice, though it may also be acquired by direct contact with infected people. Symptoms may include fever, malaise, jaundice, nausea, vomiting and abdominal pain. Most cases resolve without complications, though hepatitis A occasionally causes severe liver damage. There is no treatment. The vaccine for hepatitis A is extremely safe and highly effective.

Leishmaniasis This is transmitted by sand flies. Most cases occur in newly cleared forest or areas of secondary growth; the highest incidence is in Talamanca. It causes slow-growing ulcers over exposed parts of the body. There is no vaccine. To protect yourself from sand flies, follow the same precautions as for mosquitoes.

Malaria Malaria is very rare in Costa Rica, occurring only occasionally in rural parts of Limón Province. It's transmitted by mosquito bites, usually between dusk and dawn. Taking malaria pills is not necessary unless you are making a long stay in the province of Limón (not Puerto Limón). Protection against mosquito bites is most effective.

Traveler's diarrhea Tap water is safe and of high quality in Costa Rica, but when you're far off the beaten path it's best to avoid tap water unless it has been boiled, filtered or chemically disinfected (with iodine tablets). To prevent diarrhea, be wary of dairy products that might contain unpasteurized milk and be highly selective when eating food from street vendors. If you develop diarrhea, be sure to drink plenty of fluids, preferably with an oral rehydration solution containing lots of salt and sugar. If diarrhea is bloody or persists for more than 72 hours, or is accompanied by fever, shaking chills or severe abdominal pain, seek medical attention.

Typhoid Caused by ingestion of food or water contaminated by a species of salmonella known as *Salmonella typhi*. Fever occurs in virtually all cases. Other symptoms may include headache, malaise, muscle aches, dizziness, loss of appetite, nausea and abdominal pain. Possible complications include intestinal perforation, intestinal bleeding, confusion, delirium or (rarely) coma. A pretrip vaccination is recommended.

Zika virus At the time of research, pregnant women are advised against traveling to Costa Rica, as the virus may be linked to microcephaly, a birth defect that affects a baby's brain development. Zika is primarily transmitted by mosquitoes, but it can also be transmitted by a man to his sexual partner or by a woman to her fetus. Be aware that symptoms are usually mild in adults, and many people may not realize that they are infected.

Chikungunya virus The newest mosquito-borne viral disease was accidentally introduced to Costa Rica from Africa, and carried from *Aedes albopictus* or Tiger mosquitoes. The symptoms are similar to those of dengue fever (high fever, joint inflammation, a skin rash, headache, muscle aches, nausea), and so are the treatments – replace fluids, reduce fever and wait it out. Unlike dengue, it's very unlikely to be fatal, and once you get it you'll probably develop an immunity. The best prevention is to cover up with long sleeves and DEET.

Environmental Hazards

Animal bites Do not attempt to pet, handle or feed any animal. Any bite or scratch by a mammal, including bats, should be promptly and thoroughly cleansed with large amounts of soap and water, and an antiseptic such as iodine or alcohol should be applied. Contact a local health authority in the event of such an injury. Rabies cases are rare but do happen.

Insect bites No matter how much you safeguard yourself, getting bitten by mosquitoes is part of every traveler's experience here. The best prevention is to stay covered up – wear long pants, long sleeves, a hat, and shoes, not sandals. Invest in a good insect repellent, preferably one containing DEET. Apply to exposed skin and clothing (but not to eyes, mouth, cuts, wounds or irritated skin). Compounds containing DEET should not be used on children under the age of two and should be used sparingly on children under 12. Invest in a bug net to hang over beds (along with a few thumbtacks or nails with which to hang it). Many hotels in Costa Rica don't have windows (or screens), and a cheap little net will save you plenty of nighttime aggravation. The mesh size should be less than 1.5mm. Dusk is the worst time for mosquitoes, so take extra precautions then.

Sun Stay out of the midday sun, wear sunglasses and a wide-brimmed hat, and apply sunblock with SPF 15 or higher, with both UVA and UVB protection. Reapply often, especially if getting in the sea or rivers. Drink plenty of fluids and avoid strenuous exercise when the temperature is high.

Tap Water

○ It's generally safe to drink tap water in Costa Rica, except in the most rural and undeveloped parts of the country. However, if you prefer to be cautious, buying bottled water is your best bet.

○ If you have the means, vigorous boiling for one minute is the most effective means of water purification. At altitudes greater than 2000m, boil for three minutes.

○ Another option is to disinfect water with iodine pills: add 2% tincture of iodine to 1L of water (five drops to clear water, 10 drops to cloudy water) and let stand for 30 minutes. If the water is cold, longer times may be required.

○ Alternatively, carry a SteriPen that destroys most bacteria, viruses and protozoa with UV light.

Insurance

It's vital that travelers purchase the right type of travel insurance before coming to Costa Rica. Basic insurance tends to cover medical expenses, baggage loss, trip cancellation, accidents and personal liability, but it's worth spending extra to make sure you're covered in the event of natural disasters. If you intend to take part in adventure sports, make sure that those particular sports are covered by your policy; for divers, some policies only cover you up to a certain depth.

Worldwide travel insurance is available at www.lonelyplanet.com/travel-insurance. You can buy, extend and claim online anytime – even if you're already on the road.

Internet Access

○ The number of internet cafes in Costa Rica has greatly decreased with the advent of smartphones, and wi-fi in restaurants and cafes.

○ Expect to pay US$1 to US$2 per hour at internet

cafes in San José and tourist towns.

○ Wi-fi is common in all mid-range and top-end hotels, and in the vast majority of budget hotels and hostels. Some hostels still have computers for guest use and/or wi-fi.

Legal Matters

○ If you are arrested your embassy can offer limited assistance. Embassy officials will not bail you out and you are subject to Costa Rican laws, not the laws of your own country.

○ The use of recreational substances other than tobacco and alcohol is illegal in Costa Rica and punishable by imprisonment.

Maps

Unfortunately, detailed maps are hard to come by in Costa Rica, so it's best to purchase one online before your trip.

○ The excellent, water-resistant 1:350,000 *Costa Rica Adventure Map* published by National Geographic also has an inset map of San José. Available online or in various book and gift shops in San José.

○ Another quality option is the 1:330,000 *Costa Rica* sheet produced by

Dollars versus Colones

While colones are the official currency of Costa Rica, US dollars are legal tender. Case in point: most ATMs in large towns and cities will dispense both currencies. However, it pays to know where and when you should be paying with each currency.

In Costa Rica you can use US dollars to pay for hotel rooms, midrange to top-end meals, admission fees for sights, tours, domestic flights, international buses, car hire, private shuttle buses and big-ticket purchases. Local meals and drinks, domestic bus fares, taxis and small purchases should be paid for in colones.

○ In US-dollar transactions the change will usually be given in colones.

○ Newer US dollars are preferred throughout Costa Rica; if your note has a rip in it, it may not be accepted.

○ When paying in US dollars at a local restaurant, bar or shop the exchange rate can be unfavorable.

International Travel Map, which is waterproof and includes a San José inset.

○ **Fundación Neotrópica** (📞2253-2130; www. neotropica.org) publishes a 1:500,000 map showing national parks and other protected areas; it's available online and in San José bookstores.

○ The Instituto Costarricense de Turismo (ICT) publishes a 1:700,000 *Costa Rica* map with a 1:12,500 *Central San José* map on the reverse; it's free at the ICT office in San José.

○ **Maptak** (www.maptak. com) has maps of Costa Rica's seven provinces and their capitals.

○ Few national-park offices or ranger stations have maps for hikers.

○ **Instituto Geográfico Nacional** (IGN; 📞2202-0777; 215, Zapote; ⊙8:30am-3:30pm Mon-Fri) in San José has topographical maps available for purchase.

○ Incafo formerly published the *Mapa-Guía de la Naturaleza Costa Rica*, an atlas that included 1:200,000 topographical sheets, as well as English and Spanish descriptions of Costa Rica's natural areas. Used copies can be purchased online.

Money

○ The Costa Rican currency is the colón (plural colones), named after Cristóbal Colón (Christopher Columbus).

○ Bills come in 1000-, 2000-, 5000-, 10,000-, 20,000- and 50,000-colón notes, while coins come in denominations of five, 10, 20, 25, 50, 100 and 500 colones.

○ Paying for things in US dollars is common, and at times is encouraged, since the currency is viewed as being more stable than the colón.

ATMs

ATMs are ubiquitous, typically dispensing colones; many dispense US dollars. They are not easily found in rural and remote areas.

Changing Money

All banks will exchange US dollars, and some will exchange euros and British pounds; other currencies are more difficult. Most banks have excruciatingly long lines, especially at the state-run institutions (Banco Nacional, Banco de Costa Rica, Banco Popular), though they don't charge commissions on cash exchanges. Private banks (Banex, Banco Interfin, Scotiabank) tend to be faster. Make sure the bills you want to exchange are in good condition or they may be refused.

Credit Cards

○ Cards are widely accepted at midrange and top-end hotels, as well as at top-end restaurants and some travel agencies; they are less likely to be accepted in small towns and in remote areas.

• A transaction fee (around 3% to 5%) on all international credit-card purchases is often added.

• Holders of credit and debit cards can buy colones in some banks, though expect to pay a high transaction fee.

• All car-rental agencies require drivers to have a credit card. It's possible to hire a car with just a debit card, but only on the condition that you pay for full insurance and leave a deposit for traffic violations.

Exchange Rates

Australia	A$1	₡419
Canada	C$1	₡430
Euro zone	€1	₡663
Japan	¥100	₡506
New Zealand	NZ$1	₡384
UK	£1	₡749
USA	US$1	₡568

For current exchange rates, see www.xe.com.

Tipping

Restaurants Your bill will usually include a 10% service charge. If not, you might leave a small tip.

Hotels Tip the bellhop/porter US$1 to US$5 per service and the housekeeper US$1 to US$2 per day in top-end hotels, less in budget places.

Taxis Tip only if some special service is provided.

Guides Tip US$5 to US$15 per person per day. Tip the tour driver about half of what you tip the guide.

Opening Hours

The following are high-season opening hours; hours will usually shorten in the shoulder and low seasons. Generally, sights, activities and restaurants are open daily.

Banks 9am to 4pm Monday to Friday, sometimes 9am to noon Saturday.

Bars and clubs 8pm to 2am.

Government offices 8am to 5pm Monday to Friday. Often closed between 11:30am and 1:30pm.

Restaurants 7am to 9pm. Upscale places may open only for dinner. In remote areas, even the small *sodas* (inexpensive counters) might open only at specific meal times.

Shops 8am to 6pm Monday to Saturday.

Public Holidays

Días feriados (national holidays) are taken seriously in Costa Rica. Banks, public offices and many stores close. During these times, public transport is tight and hotels are heavily booked. Many festivals coincide with public holidays.

New Year's Day January 1

Semana Santa (Holy Week; March or April) The Thursday and Friday before Easter Sunday is the official holiday, though most businesses shut down for the whole week. From Thursday to Sunday bars are closed and alcohol sales are prohibited; on Thursday and Friday buses stop running.

Día de Juan Santamaría (April 11) Honors the national hero who died fighting William Walker in 1856; major events are held in Alajuela, his hometown.

Labor Day May 1

Día de la Madre (Mother's Day; August 15) Coincides with the annual Catholic Feast of the Assumption.

Independence Day September 15

Día de la Raza (Columbus Day) October 12

Christmas Day (December 25) Christmas Eve is also an unofficial holiday.

Last week in December The week between Christmas and New Year is an unofficial holiday; businesses close and beach hotels are crowded.

Safe Travel

Costa Rica is a largely safe country, but petty crime (bag snatchings, car break-ins etc) is common and muggings do occur, so it's important to be vigilant.

• Many of Costa Rica's dangers are nature related: riptides, earthquakes and volcanic eruptions are among them.

• Predatory and venomous wildlife can also pose a threat, so a wildlife guide is essential if trekking in the jungle.

Smoking

Smoking is banned in all public places, restaurants, bars and casinos and on public transport. There are no separate 'smoking areas.' Some hotels in Costa Rica are non-smoking only.

Telephone

○ Mobile service now covers most of the country and nearly all of the country that is accessible to tourists.

○ Public phones are found all over Costa Rica, and chip or Colibrí phonecards are available in 1000-, 2000- and 3000-colón denominations.

○ Chip cards are inserted into the phone and scanned. Colibrí cards (more common) require you to dial a toll-free number (199) and enter an access code. Instructions are provided in English or Spanish.

○ The cheapest international calls from Costa Rica are direct-dialed using a phonecard. To make international calls, dial '00' followed by the country code and number.

○ Pay phones cannot receive international calls.

○ To call Costa Rica from abroad, use the country code (506) before the eight-digit number.

○ Due to the widespread popularity of voice-over IP services such as Skype, and more reliable ethernet connections, traveling with a smartphone or tablet can be the cheapest and easiest way to call internationally.

Time

Costa Rica is six hours behind GMT, so Costa Rican time is equivalent to Central Time in North America. There is no daylight-saving time.

Toilets

○ Public restrooms are rare, but most restaurants and cafes will let you use their facilities, sometimes for a small charge – never more than 500 colones.

○ Bus terminals and other major public buildings usually have toilets, also at a charge.

○ Don't flush your toilet paper. Costa Rican plumbing is often poor and has very low pressure.

○ Dispose of toilet paper in the rubbish bin inside the bathroom.

Tourist Information

○ The government-run tourism board, the **ICT** (www.ict.go.cr/es), has an office in the capital; English is spoken.

○ The ICT can provide you with free maps, a master bus schedule, information on road conditions in the hinterlands, and a helpful brochure with up-to-date emergency numbers for every region.

○ Consult the ICT's English-language website for information.

○ From the US, call the ICT's toll-free number for brochures and information.

Travelers with Disabilities

Independent travel in Costa Rica is difficult for anyone with mobility constraints. Although Costa Rica has an equal-opportunity law, the law applies only to new or newly remodeled businesses and is loosely enforced. Therefore, very few hotels and restaurants have features specifically suited to wheelchair use. Many don't have ramps, and room or bathroom doors are rarely wide enough to accommodate a wheelchair.

Streets and sidewalks are potholed and poorly paved, making wheelchair use frustrating at best. Public buses don't have provisions to carry wheelchairs, and most national parks and outdoor tourist attractions don't have trails suited to wheelchair use. Notable exceptions include **Parque Nacional Volcán Poás** (🖉2482-1226; US$15; ⊗8am-3:30pm), which was closed at the time of research due to volcanic activity, and the **Rainforest Aerial Tram** (🖉2257-5961, in USA 1-866-759-8726; www. rainforestadventure.com; adult/student & child tram US$60/30, zipline US$50/35; ⊗7:30am-2pm; 🖈).

Download Lonely Planet's free Accessible Travel guide from http://lptravel.to/ AccessibleTravel.

Visas

Passport-carrying nationals of the following countries are allowed 90 days' stay with no visa: Argentina, Australia, Canada, Chile, Iceland, Ireland, Israel, Japan, Mexico, New Zealand, Panama, South Africa, the US and most Western European countries.

Most other visitors require a visa from a Costa Rican embassy or consulate.

For the latest info on visas, check the websites of the Instituto Costarricense de Turismo (ICT; www.ict. go.cr/es) or the Costa Rican Embassy (www.costarica -embassy.org).

Women Travelers

Most female travelers experience little more than a *'mi amor'* ('my love') or an appreciative glance from the local men. But, in general, Costa Rican men consider foreign women to have looser morals and to be easier conquests than Ticas (female Costa Ricans). Men will often make flirtatious comments to single women, particularly blondes, and women traveling together are not exempt. The best response is to do what Ticas do: ignore it completely. Women who firmly resist unwanted verbal advances from men are normally treated with respect.

○ In small highland towns, dress is usually conservative. Women rarely wear shorts, but belly-baring tops are all the rage. On the beach, skimpy bathing suits are OK, but topless and nude bathing is not.

○ Solo women travelers should avoid hitchhiking.

○ Do not take unlicensed 'pirate' taxis (licensed taxis are red and have medallions), as there have been reports of assaults on women by unlicensed drivers.

○ Birth-control pills are available at most pharmacies without a prescription.

○ As with most countries in the world, sanitary products can be found at any pharmacy.

Transport

Getting There & Away

Costa Rica can be reached via frequent, direct international flights from the US and Canada and from other Central American countries. You can also cross a land border into Costa Rica from Panama or Nicaragua. Flights, cars and tours can be booked online at lonely planet.com/bookings.

Air

Costa Rica is well connected by air to other Central and South American countries, as well as the US.

Airports & Airlines

Aeropuerto Internacional Juan Santamaría (🖉2437-2400; www.fly2sanjose.com) International flights arrive here, 17km northwest of San José, in the town of Alajuela.

Aeropuerto Internacional Daniel Oduber Quirós (LIR; www.liberiacostaricaairport. net) This airport in Liberia also receives international flights from the US, the Americas and

Canada. It serves a number of American and Canadian airlines and some charters from London, as well as regional flights from Panama and Nicaragua.

Avianca (part of the Central American airline consortium Grupo TACA; www.avianca.com). The Colombian-owned airline is regarded as the national airline of Costa Rica and flies to the US and Latin America, including Cuba.

Departure Tax

o There is a US$29 departure tax on all international outbound flights, payable in dollars or colones, though most carriers now include it in the ticket price.

o At the Juan Santamaría and Liberia airports this tax can be paid in cash or by credit card; Banco de Costa Rica has an ATM by the departure-tax station. Note that credit-card payments are processed as cash advances, which often carry hefty fees.

o If fees are not included in your ticket, travelers will not be allowed through airport security without paying.

Sea

Cruise ships stop in Costa Rican ports and enable passengers to make a quick foray into the country. Typically, ships dock at either the Pacific ports of Caldera, Puntarenas, Quepos and Bahía Drake, or the Caribbean port of Puerto Limón.

It is also possible to arrive in Costa Rica by private yacht.

Getting Around

Air

o Costa Rica's domestic airlines are **Nature Air** (☎2299-6000, in USA 1-800-235-9272; www.natureair.com) and **Sansa** (☎2290-4100, in USA 877-767-2672; www.flysansa.com). Sansa is linked with the Grupo TACA consortium.

o Both airlines fly small passenger planes; check your allowance, as some allow no more than 12kg.

o Space is limited and demand is high in the dry season, so reserve and pay for tickets in advance.

o In late 2017 two airplanes operated by Nature Air crashed, resulting in a total of 14 deaths. The Civil Aviation Administration temporarily suspended the airline shortly after the second crash, reportedly due to personnel shortages and route changes. Nature Air began flying passengers again in February 2018, and at the time of research, investigations into the causes of the crashes were ongoing.

Charter Flights

o Travelers on a larger budget or in a larger party should consider chartering a private plane, which is by far the quickest way to travel around the country.

o It takes under 90 minutes to fly to most destinations, though weather conditions can significantly speed up or extend travel time.

o The two main charters in the country are **Nature Air** (☎2299-6000, in USA 1-800-235-9272; www.natureair.com) and **Alfa Romeo Aero Taxi** (☎2735-5353, 8632-8150; www.alfaromeoair.com). Both can be booked directly through the company, a tour agency or some high-end accommodations.

o Luggage space on charters is extremely limited.

Bicycle

With an increasingly large network of paved secondary roads and heightened awareness of cyclists, Costa Rica is emerging as one of Central America's most comfortable cycle-touring destinations. That said, many roads are narrow, potholed and winding and there are no designated cycle lanes, so there's an element of risk involved.

Mountain bikes and beach cruisers can be rented in towns with a significant tourist presence for US$10 to US$20 per day. A few companies organize bike tours around Costa Rica.

Boat

o In Costa Rica there are some regular coastal services, and safety standards are generally good.

○ Ferries cross the Golfo de Nicoya, connecting the central Pacific coast with the southern tip of the Península de Nicoya.

○ The **Coonatramar Ferry** (☏2661-1069; www.coonatramar.com; adult/child/car/motorcycle/bicycle US$2/1/18/6/4) links the port of Puntarenas with Playa Naranjo five times daily. The **Ferry Naviera Tambor** (☏2661-2084; www.navieratambor.com; adult/child/car/motorcycle/bicycle US$1.65/1/23/7/4) travels between Puntarenas and Paquera six times a day, for a bus connection to Montezuma.

○ On the Golfo Dulce a daily passenger ferry links Golfito with Puerto Jiménez on the Península de Osa. On the other side of the Península de Osa, water taxis connect Bahía Drake with Sierpe.

○ On the Caribbean coast there are various bus and boat services that run several times a day, linking Cariari and Tortuguero via La Pavona, while another links Parismina and Siquirres (transfer in Caño Blanco).

○ Boats ply the canals that run along the coast from Moín to Tortuguero; although no regular service exists, tourists can pre-book water taxis to transport them around these waterways.

Climate Change & Travel

Every form of transportation that relies on carbon-based fuel generates CO2, the main cause of human-induced climate change. Modern travel is dependent on airplanes, which might use less fuel per kilometer per person than most cars but travel much greater distances. The altitude at which aircraft emit gases (including CO2) and particles also contributes to their climate change impact. Many websites offer 'carbon calculators' that allow people to estimate the carbon emissions generated by their journey and, for those who wish to do so, to offset the impact of the greenhouse gases emitted with contributions to portfolios of climate-friendly initiatives throughout the world. Lonely Planet offsets the carbon footprint of all staff and author travel.

Bus (Shuttle)

The tourist-van shuttle services (aka gringo buses) are a pricier alternative to the standard intercity buses. Shuttles are provided by **Gray Line** (☏2220-2126, in US 800 719-3905; www.graylinecostarica.com), **Easy Ride** (☏8812-4012, in USA 703-879-2284; www.easyridecostarica.com), **Monkey Ride** (☏2787-0454; www.monkeyridecr.com), **Tropical Tours** (☏2640 190; www.tropicaltoursshuttles.com) and **Interbus** (☏6050-6500, 4100-0888; www.interbusonline.com).

○ All four companies run overland transportation from San José to the most popular destinations, as well as directly between other destinations (see the websites for the comprehensive list).

○ These services will pick you up at your hotel, and reservations can be made online or through local travel agencies and hotel owners.

○ Popular destinations include Quepos, Monteverde/Santa Elena, Manuel Antonio, Dominical, Uvita, Puerto Jiménez, Arenal, Montezuma and Mal País.

○ Easy Ride offers international services directly from Monteverde to Managua.

Car & Motorcycle

○ Drivers in Costa Rica are required to have a valid driver's license from their home country. Many places will also accept an International Driving Permit (IDP), issued by the automobile association in your country of origin. After 90 days, however, you will need to get a Costa Rican driver's license. Drivers should carry their passport and driver's license at all times.

○ Gasoline (petrol) and diesel are widely available, and 24-hour service stations are along the Interamericana. At the time of research, fuel prices averaged US$1.02 per liter.

○ In more remote areas, fuel will be more expensive and might be sold at the neighborhood *pulpería* (corner store).

○ Spare parts may be hard to find, especially for vehicles with sophisticated electronics and emissions-control systems.

○ If you have an accident, call the police immediately to make a report (required for insurance purposes).

○ Leave the vehicles in place until the report has been made and do not make any statements except to members of law-enforcement agencies.

Rentals & Insurance

○ There are car-rental agencies in San José and in popular tourist destinations on the Pacific coast.

○ All of the major international car-rental agencies have outlets in Costa Rica, though you can sometimes get better deals from local companies.

○ Due to road conditions, it's necessary to invest in a 4WD unless travel is limited to the Interamericana.

○ Many agencies will insist on 4WD in the rainy season, when driving through rivers is a matter of course.

○ To rent a car you'll need a valid driver's license, a major credit card and a passport. The minimum age for car rental is 21 years. It's also possible to rent if you've only got a debit card, but you must agree to leave a deposit for traffic violations and pay full insurance.

○ Carefully inspect rented cars for minor damage and make sure that any damage is noted on the rental agreement. If your car breaks down, call the rental company. Don't attempt to get the car fixed yourself – most companies won't reimburse expenses without prior authorization.

○ Prices vary considerably; on average you can expect to pay more than US$200 per week for a standard SUV, including *kilometraje libre* (unlimited mileage). Economy cars are much cheaper: as little as US$80 a week. The price of mandatory insurance makes this more expensive, often doubling the rate.

○ Costa Rican insurance is mandatory, even if you have insurance at home. Expect to pay about US$10 to US$30 per day. Many rental companies won't rent you a car without it. The basic insurance that all drivers must buy is from a government monopoly, the Instituto Nacional de Seguros. This insurance does not cover your rental car at all, only damages to other people and their car or property.

It is legal to drive with this insurance only, but it can be difficult to negotiate with a rental agency to allow you to drive away with just this minimum standard. Full insurance through the rental agency can be up to US$50 a day.

○ Some roads in Costa Rica are rough and rugged, meaning that minor accidents or car damage are common.

○ Note that if you pay basic insurance with a gold or platinum credit card, the card company may take responsibility for damage to the car, in which case you can forgo the cost of the full insurance. Make sure you verify this with your credit-card company ahead of time.

○ Most insurance policies do not cover damage caused by flooding or driving through a river, so be aware of the extent of your policy.

○ Rental rates fluctuate wildly, so shop around. Some agencies offer discounts for extended rentals. Note that rental offices at the airport charge a 12% fee in addition to regular rates.

○ Thieves can easily recognize rental cars. Never leave anything in sight in a parked car – nothing! – and remove all luggage from the trunk overnight. If possible, park the car in a guarded parking lot rather than on the street.

○ Motorcycles (including Harley-Davidsons) can be rented in San José and Escazú, but considering the condition of the roads it's not recommended.

Road Conditions & Hazards

○ The quality of roads varies, from the quite smoothly paved Interamericana to the barely passable.

○ Many roads are single-lane and winding; mountain roads have huge gutters at the sides and lack hard shoulders; other roads are rock-strewn, dirt-and-mud affairs that traverse rivers.

○ Drive defensively and expect a variety of obstructions, from cyclists and pedestrians to broken-down cars and cattle. Unsigned speed bumps are placed on some stretches of road.

○ Roads around major tourist areas are adequately marked; all others are not.

○ Always ask about road conditions before setting out, especially in the rainy season, when a number of roads become impassable.

Road Rules

○ There are speed limits of 100km/h to 120km/h or less on highways; limits will be posted. The minimum driving speed on highways is 40km/h. The speed limit is 60km/h or less on secondary roads.

○ Traffic police use radar, and speed limits are sometimes enforced with speeding tickets.

○ Tickets are issued to drivers operating vehicles without a seat belt.

○ It's illegal to stop in an intersection or make a right turn on a red.

○ At unmarked intersections, yield to the car on your right.

○ Drive on the right. Passing is allowed only on the left.

○ Police have no right to ask for money, and they shouldn't confiscate a car unless the driver cannot produce a license and ownership papers, the car lacks license plates, the driver is drunk or the driver has been involved in an accident causing serious injury.

Taxis

In San José, taxis have *marías* (meters) and it is illegal for drivers not to use them. Outside San José, however, most taxis don't have meters and fares tend to be agreed upon in advance. Bargaining is quite acceptable.

Language

Spanish pronunciation is not difficult as most of the sounds are also found in English. You can read our pronunciation guides below as if they were English and you'll be understood just fine. And if you pronounce 'kh' in our guides as a throaty sound and remember to roll the 'r,' you'll even sound like a real Costa Rican.

To enhance your trip with a phrasebook, visit **lonelyplanet.com**. Lonely Planet iPhone phrasebooks are available through the Apple App store.

Basics

Hello.
Hola.   o·la

How are you?
¿Cómo está? (pol)   ko·mo es·ta
¿Cómo estás? (inf)   ko·mo es·tas

I'm fine, thanks.
Bien, gracias.   byen gra·syas

Excuse me. (to get attention)
Con permiso.   kon per·mee·so

Yes./No.
Sí./No.   see/no

Thank you.
Gracias.   gra·syas

You're welcome./That's fine.
Con mucho gusto.   kon moo·cho goo·sto

Goodbye./See you later.
Adiós./Nos vemos.   a·dyos/nos ve·mos

Do you speak English?
¿Habla inglés? (pol)   a·bla een·gles
¿Hablas inglés? (inf) a·blas een·gles

I don't understand.
No entiendo.   no en·tyen·do

How much is this?
¿Cuánto cuesta?   kwan·to kwes·ta

Can you reduce the price a little?
¿Podría bajarle el   po·dree·a ba·khar·le
el precio?   el pre·syo

Accommodations

I'd like to make a booking.
Quisiera reservar   kee·sye·ra re·ser·var
una habitación.   oo·na a·bee·ta·syon

Do you have a room available?
¿Tiene una habitación? tye·ne oo·na a·bee·ta·syon

How much is it per night?
¿Cuánto es por noche? kwan·to es por no·che

Eating & Drinking

I'd like ..., please.
Quisiera ..., por favor. kee·sye·ra ... por fa·vor

That was delicious!
¡Estuvo delicioso!   es·too·vo de·lee·syo·so

Bring the bill/check, please.
La cuenta, por favor. la kwen·ta por fa·vor

I'm allergic to ...
Soy alérgico/a al ... (m/f) soy a·ler·khee·ko/a al ...

I don't eat ...
No como ...   no ko·mo ...
  chicken   *pollo*   po·yo
  fish   *pescado*   pes·ka·do
  (red) meat *carne (roja)* kar·ne (ro·kha)

Emergencies

I'm ill.
Estoy enfermo/a. (m/f) es·toy en·fer·mo/a

Help!
¡Socorro!   so·ko·ro

Call a doctor!
¡Llame a un doctor!   ya·me a oon dok·tor

Call the police!
¡Llame a la policía!   ya·me a la po·lee·see·a

Directions

Where's a/the ...?
¿Dónde está ...?   don·de es·ta ...
  bank
  el banco   el ban·ko
  ... embassy
  la embajada de ... la em·ba·kha·da de ...
  market
  el mercado el mer·ka·do
  museum
  el museo   el moo·se·o
  restaurant
  un restaurante oon res·tow·ran·te
  toilet
  el baño   el ba·nyo

Behind the Scenes

Acknowledgements

Climate map data adapted from Peel MC, Finlayson BL & McMahon TA (2007) 'Updated World Map of the Köppen-Geiger Climate Classification', Hydrology and Earth System Sciences, 11, 163344.

This Book

This 2nd edition of Lonely Planet's *Best of Costa Rica* guidebook was researched and written by Ashley Harrell, Jade Bremner and Brian Kluepfel. The previous edition was written by Mara Vorhees, Ashley Harrell and Anna Kaminski. This guidebook was produced by the following:

Destination Editors Bailey Freeman, Alicia Johnson

Senior Product Editor Saralinda Turner

Product Editor Rachel Rawling

Senior Cartographer Corey Hutchison

Book Designer Jessica Rose

Assisting Editors Sarah Bailey, Lucy Cowie, Andrea Dobbin, Emma Gibbs, Victoria Harrison, Tamara Sheward, Gabrielle Stefanos, Sarah Stewart

Cover Researcher Wibowo Rusli

Thanks to Imogen Bannister, Heather Champion, Sandie Kestell, Kate Kiely, Kathryn Rowan

Send Us Your Feedback

We love to hear from travelers – your comments keep us on our toes and help make our books better. Our well-traveled team reads every word on what you loved or loathed about this book. Although we cannot reply individually to postal submissions, we always guarantee that your feedback goes straight to the appropriate authors, in time for the next edition. Each person who sends us information is thanked in the next edition, the most useful submissions are rewarded with a selection of digital PDF chapters.

Visit lonelyplanet.com/contact to submit your updates and suggestions or to ask for help. Our award-winning website also features inspirational travel stories, news and discussions.

Note: We may edit, reproduce and incorporate your comments in Lonely Planet products such as guidebooks, websites and digital products, so let us know if you don't want your comments reproduced or your name acknowledged. For a copy of our privacy policy visit lonelyplanet.com/privacy.

Index

A

B

C

LONELY PLANET IN THE WILD

Send your 'Lonely Planet in the Wild' photos to social@lonelyplanet.com
We share the best on our Facebook page every week!